The Springer Series on Human Exceptionality

Donald H. Saklofske, Ph.D.
Division of Applied Psychology
University of Calgary, Canada

Moshe Zeidner, Ph.D.
Center for Interdisciplinary Research on Emotions
Department of Human Development and Counseling
Haifa University, Israel

For further volumes, go to:
www.springer.com/series/6450

Zipora Shechtman

Treating Child and Adolescent Aggression Through Bibliotherapy

 Springer

Zipora Shechtman
University of Haifa
Mount Carmel
Israel

ISSN: 1572-5642
ISBN: 978-0-387-09743-5   e-ISBN: 978-0-387-09745-9
DOI 10.1007/978-0-387-09745-9

Library of Congress Control Number: 2008938332

Printed on acid-free paper

springer.com

To my dear family
The source of my energy and support
With love

To the many students who applied the
method of bibliotherapy
The source of the case studies and
illustrations
With appreciation

Preface

Aggression among children and adolescents is a highly disturbing behavior, whether it takes place at home, in the school, on the playground, or in the community. Attempts have been made to prevent aggression through disciplinary action ("Zero Tolerance" approach) and social enhancement ("Well-Being" approach), but while they often do result in decreased aggression, they don't work for everyone. Owing to various individual differences (temperament, family circumstances, developmental difficulties, etc.), some children remain aggressive despite those efforts. Classroom and school-based educational programs to reduce aggression are often of a primary prevention type, targeted toward the normative population in the school. But the children and adolescents who are at high risk for aggressive behavior need a secondary prevention treatment, one that addresses the unique difficulties of aggressive young people.

Take, for example, the recent shooting at Virginia Technical University, in which a college student killed 32 peers and professors and then committed suicide. This was an act of one very angry and lonely young man, as were other mass shootings in schools in the United States. It is this anger, loneliness, and sense of rejection that need to be addressed in the treatment of these children, starting at an early age.

Ignoring the needs of the aggressor is typical of our society. Paradoxically, the more prevention attempts are made the more difficult becomes the situation for such children and youth. Prevention programs enhance awareness of the norms, rules and regulations expected in a certain setting, and any deviation from them arouses antagonism and anger. Because aggressive children demonstrate deviant behavior that does not adhere to group rules, and because they are a threat to others, they are rejected by their peers and by adults. Indeed, adults are often quite helpless in facing the challenges these youngsters pose. Teachers even feel unsafe in schools and often don't know how to cope with highly aggressive students. As a result, they punish rather than treat them.

It makes sense to punish those who inflict harm on others, who use force to achieve their goals, and who take advantage of their power against victims. We can even rationalize the punishment by arguing that we are protecting the weak. But is this effective in reducing aggression of the perpetrators? The argument I make in this book is that rejecting and punishing aggressive children perpetuates those very life experiences that made them aggressive individuals in the first place. If we want to break the cycle of aggression, we need to help them. Aggression is the symptom, not the cause of the behavior. Rather than pushing them away from the social mainstream, we need to understand their difficulties, try to address their special needs, and bring them back to society.

Think for a moment about driving on a wet road, when suddenly the car veers to the right. Your first instinct is to turn the wheel in the same direction, but actually you should turn it the other way. So, too, with aggressive youth, we need to act against our basic instincts, to love rather than hate, to accept rather than reject, to nurture rather than punish, and to reach out rather than avoid.

Efforts to change aggressive behavior are commonly based on cognitive restructuring, because aggressive children exhibit distorted social information processing. They tend to ascribe hostile meaning toward them and react aggressively in defense without considering alternative behavior. Although the deficit in information processing is clear, treatment that focuses solely on this deficit may be insufficient, because emotional factors play an important role in their aggressive behavior. Aggressive children are frustrated, dissatisfied, angry, and lonely. They feel that they need to protect themselves from further disrespect, intimidation, and attacks. Most of the time, they are unaware of the problems their behavior is causing to others. They rather see themselves as victims of others' aggression and their own behavior as an "innocent" attempt to defend themselves. Even when they do have some awareness of their antisocial behavior, these vulnerable children will not easily abandon their aggression, as it provides them with a sense of power that they need for their survival. This is why aggression is so resistant to change.

Changing aggressive behavior is not an easy task. It requires promoting the development of self-awareness without frightening the child. We must engage the child in an empowering process and enhance his/her motivation to make a change. And we must offer an alternative to aggression. All these require an environment of care, recognition, respect, and support. These are the necessary conditions for any successful therapy, but they are insufficient conditions for treatment of aggression. In addition, we need to apply special methods and techniques that help us capture the child's attention, raise the motivation to change, increase cooperation with the therapist in the change process, and reduce self-defensiveness.

I offer bibliotherapy as an adjunct to a therapeutic process based on an integrative theory of treatment. Telling stories that are relevant to aggressive behavior present an indirect treatment for the child, one that minimizes self-defensiveness. It permits children to understand their behavior without focusing directly on themselves. Through identification with the characters in the story, they can learn about the reasons for aggression and its consequences without having to feel ashamed, guilty, or threatened. In the process of discussing alternative behaviors to aggression for the character, they become aware of their own alternatives to aggression. All this is done in an indirect way, so that the children are not quite aware of the pressure to change. Indeed, reducing external pressure to change is the key; it is of utmost importance for aggressive children and youth because of the oppositional nature of their disturbance.

Bibliotherapy entails the use of literature for therapeutic purposes and it includes listening to stories and poems, watching films, and looking at pictures. It is a playful, engaging, and fun process. In a safe climate, children eventually make the connection to their own feelings and behavior and become ready to take charge of their lives.

The integrative theory that we apply entails the treatment of aggressive children in stages. First, we use humanistic principles to create the necessary conditions for change: bonding with the therapist (individual therapy) or with the therapist and other children (group therapy), and creating a safe social and emotional climate in which self-disclosure is promoted. Next, in the working stage, through the use of stories, poems, pictures, and films, we apply psychodynamic principles to develop awareness of their unconscious behavior. Finally, we use cognitive-behavioral principles to develop processes in which the children consider the pros and cons of aggressive behavior, and make a commitment to change their behavior.

The method is most often used in the school, but it can equally be used at home, in private clinics, and in corrective facilities, among others. With some modifications and adjustments of the literature, it can be applied to specific types of aggression (relational, reactive, and proactive) and in unique areas (e.g., sexual aggression, addictions, and animal abuse).

Over the past 10 years, my colleagues and I have worked successfully with this method with hundreds of children, in both individual and group formats. Through a series of empirical studies, we were able to show that the method is effective in reducing aggression and increasing empathy—the flip side of aggression. We also were able to learn a great deal about the change processes that the children undergo.

I would like to share this knowledge and understanding with professionals who struggle with aggressive behavior. These include teachers, school counselors, psychologists, social workers, and other mental health employees. Parents, who are currently quite helpless in conflict situations at home, may also find this approach amenable to their needs.

Contents

Chapter 1
The Nature of Aggressive Children

The Problem

Aggressive behavior is defined as any "intentional act to hurt others, physically or psychologically" (Moeller, 2001). While "aggression" is often used interchangeably with "violence," the latter term connotes more serious and extreme forms of behavior. Clinically defined, aggression and violence are typically parts of the symptom patterns presented by children with DSM-IV diagnoses of oppositional defiant disorder (ODD) or conduct disorder (CD) (American Psychiatric Association, 1994). Such disturbances are usually manifested in high-level aggression, such as violent criminal acts, shooting, and murder.

However, current literature on anger and aggression suggests "that the field go beyond diagnostic categories and include a range of other important individual, group, and cultural characteristics" (Deffenbacher, Oetting, & DiGiuseppe, 2002, p. 266). Hence, while violent acts have become a major topic of concern in the general public, they are relatively rare. It is low-level aggressive behavior that actually captures our attention currently, because it is more frequent and disquieting in everyday life, and more than ever, we are aware of the lasting effect of mild aggression on both victims (Olweus, 1993) and perpetrators (Farrington, 1994). Thus, when the current literature reports on the rates of aggression, it refers to a wide range of acts from severe physical aggression and violence to such mild behaviors as pushing and kicking, and to verbal aggression, including insults and name calling.

Reported rates of mild and low-level school aggression are extremely high. Some researchers indicate that every second boy and every fourth girl in school is involved in physical conflict (Horne, Stoddard, & Bell, 2007), while others report even higher rates. For example, Benbenishty and Astor (2005) found that 20% of students endured severe physical aggression, 60% suffered from mild physical aggression, and the rates of verbal aggression were even higher (about 80%). These findings suggest that, for many children and adolescents, safety in their environment (e.g., school, school bus, and playground) is a daily concern (Connor, 2002; Goldstein, 1999). Whether

Z. Shechtman, *Treating Child and Adolescent Aggression Through Bibliotherapy*,
The Springer Series on Human Exceptionality, DOI 10.1007/978-0-387-09745-9_1,
© Springer Science+Business Media, LLC 2009

aggression is present in the school or elsewhere, it violates one of the basic needs of children (and adults)—the need for safety (Maslow, 1998).

These findings are particularly troublesome, owing to the evident stability of aggressive behavior over time, and because aggressive behavior has become a notable risk marker for a variety of adolescent problem behaviors. Aggressive behavior implies disrespect, and is threatening, intimidating, belittling, and hurtful, leaving the victim helpless and hopeless. Such behaviors create a toxic climate that bears short-term and long-term consequences. An aggressive climate interferes with the victims' immediate functioning in their academic and social life (Elias & Arnold, 2006), and it has a marked impact on the children's self-esteem and social adjustment at later stages (Olweus, 1993).

Interestingly, the aggressors are also affected negatively by their own behavior, in both the short- and the long-run. The immediate response to aggressive children is social rejection and punishment, which only makes them angrier, more rebellious, and more aggressive. Moreover, because aggressive behavior is quite stable, it is associated with poor longitudinal outcomes across a variety of domains, including scholastic difficulties, violent crimes, partner assault, alcoholism, drug abuse, unemployment, divorce, abusive parenting, and mental-health disorders (Connor, 2002; Woodward & Fergusson, 2000).

Because we are currently aware, more than ever, of the consequences of aggressive behavior on nonaggressive children, we try to decrease aggression through various prevention programs, some more successful than others (for a review, see Horne et al., 2007). Most of the prevention programs take an ecological perspective (Bronfenbrenner, 1979; Espelage & Swearer, 2004) and are aimed at improving school and classroom climate, increasing mutual respect, and teaching resolution skills to the children in conflict. Support for such interventions was obtained from a recent study that investigated the association between classroom climate, life skills, and the level of classroom aggression, in a population of about 10,000 elementary-school children. Results showed that the more positive the classroom climate, and the more skilled children are in conflict resolution, the less aggression there is in the classroom. Of particular importance were the factors of bonding with classmates and classroom involvement; the higher the social involvement, and the closer the relationships with peers and teacher, the lower the level of aggression in the classroom (Shechtman, 2006b).

However, even with the best programs implemented in classes and schools, there will always remain a core of youngsters (about 5–10%) who continue to demonstrate aggressive behavior. We tend to think that aggression is especially high in adolescence, but the literature suggests that children who are highly aggressive during elementary school years are at greatest risk of physical aggression during adolescence and adulthood (Broidy et al., 2003). This implies that we need to start interventions to reduce aggression from the early age of preschool and continue our efforts in elementary school and through adolescence. But, before we get into treatment, we need to understand the various types of aggression, because each type may need a certain adjustment in respect to treatment.

Types of Aggression

Aggressive behavior can be expressed in three forms: physical, verbal, and relational. All these forms can be manifested in different types of aggression, such as bullying, reactive aggression, and proactive aggression. I will first explain the three forms of aggression, with an emphasis on relational aggression, which is relatively less known in conceptual terms, after which I will explore the three types of aggression in depth.

Physical aggression includes activities in which actual physical harm is intentionally done to a person, animal, or object. Examples are hitting, kicking, stabbing, shooting, pushing and shoving, throwing objects, breaking windows, and setting fires. Verbal aggression involves the use of words to harm another, and it includes behaviors such as making threats or writing threatening notes, calling names, cursing, and teasing. Recently, a third type called "relational aggression" has been suggested, defined as behaviors that harm others through damage to social relationships or feelings of acceptance, friendship, or group inclusion (Crick, Grotpeter, & Bigbee, 2002). Spreading gossip, snubbing a party invitation, and ostracizing are a few examples. While relational aggression tends to be more indirect than other types of aggression, it is just as aversive and cruel.

Relational aggression is more common among girls, because their same-sex interpersonal relationships are based on close friendships and driven by values of intimacy. Some research suggests that girls are more emotionally aggressive than boys (French, Jansen, & Pidada, 2002). Girls also internalize the feminine role and societal values, characterizing them as delicate and nonaggressive. Yet, relationally aggressive girls share many of the features characterizing aggressive boys (e.g., hostile attributional biases). Moreover, recent research suggests that many boys are using relational aggression toward girls (Peets & Kikas, 2006; Salmivalli & Kaukiainen, 2004).

All these forms of aggression can be included in bullying, reactive aggression, and proactive aggression. Bullying is the use of repetitive force on vulnerable victims. Proactive aggression (also called instrumental aggression) involves the use of force to obtain predetermined goals. Finally, reactive aggression is a response to some provocative event or behavior. It should be noted that Dodge and colleagues (1997) refer to bullying as a behavior typical of proactive aggression. Nonetheless, I have chosen to treat it as a separate type of aggression, because it is so common in school and there is a wide range of literature on bullying that point to unique characteristics of this type of aggression.

Bullying

Bullying is the most frequent type of aggression and victimization among children and adolescents, particularly in the school (Horne et al., 2007; Orpinas &

Horne, 2006). Olweus (1993), who first brought this concept to public attention, suggests that bullying can take the form of emotional and physical aggression, direct or indirect, but what differentiates it from general aggressive behavior is that it is a repetitive behavior against a victim that takes advantage of his/her physical or psychological weakness. Horne and colleagues refer to the characteristics of bullying behavior as the "PIC" criteria; that is, it is Purposeful, there is an Imbalance in power, and it is Continual.

Bullies share some characteristics with other types of aggressors, but they also have unique characteristics. They are usually strong, quite confident emotionally and socially, and self-controlled. They deliberately choose to attack their victims to get some excitement, to gain social power, or simply to inflict pain on someone (a hostile act). Similar to other aggressors, and perhaps even more than others, they lack the skills of perspective-taking, empathy, and moral judgment. Their lack of empathy prevents them from feeling remorse or sorrow for the emotional and physical pain they cause. Because bullying is demonstrated by quite normally developed youngsters, their behavior is often overlooked by adults and misinterpreted as a childhood prank. However, bullying has far-reaching consequences for the victims (Natvig, Albrektsen, & Qvarnstrom, 2001; Olweus, 1993; Sullivan, 2000) and the bullies alike (Boulton & Smith, 1994).

Bullying can take the form of physical or verbal aggression. The following is an example of a combination of physical and verbal bullying:

> Simon, a child from a religious family, is the only student in the class to wear a "kipa" (a head covering worn by orthodox Jews). Every morning when he enters class, a group of classmates make fun of him, calling him "the kipa man" and sometimes adding a smack to his head that can really hurt. Simon hates to go to school; he is often absent, presenting psychosomatic complaints, and lately he has asked his parents to be transferred. His only fault is that he is different and weaker than his bullies. For the bullies it means excitement, power, and the overt and silent support of their classmates.

Or it can take the form of relational aggression:

> Leslie is a highly competitive and domineering girl, the "queen" of her class. She decides who is going to be invited to a game, activity, or party, and who is not. One day, Debra received a better grade in math. The same weekend Debra had a birthday party. Leslie sent out e-mails, telling all the girls in class not to attend the party and most did what she asked. When questioned about her actions, Leslie responded: "They have their own opinion and I just expressed mine." The other girls, though, confessed that they were afraid of her, "because you never know when she will turn against you."

And although bullying through relational aggression is mainly attributed to girls, it is also practiced by boys:

> Bobby put up a picture of Myra, the best student in his class, on the Internet, announcing that she invites any handsome boy to have sexual relationships with her. The next day the whole class mocked her. Myra became so depressed and hurt that she stopped going to school for a long while.

A major problem regarding bullying is that bullies get direct and indirect support from several other children and from bystanders. In every class there is a group of children, who do not have the power to hurt someone, but who worship the power of those who carry out their hidden wishes and like the excitement that goes along with scapegoating another child. Even more meaningful is the indirect support received from the majority of the class, who play the role of the silent audience (Salmivalli, Lagerspetz, Bjorkquist, Osterman, & Kaukiainen, 1994). The fact that the social group does not object serves as reinforcement for the bullies to continue their destructive behavior. This scenario creates a sense of terrible loneliness and helplessness for the single victim who, in addition to being hurt by the bully, feels that nobody cares about him or her. The lack of social support in such a situation may be even more harmful than the aggressive act itself. It has a devastating effect on one's emotional and physical wellbeing (Natvig et al., 2001). The aggressors get mixed reactions: they are often admired by their close peer group, but at the same time they are also rejected by many others.

Bullies are often treated in a group context, and rightly so. Changing the group norms, so that endorsement of aggression is reduced probably does decrease bullying, as no support for their behavior will be received (Olweus, 1993). However, this does not mean that bullies do not need to be treated directly with the aim of changing their behavior. They certainly have an anti-social approach to life, a poor value system, and a lack of empathy—all of which can be treated through the approach presented in this book.

Reactive and Proactive Aggression

Bullying cannot explain the entire spectrum of aggressive behavior in the school. There are aggressive acts that do not involve systematic misuse of power. Physically weak children often act aggressively, even when it is clear that they have no chance of winning. There are perpetrators who attack strong children and even adults, if it serves their purpose. Along these lines, Dodge and colleagues (1997) have suggested a distinction between two types of aggression: reactive and proactive.

Reactive aggression is an angry retaliatory response to a perceived provocation. It is a "'hot-blooded' behavior that is motivated by underlying states of anger and frustration" (Dodge et al., 1997, p. 38). Observations of peer groups, made up of young children, showed that reactive aggression includes expressions of anger, temper tantrums, and vengeful hostility. This type of aggression has theoretical roots in the frustration-aggression model (Berkowitz, 1963; Dollard, Doob, Miller, Mowrer, & Sears, 1939).

> Dan is a 12-year-old boy who looks much younger. He is restless and hyperactive, often angry at his teachers and classmates, and constantly complains of being picked on. One morning a classmate bumped into his desk in passing. Dan became furious, jumped on the boy and knocked him to the ground. The fact that his victim was much stronger did not prevent the attack, which took place in the classroom in the presence of a teacher. When asked why he did it, Dan explained that his classmate had intentionally hit his

desk to put him down in front of the whole class. This was an unfortunate misinter-
pretation, resulting from Dan's perception of the event as a threat. Dan did not
accurately read the social event; his encoding of cues was limited, and his interpretation
was based on attribution of hostile intentions to the other child.

In contrast, proactive aggression is a "cold blooded" (Dodge et al., 1997,
p. 38) planned response to achieve certain goals, mostly instrumental, in a social
situation, and does not involve underlying states of anger. Observations of
children's peer groups revealed that proactive aggression was manifested
through domination, teasing, name-calling, and coercive acts. This understanding of aggression is rooted in social-learning theories (Bandura, 1983), which
explain aggressive behavior as highly influenced by an aggressive environment.
Children who behave in this way endorse power and believe that aggression
leads to positive outcomes (Perry, Perry, & Rasmussen, 1986). They are more
likely to be found in poverty populations and among delinquent youth.

Ron is a 13-year-old student in a special education vocational school. One day a
policeman came to school to question him about a break-in at a toy store. He
immediately admitted that he had done it, explaining that he wanted a ball that was
displayed in the store window so he could get some friends to play with him. Although
he was a boy of average intelligence, he did not think of his behavior as wrong. He knew
that this was the only way he could get the ball and gain friends. In a later counseling
session, he understood what was wrong, but pleaded to me: "Please get me out of this
neighborhood, because as long as I remain there, I will join my friends, as I need friends
to play with."

Studies support this distinction. Reactively aggressive children seem to be
more prone to hostile attributional biases than proactively aggressive children,
while the latter hold more positive expectancies for aggressive behavior than the
former (Crick & Dodge, 1996; Dodge & Coie, 1987). Reactive aggression is
correlated with peer victimization, whereas proactive aggression is correlated
with social dominance (Schwartz et al., 1998). Reactive aggression starts early
in life, is affected by harsh circumstances, and is correlated with overall impairment in school-age years (Waschbusch, Willoughby, & Pelham, 1998). In contrast, instrumental aggressors are mainly a product of their harsh environment,
and their aggression is manifested in delinquent behavior along the lifespan
(Dodge et al., 1997).

It is not always easy to distinguish between the two types of aggression. In
many children we witness behavior that is a combination of reactive and
proactive aggression (Connor, 2002). Dodge and colleagues (1997) refer to
this group as pervasively aggressive. They found elements of both types of
aggression and historical factors typical of both types among such children.
For instance, pervasive aggressors not only have a history of child abuse and
other stressful events in early childhood (reactive aggression), but also have
aggressive role models at home, in the neighborhood, and/or among peers
(proactive aggression).

At a boarding school for troubled youth, Mark came in after a weekend at home in an
extremely vulnerable mood. At recess, the kids were playing soccer but refused to

include him in the game. In response, he took the ball away from them. The counselor who was present at the scene tried to intervene, but despite the good relationship she had with him, Mark continued fighting, totally out of control, hitting the counselor and breaking her finger. When he was later questioned about the event, he stated: "You would never understand, because you have not been to my home."

The goal was to take the ball and to be part of the game. Coming from a family of physical abuse, using force is the only way Mark knows to achieve his goal. So far, this is a typical case of proactive aggression. Yet, one cannot ignore the tremendous amount of anger and frustration that this boy accumulated during his weekend at home, as well as throughout his whole life. This makes it hard to classify him into either category of aggression.

As we have seen, there are common characteristics among bullies, proactive aggressors, and reactive aggressors. Moreover, physical, verbal, and relational aggressions also have much in common, and there are similarities between the aggressive behavior of boys and girls as well. When treating aggressive young people, we need to pay attention to all these types. But first we need to understand the origins of aggressive behavior, as aggression is a complicated behavior with multiple causes. Understanding these causes can help us offer more effective treatments.

Causes of Aggression

Regardless of the type of aggression, a central question is why children come to behave that way. What makes a child or adolescent angry and aggressive? The answer is complex, says Potter-Efron (2005). Apparently, a confluence of risk factors work together, creating a situation in which aggressive behavior is over-determined and over-learned, turning children into aggressors (Moeller, 2001). These risk factors include certain biological traits, family features, ineffective parenting, poor schools, a rejecting peer group, affiliation with antisocial peers, and contextual factors such as poverty, stressful life events, and access to weapons (Bloomquist & Schnell, 2002; Capuzzi & Gross, 2000; Loeber & Farrington, 2000; Moeller, 2001).

Genetic, Biological, and Temperamental Factors

A large and growing body of evidence (Connor, 2002) suggests that a substantial part of children's aggressiveness is due to internal biological and physiological processes, which, if not innate, emerge within the first few years of life. In particular, studies have shown a positive relationship between uninhibited temperament in infancy and subsequent aggression, delinquency, and violence in childhood and adulthood. Furthermore, minor physical anomalies, unique brain waves, and early neurological impairment have been found to be related to later aggression, particularly to its more violent forms. Some research indicates that complications before and during birth might affect later aggression. For example, minor physical anomalies, which are linked to prenatal adversity, have been shown to be correlated with childhood disorders and violent offenses in adulthood. Further, birth complications were found to predict conduct disorder. But such factors take effect only when in interaction with other environmental variables, such as maternal rejection or overall stressful family circumstances (Moeller, 2001).

The research in this area is underdeveloped. It is likely that some children are born with a predisposition to develop aggression and violence, but environmental factors may also be important in determining to what extent this predisposition develops into actual behavior (Moeller, 2001). One of the most major influences on aggression, for which consensus has been established, is the family.

Family Factors

Violent parents tend to have violent children. Hence, it is clear that violence is transmitted intergenerationally. However, the interpretation of how the family influences the child's behavior varies from one psychological orientation to another.

A clear and direct explanation, widely supported by research, is offered by *cognitive-behavioral theory*. Accordingly, children who live in a violent home climate learn, through observation, the models for conflict resolution their parents present to them. The theoretical context of this theory is social knowledge (Huesmann, 1988). Huesmann proposed that social behavior is controlled by programs learned during the individual's early development. These programs are cognitive scripts stored in memory and used as guides for behavior and social problem solving. Scripts of aggression are learned through observation, reinforcement, and personal experience of situations in which aggression is a salient behavior. These scripts become encoded, rehearsed, stored, and retrieved, like any other strategy for behavior. Once stored, they become resistant to change (Huesmann & Reynolds, 2001). Several studies have indicated that aggressive children have limited scripts, their content is more aggressive, and they behave according to the scripts automatically (Eron, 1997).

Dodge and Schwartz (1997) expand on this cognitive-behavioral explanation, suggesting that the social information processing of aggressive children differs from that of nonaggressive children (see also a detailed explanation later in this chapter). It is not just that they act automatically based on internalized scripts, their very thought process is impaired. In a provoking social event, they perceive minimal cues, attribute hostile intent to the provocator, select aggressive goals from a limited repertoire of responses, evaluate aggression as positive, and thus act aggressively. In short, it is more than internalized scripts that aggressive children act on. In addition to what they have learned through observation, identification processes, and reinforcements, they come to appreciate and endorse aggression, and therefore select it as a promising response in a social conflict (Dishion & Patterson, 1997; Dodge, 2002).

Such distorted information processing results not only from social learning based on observation and modeling, as suggested by cognitive psychology (e.g., Bandura, 1983), but also from lack of parental supervision and monitoring. Parental neglect is one of the best predictors of later aggression and delinquency, because children with no consistent disciplinary action suffer from an incomplete process of learning. Thus, it is not surprising that, when they face a conflict, they use the methods that they know best to resolve it and that they endorse power and believe that attacking the "enemy" will bring the best results. Recall Ron who hit his counselor in the midst of a fight. He had many reasons to be frustrated at home and to be mistrustful of his friends, and he probably learned from his family that aggression is the proper way to deal with stress. Ron comes from a very poor inner-city family. Indeed, research suggests that, on average, socioeconomically disadvantaged boys, particularly those living in urban neighborhoods, are more disruptive and aggressive than their peers (Loeber & Farrington, 2000).

However, not all poor families raise aggressive children, and there are aggressive children in growing numbers in well-to-do families. Hence, learning processes, although important, cannot be the sole explanation of aggressive behavior. *Attachment theory* (Ainsworth, Blehar, Waters, & Wall, 1978; Bowlby, 1969) provides an alternative explanation to childhood aggression. According to it, children develop one of the three attachment styles—secure, anxious, or avoidant—depending on the quality of their relationships with their primary caregiver, usually the mother. Responsive parents who are attuned to their child's needs raise securely attached children, whereas nonresponsive parents raise insecure (anxious or avoidant) children. This parent-child interaction, which develops at a very early age, predicts future social relationships in school and with peers. On the whole, securely attached children were found to be more prosocial and less aggressive than anxious or avoidant children (Cassidy & Berlin, 1994; Thompson, 1999). Insecure children were anxious, lonely, hostile, and aggressive (Shechtman & Dvir, 2006).

Gilliom, Shaw, Beck, Schonberg, and Lukon (2002) use attachment theory to explain excessive anger and aggression among children. Accordingly, most young children have not developed the ability to self-regulate their emotions effectively, and so are dependent on their parents' reaction to stressful situations. When parents are responsive to their children's needs and calm the situation down, children learn to control themselves and trust that adults in their environment will come to their rescue, if needed. However, when parents are unresponsive to children's needs, children become disorganized in a stressful situation and unable to trust themselves or others. That is, securely attached children learn through their socialization process to trust, respect, love, and be sensitive to others, while insecure children are distrustful, defensive, and aggressive in social situations (Potter-Efron, 2005). Furthermore, children who are initially highly irritable and whose frustration is exacerbated by harsh, restrictive parenting will exhibit particular difficulties in self-regulation and become more aggressive. It appears that parents' attachment style lays the foundation for those parenting behaviors that increase aggression among their children: lack of warmth, harsh control, physical punishment, and emotional and physical abuse.

Adlerian theorists also argue that the family is the major source of influence on children's aggression, but focus on the sense of inferiority as the critical cause of aggression. They explain that aggressive children select a pattern of life based on this sense of inferiority. Children, who grow up under conditions of disrespect, neglect, and rejection or, conversely, are pampered and overprotected, are likely to develop a pattern of aggressive behavior, because it best suits their need for superiority. By overcoming their victims, maltreated or traumatized children regain the power they have lost in the family. Indeed, research suggests that harsh discipline and high psychological parental control affect children's level of aggression and delinquent behavior (Dodge, 2002). By a similar token, spoiled and overprotected children tend to expect immediate attention or reward. Because they get what they want so effortlessly, they develop a sense of helplessness. Moreover, they are centered on their own needs and have little interest, empathy, or responsibility for others. They, too, tend to overcome feelings of inferiority through aggression toward others, which restores their sense of power.

Related to the above approach is *humanistic psychology*, which stresses the emotional climate in the family. When basic needs for security, sense of belonging, love, and respect are not met, the child becomes unhappy, depressed, and/or aggressive. A great deal of research has shown that families of aggressive children are characterized by a low level of emotional warmth and a high level of mutual hostility (Loeber & Dishion, 1984). Emotional hostility is positively associated with antisocial and aggressive behavior, whereas an emotionally warm relationship seems to protect children against externalizing behavior (Rothbaum & Weisz, 1994). Under hostile circumstances, children grow up mistrusting themselves and others, and they accumulate anger that is manifested in stressful social situations.

While some of the above theories provide a better explanation than others for specific forms of aggression, on the whole, they all explain aggression as resulting from harsh family conditions. "Severe discipline is a seed for bad behavior," says Dodge (2002**).** Maltreatment teaches children to adapt their behavior and thinking to the harsh fact that those who are in charge of caring for them are the very same people who hurt, ignore, and attack them. They learn to understand the world through the lens of their own abuse. As a result, children become hypersensitive to negative social cues and oblivious to positive social cues. Further, they develop a repertoire of aggressive behavior and draw the conclusion that aggression is a successful way to get what they want.

Social Influences

Although the family plays a central role in the development of childhood aggression, it is definitely not the only source. Social influences at the macro and the micro level have a great impact on the socialization processes of children and adolescents.

At the macro level culture, social norms, and values have considerable influence on children's socialization. Some cultures endorse aggression more than others, influencing families and children to act in an aggressive way.

> At an early stage of my teaching career, I worked with children of new immigrants to Israel who originated from African countries. The parents of my students encouraged me to "use my authority properly" and apply corporal punishment, just as they did. The children, too, upon my first entrance into the classroom, pointed to a long stick that was placed near the blackboard and said: "You will never have quiet here unless you use this stick." I told them that I did not choose a teaching career in order to hit students, and that we would have to find another method of communication. They were quite skeptical about my approach, as they were not familiar with any other way. However, just as they learned in their family and community that aggression is a common language, they were able over time to learn a new mode of communication, mostly through the corrective positive experiences that they had in our classroom relationships.

The norms of subcultures vary by community. For example, inner cities have their "street code" that is manifested in concepts such as respect, loosely defined as being treated "right." To get this type of respect is even worth dying for. Under such codes, violence seems justified (Moeller, 2001). Although high rates of aggression and violence can be found in the inner city and in poor neighborhoods, norms that endorse aggression can be found anywhere.

Several clinicians suggest that much male aggression in the United States results from cultural norms that encourage boys to be aggressive. Pollack, a psychiatrist who observed children from a very early age, concluded that the American culture promotes a "boy code" that favors male stoicism and makes boys ashamed to express weakness or vulnerability. They are forced to wear a "mask of masculinity" and a "straitjacket of gender." Pollack noted the discrimination of kindergarten-aged boys: when a girl cried on the first day of school, the teacher allowed her mother to stay with her daughter a bit longer, but when a boy cried, she asked the mother to leave and let him cope with the stress alone. Boys have to repress their feelings of fear and anxiety and fight the accompanying sense of shame. Society makes boys disconnect from their loved ones and sacrifice that part within themselves that is loving, caring, and affectionate. They react with aggression to cover their real feelings of fear, humiliation, and failure; those who do not react with aggression are drawn to isolation, depression, and despair. This, he explains, is one of the ways that culture makes boys wear their mantle of manhood (Pollack, 1998, 2000).

Garbarino (1999) has a similar understanding of boys' aggression. Interviewing delinquent youth, he learned that these boys appear tough on the outside, but actually are extremely vulnerable. Anger over neglect and maltreatment is often disguised by male depression. This potential for depression is actualized when a boy's experience of abandonment combines with the cultural messages he receives about masculinity—messages that devalue the direct expression of feelings, particularly those of emotional connection, vulnerability, and softness.

On the micro level, school and classmate ecology affect children's social behavior. Individual tendencies coupled with academic failure and peer rejection increase aggressive behavior (Dishion & Patterson, 1997). The socialization processes in a classroom resemble those of the family. Children learn norms from others and act on them to be socially accepted. If those norms endorse aggression, even the less aggressive child is tempted to act aggressively.

> I recall a case in which an adolescent was explaining his violent behavior to his therapist. Dimitri said: "I was passing by a group of strangers with my friends, when someone called me 'Hey Russian.' If I were alone, I would just ignore it, but I could not lose face in front of my friends." "You know," he continued, "I come from a good family in which violence is forbidden, but here my friends' expectations were to react with all my force."

In this case, the effect of the norms established in his peer group had a stronger influence on Dimitri's behavior than those of his family. This is not surprising, considering the boy's age. At adolescence, one main task is to find a niche in one's peer group, to be accepted, and to belong. Acting against peer expectations does not help one to be accepted. Yet, many adolescents are not accepted in the mainstream social group due to racism, stereotypes, and prejudice. Bronfenbrenner (1979) refers to these phenomena as social poisons, which have a devastating impact on vulnerable children, as they lead to a sense of alienation and loneliness. When a teenager is rejected by the mainstream, he or she is liable to seek an alternative, often turning to a deviant, antisocial gang, which may be very dangerous.

> I have read about an incident in which a gang made one of its new members kill his girlfriend. This was a particularly shocking story, because the boy was an honor student of Chinese origin. Violence was certainly not a normative behavior in his community and did not fit his personality. The gang leader made him perform this horrible crime as a test of acceptance to the gang. When questioned, the boy explained that he did not belong to the mainstream of classmates, that he needed to belong to some group and be accepted by someone.

Close friends are particularly influential in this respect. They are the most important source of support, which is, of course, very positive. But, if the friend is violent, it can lead to disaster.

> A horrible crime was committed in which two 13-year-old boys shot and killed a taxi driver. These two very close friends were a nightmare in their school: they bullied others, stole money from a school kiosk, vandalized, beat a classmate half to death, were cruel to animals, and eventually got hold of a pistol and killed a taxi driver whose only crime was to suggest taking them home at no charge. Of the two, one was the leader, a cruel domineering psychopath from a very affluent family, while the other was his blind follower from a single-parent family, who simply complied with his friend's commands. Neither their parents nor the school authorities could separate them, although they realized what a dangerous friendship it was.

Learning Disabilities

Anger and aggression are often associated with psychological diagnoses, such as attention deficit disorder (ADD), attention deficit and hyperactivity disorder (ADHD), anxiety disorders, antisocial personality disorders, depression, and post-traumatic stress disorder (PTSD) (Lochman, Fitzgerald, & Whidby, 1999; Potter-Efron, 2005). As learning disabilities receive considerable attention nowadays in schools, and because ADHD is closely related to reactive aggression (Dodge et al., 1997), this sub-group deserves unique attention in the discussion of childhood aggression.

A large portion of the research on children with learning disabilities (LD) indicates that they are lonelier than non-LD children, have more social difficulties, are less attachment-secure, and have difficulties in information processing and with self-control (Al-Yagon & Mikulincer, 2004; Tur-Kaspa, 2004). All these are conditions that increase the likelihood of aggressive behavior.

These difficulties are even more salient among children with ADHD (Barkley, 2002). Studies on this population consistently point to antisocial, impulsive, hostile, and aggressive behavior. According to several reviews, 30–50% of hyperactive children are prone to high-levels of anger (Miranda & Presentacion, 2000), behavioral disorders, and aggression (Hinshaw & Melnick, 1995). One explanation for these high rates of aggression is that many of these children also suffer from conduct disorder (Connor, 2002). However, this dual diagnosis explains only some of the high rates of aggression; other studies show that children identified only with ADHD (without CD) also demonstrate high-levels of aggression. The alternative explanation for these high rates of aggression is the hyperactivity-impulsivity factor itself. For example, Taylor, Chadwick, Heptinstall, and Danckaerts (1996), who followed a large sample of ADHD children from the age of 6–7 to the age of 16–18, concluded that hyperactivity alone was a major risk factor for later development, including poor peer relationships, violent disruptive behavior, lack of social involvement, and poor academic achievements. Other researchers (Rebok, Hawkins, Krener, Mayer, & Kellem, 1996) attribute the high rates of aggression to the symptom of inattention; concentration problems predicted increased aggression problems in the classroom. Overall, ADHD appears to be a high-risk factor for the development of aggressive behavior. Whether the result of neurological problems or developmental and social difficulties, this group requires special attention in the treatment of aggression.

In the above literature review, I have separated the risk factors to facilitate the reader's understanding of the origins of aggressive behavior. In reality, however, risk factors rarely exist in isolation. They are generally multiple, interacting in complicated transactions over the course of the child's development. The current perspective is that there is an interplay of genetic and psychological factors influencing aggression. Conduct disorders and ADHD are good examples of such combinations of factors. Also of great importance is the cumulative nature of risk factors. Thus, the specific type of risk factor is less important than the total number of factors. Parental psychopathology, poor parental practices, low SES, adverse life events, and biological factors usually go hand-in-hand, and have a far more serious impact on children's aggression (Connor, 2002).

Characteristics of Aggressive Children

Even though some life circumstances influence a certain type of aggressor more than another (e.g., poverty may affect an instrumental type of aggressor more, while parental neglect may have greater impact on a reactive type of aggressor), aggressive children and adolescents share some common characteristics. Several psychological qualities may be associated with aggressive behavior: difficulties in verbalization of emotions, deficits in information processing, lack of empathy, and lack of self-control.

Verbalization of Emotions

Some research suggests an association between low intelligence and aggressive behavior. For example, antisocial youth have IQs that are about 10 points below the mean (Wilson & Herrnstein, 1985), and childhood IQ predicts violent behavior in the future. For example, West and Farrington (1973) found that low nonverbal IQ at the age of 8–10 predicted delinquency in adolescence. Stattin and Klackenberg-Larsson (1993) found that low IQ at age 3, significantly predicted offensiveness in males up to the age of 30.

Specifically, aggressive children were found to suffer from verbal deficits (Connor, 2002). One explanation of the relationship between verbal deficits and aggression can be the difficulties of such children to express their needs and explain themselves (Moeller, 2001), resulting in impulsiveness and an inability to control themselves. This can be observed in very young children. Toddlers, for example, may scream, bite, push, and hit when they want something, because they lack the ability to express their needs verbally. Unfortunately, some older children remained fixated in this regressive stage. Unable to articulate their needs and emotions, they express themselves in a physical manner.

Some clinicians point to a deeper level of verbal deficits, suggesting that they are related not to IQ, but to the ability to identify, recognize, and connect to one's feelings. In his book *Lost Boys*, Garbarino (1999) writes: "Some of the aggressive boys appear very tough on the outside, but when I get a glimpse of their inner life, I am deeply touched by their vulnerability and pain, and I come to see their toughness as a survival strategy" (p. 22). One of the characteristics I have found in aggressive children is their difficulty in dealing with emotions. They act cool, as if nothing hurts them, but this is actually a defense against overwhelming emotions. Denying feelings helps them survive, despite the unfortunate circumstances of their lives, the stress, and the experiences of neglect and maltreatment. The most common emotions that aggressive children suppress are anger, shame, fear, and guilt.

Anger is perhaps the emotion most strongly associated with children's aggressive behavior. Berkowitz (1963) postulated that it results from frustration and is combined with the child's existing aggressive habits to produce a motivational readiness for aggression. Based on reviewed research, Moeller (2001) suggests that aggressive children deal with anger through direct or indirect aggression, rather than through verbal communication. Anger and aggression are usually a brain-and-body reaction to a threatening event, although the threat can be immediate or potential, real or imagined, weak or strong. Chronically angry individuals react far more often with anger to potentially threatening cues than others; in fact, anger becomes their habitual response. Anger over neglect and maltreatment is often hidden behind male depression. This potential for depression is actualized when a boy's experience of abandonment combines with cultural messages he receives about masculinity, messages that devalue the direct expression of feelings and emphasize the necessity of burying feelings, particularly feelings of emotional connection, vulnerability, and softness.

Shame is another emotion that characterizes aggressive children. They overcompensate for their sense of emptiness and worthlessness by displaying arrogance. "Abandonment is associated with shame, which begets covert depression, which begets rage, which begets violence," says Garbarino (1999, p. 44). He concludes that, as a result, these boys are "emotionally retarded" (p. 53).

Fear is yet another emotion that aggressive boys try to hide deep within themselves, as fear is a sign of vulnerability and thus invites victimization. Moreover, fear may be connected to a sense of helplessness or hopelessness, especially for those living in inner cities. If they believe that their lives can get no worse, that they have been treated unjustly, they may turn to aggression as a viable means of coping.

Finally, aggressive children show inappropriate *guilt* response. Researchers distinguish between predispositional and chronic guilt (Bybee & Quiles, 1998). The former is a reaction to a specific situation characteristic of prosocial behavior, while the latter is an ongoing condition of guiltiness, regret, and remorse, which is more typical of aggressive people. Thus, aggressive children constantly feel that they are bad.

It appears, then, that aggressive youth do not cope well with the basic feelings of anger, shame, fear, and guilt. Rather than acknowledging and expressing these feelings, they dissociate from them and this becomes a way of life. But the emotions that arise in response to rejection, abuse, and abandonment do not go away; they build up, turning into rage, so that any little event triggers violence. Moreover, because aggressive children are not attuned to their own feelings and their feelings are locked away, it is unlikely that they have a basis for feelings toward others. In other words, we would not expect to find much empathy in aggressive children and adolescents.

Empathy

Lack of empathy is one of the main characteristics of aggressive youngsters (Moeller, 2001). Empathy, generally defined as the ability to understand and share another's emotional state (Feshbach, 1997), is multidimensional. It encompasses traits (an individual's empathic tendencies), states (momentary empathic experiences elicited in a concrete situation), and interpersonal behavior (helping or comforting) (Davis, 1996). Both cognitive traits (the ability to understand another person's feelings, also known as perspective-taking skills) and affective traits (the tendency to share another person's feelings and experience an affective response) are important in buffering or inhibiting destructive behavior, including aggression. Research suggests that empathy relates positively to prosocial behavior (Miller & Eisenberg, 1988) and negatively to antisocial behavior and aggression (Kaukiainen et al., 1999; Loudin, Loukas, & Robinson, 2003).

Most research, however, focuses on cognitive skills of perspective taking, whereas affective empathy is rarely investigated. A recent study (Wied, Branje, & Meeus, 2007) investigating the relation between affective empathy and conflict behavior in close same-sex friendships found that empathy played a direct role in conflict resolution. Affective empathy was related negatively to conflict engagement and positively to problem solving. Another study (Shechtman, 2003b) comparing aggressive and nonaggressive elementary school students in terms of both cognitive and affective empathy showed that, while there was no difference in perspective-taking, there was a significant difference in affective empathy. Nonaggressive children were twice as affectively empathic than their aggressive counterparts. The study concluded that, while aggressive children may be able to understand another's situation cognitively, they cannot respond to it emotionally. This may be a result of shut-off feelings, as believed by many professionals, or a matter of motivation.

The literature suggests there is a motivational component to aggression. In other words, children can choose when to be empathic and when not to be. As aggressive children may believe that they need to appear strong and tough, showing emotions may arouse fear of losing power. Consequently, they may behave nonempathically even when they understand the situation of another person, and even when they actually feel empathy.

A relevant example can be found in a research on empathy within the context of the intergroup conflict between Arabs and Jews in Israel (Shechtman & Bashir, 2005). The study compared the level of aggression endorsement and empathy that Arab children had for Arab (in-group) and Jewish (out-group) children. Results indicated that all participants, boys and girls, supported an aggressive reaction to a child from the out-group more than to one from their in-group and exhibited a higher degree of empathy toward their own group.

In short, lack of empathy is a highly important component in aggressive behavior. Training children in perspective-taking skills and conflict-resolution skills may not be sufficient to reduce their aggression, because the affective component of empathy is missing.

Perception Problems: The Endorsement of Power

As explained earlier, social information processing (SIP) provides a common explanation for children's aggression (Dodge & Schwartz, 1997). SIP is a systematized series of sequential mental operations involving cognitive and emotional processing and reflects both conscious and unconscious operations. A child's behavior in a particular social situation occurs as a direct reflection of his/her mental processing of the situation. Competent SIP will usually result in adaptive social behavior, whereas biased, inaccurate, or ineffective processing will usually lead to maladaptive behavior, such as aggression.

The process involves six stages: encoding, interpretation, goal selection, response selection, evaluation, and behavior enactment. Research has shown that aggressive children process social information differently from their nonaggressive peers. Encoding is primarily a sensory task through which a child attends to the social stimuli in a given situation. A constructive response will occur when the child can see a wide range of stimuli and attend to the most relevant. However, hypervigilance to threatening cues limits the number of positive cues a child perceives and can lead to an automatic response of aggression.

Following encoding of the situation, the child generates an interpretation of the social situation. Nonaggressive children will try to understand the cause of the event, infer the motives of the actor, and foresee the consequences of their own actions. In contrast, a child who displays a hostile attributional bias is likely to respond with aggression. Next, the child must select a goal for reaction. An angry and frustrated child will probably choose to hurt the actor. The child then evaluates his/her selection of the goal. A child who is morally underdeveloped and believes that aggression leads to desired outcomes will probably act aggressively.

It is quite clear how aggressive children come to use such distorted information processing. The sense of loneliness, emptiness, and shame caused by consistent rejection and neglect leads to perception of the world as nongratifying, unfriendly, and dangerous. As the most meaningful persons in their lives have caused them to experience humiliation and despair, it is almost impossible to trust strangers. Hence, a hostile attribution bias develops that leads them to conclude that others harbor hostile intent toward them and therefore deserve to be attacked (Moeller, 2001). Moreover, these children are constantly on guard not to be humiliated again, and therefore must always be strong. Any sign of weakness may be exploited, they think. Even admitting to a mistake or forgiving someone is interpreted as weakness. Moreover, in the absence of moral-reasoning skills, empathy, and conflict-resolution skills, acting aggressively seems to be the only option.

Self-control

Aggressive behavior is often preceded by anger, and anger is the emotion that people have most difficulty controlling. Hence, intense uncontrolled anger arousal is a central component in antisocial and aggressive behavior (Lochman et al., 1999). Children's anger-related physiological arousal is activated by their cognitive processing of the event and of their response, and their arousal, in turn, impairs their cognitive processing. With heightened arousal, children's attention becomes more narrowly focused on aspects of the perceived threat, and they become prone to responding in an impulsive manner, spending very little time processing alternative solutions. This anger arousal model is consistent with the social information processing studies, showing that aggressive children have distorted and deficient social information processing at each of the six stages in Dodge's (Dodge & Schwartz, 1997) model.

Four child-based factors have been found to influence social cognition: social goals, prior expectations, physiological arousal, and information processing style. Aggressive children place higher value on social goals of dominance and revenge, and these goals become rigid schemas that govern future behavior. They are also quickly aroused physiologically; their heart rates increase when they face a threatening provocation, and their hostile attributions increase. In such situations, they tend to use impulsive, automatic information processing rather than deliberate information processing. In other words, they see less cues, find less solutions, and are less verbally assertive; therefore, they burst out in an aggressive act.

Self-control is developed in an early stage of child development, mostly through intensive relationships with the mother. This mother-child relationship is the initial stage of the child's socialization process. Hence, warm parenting facilitates self-regulation while authoritarian and controlling parenting leads to rigid responses to frustration. Skills such as inhibition of disruptive behavior, cooperation with others, and self-assertion have been identified as the most important elements of self-control (Bohart & Stipek, 2001). For aggressive children, inhibiting or regulating anger is of particular importance. Attenuated and supportive parents help highly irritable children to calm down and organize themselves, while harsh and restrictive parenting exacerbates frustration, leading to explosive reactions.

Summary and Implications for Treatment

Child and adolescent aggression presents a challenge to our daily lives. Children often feel unsafe and adults are often unarmed, sometimes helpless, in facing the magnitude of the problem. Very often, aggression is confused with disciplinary issues and other problems. Although some overlap can be found, aggression has its own unique definition and characteristics. The delineation of these factors is important, because the form of aggression—whether it be physical, verbal or relational, and the types of aggression—bullying, reactive, or proactive—helps us set goals for treatment. Sometimes there is a need to adjust the type of treatment to the form of aggression.

We have also seen that there are multiple causes of aggression; they, too, can affect the type of treatment that is required. Regardless of the differences in theoretical orientation, parenting and family relations seem to be the major influence on the child's aggression. Nonetheless, society and social norms also play a role. Culture and the code of ethics among boys, which encourage them to be tough and emotionless, explains much of the mild aggression found among children. School and the peer group are additional important sources of influence, as they provide failing experiences in both the academic and social arenas, which in turn increase frustration. In the absence of skills to cope with such stressful situations, children tend to use aggression as a coping mechanism.

Finally, in order to treat aggressive children, it is perhaps most important to understand their underlying characteristics. This chapter identified and discussed four main characteristics of aggressive children and adolescents: verbal deficits, lack of empathy, perceptual problems, and difficulties with self-control. Clearly, an intervention for aggressive youngsters must address all four of these components. Therapy with these children should help them reconnect to their real emotions, giving up some of their classical defensive reactions (e.g., "I am only responding to his threat"). Therapy should help children express their real emotions (e.g., "I am afraid, I am angry"). In one of our groups of aggressive children, Greg explained to the group how he felt about going to the doctor: "I hit a chair, I almost killed my sister, so afraid I was of getting a shot." An effective program should *also* help aggressive children be more empathic to the suffering of their victims, because empathy buffers aggression. You cannot hurt someone if you are aware of his suffering and care about him.

> A group I worked with included Stephanie, the perpetrator, and Patricia, her victim. In one session, Patricia was able to disclose her suffering. She went through a cathartic experience, after which several girls sided with her. She then was courageous enough to point to her perpetrator, directly accusing her of bullying. At first, Stephanie aggressively resisted the accusations and blamed Patricia for being weak, but then she revealed her own insecurities: "You bring it on yourself. You have to be strong; otherwise, people will take advantage of you. I know what it means to be in that place; I never want to go back there." She then admitted that she has chosen to be on the side of power, and that bullying others gives her that position. But following that session, she stopped bullying Patricia and actually became her protector outside the group as well. For Stephanie, two mechanisms were at work: she was able to connect to her real feelings and speak about them, and she had an opportunity to hear clear and direct emotional messages from her victim, which seem to have awakened some empathy towards her.

Perceptual problems must also be addressed in a therapeutic program with aggressive children. They need to be trained to see a social conflict from a wider perspective, to attribute nonhostile intentions to others, to respect power for what it truly is, to forgive and be forgiven, and to find better alternatives to aggression.

I know a teacher who, during an open day for parents, said to one girl who walked over to sharpen her pencil without permission: "If I looked like you, I would never get up in front of this many people." This was a terribly aggressive remark and atypical of her, so I asked: "Why did you say that?" With tears in her eyes, she responded: "When I was 12, my parents divorced. Since then, I have learned that, in the face of any threat, I have to prevent it from escalating. I guess I was worried about discipline in front of all these parents."

Finally, an effective program must help children control their behavior. This is not easy, as temperament and learned patterns of behavior are difficult to modify. This requires motivation and time. I recall many children who admitted that, though they try, it does not always work for them.

Jeff would tell his counselor every session of his success in controlling himself. One day he said: "I did not talk back to the teacher when she yelled at me. I did not hit the winning soccer team; even though I was angry, I just walked away. But, when Joe called my sister names, I couldn't stand it. I felt I had to protect her."

All these themes, will be further discussed in later chapters. However, based on this chapter, it becomes clear that reducing child and adolescent aggression is a demanding endeavor that requires us to challenge well-established attachment styles, beliefs, norms, and habits. We need to provide a corrective socialization process, corrective interpersonal experiences, new perceptions, and new skills, all to a population of clients who are not really enthusiastic about therapy. Bibliotherapy can help us achieve these goals because of its unique characteristics. In the next chapter, I discuss the method of bibliotherapy, which I offer here as a major adjunct to psychotherapeutic treatment of aggressive children and youth.

Chapter 2
Bibliotherapy as a Method of Treatment

Introduction

The idea of healing through books is not new; it can be traced far back, to the first libraries in ancient Greece. Use of the term "bibliotherapy" goes back to the beginning of the twentieth century, when Crothes (1916) labeled it as such. Most of us recognize the power of therapeutic reading. We find ourselves entering the world described in the pages of a good book or appearing in the scenes of a good movie, and we become involved with the characters. We feel happy or sad, we cry with the character who suffers, we want the good ones to cope and the bad ones to be punished; we really care. We usually end up gaining new insights and ideas for our own lives as well. Just reading high-quality literature, then, is a healing process that can enrich our selves.

The use of books for treatment purposes received special and widespread attention following World Wars I and II. With many soldiers returning from battle with posttraumatic disorders or symptoms, bibliotherapy was considered a cost-effective treatment. Since then, the use of bibliotherapy has expanded and is currently employed in nearly every helping profession, with every age group, and with multiple populations. Bibliotherapy is used by school counselors (Gladding, 2005), social workers (Pardeck, 1998), mental health nurses (Frankas & Yorker, 1993), teachers (Kramer & Smith, 1998), and librarians (Bernstein, 1989).

A wide range of issues and problems are addressed through bibliotherapy. Many use books in character-education programs (Kilpatrick, Wolfe, & Wolfe, 1994); others use them for more specific difficulties, such as death and dying (Todahl, Smith, Barnes, & Pereira, 1998), and divorce (Kramer & Smith, 1998). Treatment of aggression in this manner, however, has not been researched earlier, and perhaps is being introduced for the first time in this book.

The term bibliotherapy is made up of two words: *biblio*, originating from the Greek word *biblus* (book), and *therapy*, referring to psychological help. Simply stated, bibliotherapy can be defined as the use of books to help people solve problems. *Webster's Dictionary* (1985, p. 148) defines it as "guidance in the solution of personal problems through reading." Berry (1978) provides a more comprehensive definition: "a family of techniques for structuring interaction

Z. Shechtman, *Treating Child and Adolescent Aggression Through Bibliotherapy*,
The Springer Series on Human Exceptionality, DOI 10.1007/978-0-387-09745-9_2,
© Springer Science+Business Media, LLC 2009

between a facilitator and a participant ... based on their mutual sharing of literature." Baker's (1987) definition is more clinical; he suggests that bibliotherapy is the use of literature and poetry in the treatment of people with emotional or mental illness.

All the above definitions share one common thread: Bibliotherapy requires some form of reading. But not all agree if the reading should be fiction or nonfiction (Pardeck, 1998), and there is a clear split among therapists regarding the amount of therapy required and therapist involvement. The amount of therapy falls on a continuum, from self-help books at one extreme, in which the book is the major therapeutic agent and the involvement of a therapist is minimal, to bibliotherapy as an adjunct to therapy, in which the therapy process is the major therapeutic agent of change, with the book serving as a helping tool, and the involvement of a therapist is critical. These differences in the amount of therapy in bibliotherapy treatment have been influenced mostly by the theoretical orientation of the therapists. Indeed, this difference in theoretical orientations is responsible for the split between two major schools of bibliotherapy: "cognitive" and "affective."

As cognitive therapists perceive learning processes as the major mechanisms of change, nonfiction written material for educating individuals has been elected as the form to treat people. It can be a written program, even a computerized program, as long as it guides individuals to improve their functioning and to solve their problems (Tallman & Bohart, 1999), and it is usually administered as a self-help therapy, with no therapist involved or with minimal therapist contact.

In contrast, affective bibliotherapy originates from psychodynamic theories that can be traced back to Freud. It refers to the use of written materials to uncover repressed thoughts, feelings, and experiences. It is assumed that while the character works through a problem, readers are emotionally involved in the struggle and ultimately achieve insight into their own situation (Shrodes, 1957). Strong emphasis is placed on the promotion of emotional responses through identification with the experiences that the literary figures undergo. To permit such identification processes to happen, fictional literature is needed—fiction of literary merit, so that it can mirror a person's dilemmas, and help him or her to connect to the emotions and pain with minimum fear (Gersie, 1997; Gladding, 2005). High-quality literature is essential, as a poorly written novel with stereotyped characters and simplistic answers to complex questions is probably worse than no reading at all. As affective bibliotherapy deals with deep emotions and experiences, it cannot be a self-help treatment and definitely requires the involvement of a therapist.

Cognitive Bibliotherapy

It is not surprising that cognitive bibliotherapy is getting so much attention nowadays. We are functioning in a world in which cognitive-behavioral therapies dominate the field of psychology. This is particularly because they produce more empirical data, thus establishing them as evidence-based therapies—which is sought now, more than ever (Norcross, Beutler, & Levant, 2006).

Cognitive bibliotherapy is an old practice that started at the beginning of the 20th century, with psychiatrists and librarians cooperating in efforts to help clients with psychological problems. They would offer patients' books that fit their unique difficulties, assuming that these people would learn from the process and apply it to their own lives. This could be the sole treatment or in conjunction with medication. It could also be completely self-help or followed by occasional meetings to discuss the book. However, the main focus was on the content presented in the book and its relevance to a person's difficulties or problems.

The basic assumption of cognitive-behavioral therapies is that all behaviors are learned, and therefore can be relearned with proper guidance. These theories, thus, rely on learning as the ultimate catalyst of behavior change. Along these lines, cognitive bibliotherapy is the process of learning from high-quality written material (not necessarily literature) for therapeutic benefit (Glasgow & Rosen, 1978). This is perceived as an educationally oriented form of intervention, in which mastering information and acquisition of skills are the main goals. In principle, cognitive bibliotherapy is a self-help intervention in which the absence or minimization of the therapist is a major characteristic. It can be a no-contact intervention, which mirrors what happens in the real world of the reader, or it can be a minimal-contact intervention involving telephone calls or occasional visits to a clinic, with the understanding that the major therapeutic work is to be done by participants on their own (Glasgow & Rosen, 1978). There are thousands of self-help books on the market and many consumers use them, but not every self-help book is considered bibliotherapy. Only when a specific program or treatment exists is it considered bibliotherapy material (McKendree-Smith, Floyd, & Scogin, 2003).

Studies of Cognitive Bibliotherapy Treatments

A major area of cognitive bibliotherapy practice is in the treatment of depression. When treating depression, it is crucial that clients learn to understand and modify their cognition and behavior. A book that is often used with depressed clients is *Feeling Good* (Burns, 1980). This is an informative book, and the assumption is that clients will be guided by the knowledge presented within it. Indeed, most of the empirical work on cognitive bibliotherapy was conducted with clients with depression, using this particular book. The first study (Scogin, Jamison, & Gochneaur, 1989) compared three groups: Experimental (clients read *Feeling Good*), placebo (clients read *Man's Search for Meaning*; Frankl, 1959), and no treatment. The first group improved significantly more in terms of reduction of depression symptoms. Two additional studies (Floyd et al., 2004) compared cognitive bibliotherapy treatment with 15 sessions of individual treatment and with wait-list participants (control group). In both studies, bibliotherapy was found superior to control, with no differences between the treatment types. A follow-up measurement 2 years later indicated that treatment effects were durable and there was no decline in scores from posttreatment to follow-up. However, in the bibliotherapy treatment, participants had significantly more recurrences of depression during the follow-up period.

The comparison of bibliotherapy with individual treatment is important, as it points to the effectiveness and cost effectiveness of the former intervention. If we can replace 15 sessions of treatment with a self-help book, that is impressive. But the first study (Scogin, Jamison, & Gochneaur, 1989) is even more important, as it argues that not every book can be helpful. Even an inspiring book like Frankl's had a lessened effect on participants. This supports the basic assumption of cognitive bibliotherapists that the book has to be informative and directly relevant to the difficulties of the treated persons. More importantly, it suggests that the book itself makes a unique contribution to the healing process. Despite the less stable effect of bibliotherapy, the general conclusion of these studies is that cognitive bibliotherapy is an efficacious method of treatment, particularly with issues of depression in adults (see review by McKendree-Smith et al., 2003).

Other areas in which cognitive therapy has been investigated include smoking and drinking, but the effect of bibliotherapy in these areas is less clear. In a review of the literature, Mains and Scogin (2003) conclude that treatment of depression via cognitive bibliotherapy is supported more than habit-control problems. However, these results pertain to an adult population, actually elderly patients. The results cannot be generalized to children and adolescents.

There is one study that was conducted on adolescents with depression symptoms (Ackerson, Scogin, McKendree-Smith, & Lyman, 1998), using the same book (*Feeling Good*) read in the previous studies. Compared to a delayed-treatment control condition, the treatment adolescents improved more on depression symptoms, and this effect was sustained at the 1-month follow-up. However, no change in actual behavior, as assessed by parents, was found. Moreover, 8 of the 30 participants did not complete the study. Thus, although the researchers conclude that cognitive bibliotherapy is a promising avenue for treatment of adolescent depression, this must be stated with reservations.

With the exception of the work produced by Scogin and colleagues, which indicated positive results of cognitive bibliotherapy, existing reviews of the literature on self-help bibliotherapy show mixed results (for a review, see Pardeck, 1998; Riordan & Wilson, 1989). Several studies suggest that self-help books were effective in changing ineffective adolescent behavior, while others did not find improvement in the very same areas of functioning. What resounds more loudly than the outcomes is the drop-out rates of self-help treatments. Glasgow and Rosen (1978) reported a drop-out rate of 50% of the patients. Zeiss (1978) went much further, reporting that none of the self-help treatment patients completed the program in his study. This is a major concern for therapists who treat children and adolescents.

Drawbacks of Cognitive Bibliotherapy

Self-directed treatments place more of the treatment responsibility on the client. Thus, the ability to utilize written materials and work independently is critical. Indeed, poorly educated clients had higher rates of discontinuation, and those with higher levels of learned resourcefulness did much better (Scogin, Hamblin, & Beutler, 1989). Moreover, individuals with an externalizing style of coping did worse in the self-directed treatment (Beutler et al., 1991). This method is also unsuitable for individuals with extensive interpersonal problems, emotional avoidance, and severe symtomatology (Mains & Scogin, 2003).

Motivation is another key factor in treatment success with self-help books. One really needs to want to overcome the difficulties, long-term habits, and temptations in order to make use of what the written material teaches. This precondition is unlikely to hold in the treatment of aggression. Motivation to change is low, as aggression often serves the aggressor as a vehicle for catharsis. Moreover, the aggressor is likely to perceive giving up aggression as surrendering power, a main component of the aggressive behavior.

Another difficulty with cognitive bibliotherapy is that comprehension of the written material requires intellectual and emotional maturity, and distortion of perceptions may result. Even the reading level may be a problem for some. Mains and Scogin (2003) indeed recommend that cognitive bibliotherapy of a self-help type be best seen as a "first step" in the provision of mental health services.

Another criticism raised against self-help bibliotherapy is the quality of the books. *Feeling Good* was the book most frequently used, and the conclusion regarding this particular book is that it is effective and does not harm readers. Yet, many books lack adequate validation, and some of them may even be dangerous, claims Rosen (1981). We don't know yet how readers are affected by a certain book—positively, negatively, or no change. We also don't know which books are effective and which are not.

Because of the disadvantages outlined above, most therapists prefer some type of contact with clients, and this is particularly true in working with children. Indeed, very little pure self-help cognitive bibliotherapy has been used with children and adolescents. Instead, most of the cognitive bibliotherapy relevant to children has been targeted to training the parents of children with problems, such as conduct disorder (Webster-Stratton, Hollinsworth, & Kolpacoff, 1989), rather than the children themselves. This is quite understandable. Children may not have the cognitive and emotional ability to learn from reading on their own. They often do not have the motivation to change, and they have not yet developed a strong enough ego that can help them control their behavior. Monitoring by a therapist is required to help them gain the most out of their reading materials. It is recommended, therefore, to use bibliotherapy in the treatment of children and adolescents only as an adjunct to the therapist's treatment, and not as a replacement (Elgar & McGrath, 2003; Gladding, 2005; Holman, 1996).

Affective Bibliotherapy

Most of the existing literature on bibliotherapy with children is of affective bibliotherapy (Gladding, 2005). Affective bibliotherapy uses fiction and other high-quality literature to help the reader connect to emotional experiences and human situations through the process of identification. In contrast to cognitive bibliotherapy, affective bibliotherapy relies on psychodynamic theories, some tracing back to Sigmund and Anna Freud. The basic assumption in affective bibliotherapy is that people use defense mechanisms, such as repression, to protect themselves from pain. When such defenses are activated often, individuals become disconnected from their emotions, unaware of their true feelings, and therefore unable to resolve their problems constructively. Stories are helpful in offering insight into personal problems (Forgan, 2002) through the creation of a safe distance, bringing the child and adolescent indirectly to the edge of sensitive issues, issues that are threatening, and probably too painful to face directly (Corr, 2003/4).

Another assumption of affective bibliotherapy is that identifying, exploring, and reflecting on emotions are important components of the therapeutic process (Greenberg, 2002; Hill, 2005). Through identification with literary characters, individuals are exposed to a wide range of emotions, of which they can recognize something in themselves, thus reconnecting to their own emotional world. Experiencing is enhanced through the richness of human life, characters, situations, and problems that the literature presents.

There is a great amount of psychological wisdom incorporated in such books. Yalom (1998) argued that psychology started long before the advent of science methods, with novelists such as Tolstoy. As Kottler (1986) stated, "Without Shakespeare's plays, Dostoyevsky's novels, or James's short stories, our knowledge of anguish and conflict would be hollow, our self-revelation would be one-dimensional" (p. 35). High-quality literature presents a wide range of human thoughts and emotions that readers can identify with, learn from, and apply to their own lives. Such literature goes beyond fictional stories. For example, a great deal of poetry expresses subtle and overt psychological insights about life situations that clients may come to personalize into their own lives. Similarly, films exhibit psychological situations, dilemmas, and conflicts that people can easily identify with.

Benefits of Affective Bibliotherapy

True self-knowledge and a greater understanding of the world may emerge following interaction with literature. Clients realize that their problems are universal, as well as unique. They learn that they share a connectedness with many other people and cultures, which provide comfort and legitimizes their feelings and thoughts (Gladding, 2005). Listening to or reading stories addresses a basic human need to discover the truth, to understand, to find an explanation for painful experiences, and even to challenge injustice or lack of meaning.

In the process, the reader or listener is believed to pass through three stages: *identification* with the character and events in the story; *catharsis*, where the reader becomes emotionally involved in the story and is able to release pent-up emotions under safe conditions; and *insight* resulting from the cathartic experience, whereby readers may become aware of their problems and of possible solutions for them. When people read or listen to a story or poem or watch a movie in which human beings display their vulnerability, weaknesses, and strengths, they tend to identify with the characters' experiences, suffering, and pain, as well as their happiness. Through this identification process, the individual shares feelings and conflicts with the characters and experiences catharsis. These stories enhance understanding of the human situation and increase empathy for the suffering of others, which eventually may help individuals understand themselves better.

This in itself can be a corrective emotional experience; such experiences are necessary for people who did not have enough positive emotional experiences in their lives or who suffered from tragic events. Particularly in situations of crisis, people become so involved in their pain that they see no meaning or resolution to their situation. The literature provides a context to explore that pain from a distance (Gersie, 1997). Looking at life's circumstances at arm's length may help individuals to deal with the complexity of their situation with less defensiveness, allowing understanding, and insight to grow. This is not merely a cognitive understanding, but rather an experiential one, based on the opening of internal-communication processes and touching repressed experiences.

> I once worked with a group of teachers, using a story about a father who had overly high expectations of his 4-year-old son to excel academically. His expectations were beyond the ability of such a young child, and although he was usually proud of his son's achievements, he also used threatening methods of education when the child did not meet his expectations. One day the father decided to test the child in telling time. His son figured out the logic of the small hand showing the hours, but had a hard time grasping the function of the large hand that showed the minutes. When he failed the test, his father became very frustrated and hit the child.

As soon as I finished reading the story, Cheryl, a group member, said:

> It is just like in my home. I work intensively with my kids on their homework and I get very frustrated when they disappoint me. I get angry at them in a very mean way, you know. I scream, I threaten, and sometimes I even hit them. . . .I can now see the horror in their eyes, and I am so ashamed of myself.

This was already an emotional experience, through which Cheryl understood how unconstructive her behavior was, but also did not feel good about herself. To turn it into a positive experience for her, the discussion had to be directed such that she would better understand why she behaves that way (develop insight), and this needed to occur in a therapeutic context, with no criticism or blame. We went on discussing the possible reasons for the father to act as he did, even though it was illogical. Cheryl interpreted his behavior as the need to show off, to show how successful he and his family is. Later, she made the connection to her own life, saying: "I teach in the same school that my kids attend. My fellow teachers know me as a very strict and demanding teacher; I cannot afford less than excellence on their part." The group's understanding and acceptance of her feelings made her reconcile her behavior at home, as her response reflects: "My children do not have to pay the price of my ambitions; I do not like what I do to them."

As we see in this illustration, the distance from the individual's problems created by the literature also nurtures constructive thinking and a basis for creative problem solving. This is one reason that legends and fairy tales make particularly good materials to help children, says Bettelheim (1977), being extremely distant from reality makes them a particularly safe ground for the exploration of one's own feelings. They also offer unexpected resolutions to serious problems, thus providing hope in extremely difficult situations, as well as alternative solutions. The next example is drawn from my experience with fairy tales.

> I once worked with Randy, a 6-year-old boy who was on probation for adoption into a family that had already adopted his older brother. He seemed to have some learning disabilities and the family was not sure they could cope, so they took him in for a one-year trial period and provided him with plenty of academic and emotional support. This poor child had six teachers and therapists, each working on a different area. But Randy was so anxious that he could hardly cooperate with any of them. He was extremely withdrawn and depressed and it was hard to communicate with him. In response, a student therapist decided to use bibliotherapy, and she read to him the story of Cinderella. When she got to the place where Cinderella worked so hard to clean and cook, Randy whispered, "it's just like me." This was the first time he could talk about his anxiety, referring to his fears that, despite all the effort he was investing, he would eventually be placed back in a foster home. He was afraid of failing the test and having to separate again from his brother.

The Need for a Therapist

Arguably, these processes of identification with literary characters, followed by cathartic experiences, insight, and action, may occur in everyday experiences without therapy. Bennett (1998) points to two things good stories provide: A code of conduct (honesty) and good examples. Books provide a ground for moral judgment and comparison, and help children sort out right and wrong. They help them develop a sense that alerts them when something is morally wrong. Books also provide models for identification. Bettelheim (1977) observed that, for a child, the question "Who do I want to be like?" is more important than "Do I want to be good?" (p. 10). Identifying with a positive model is thus an important step in child development.

However, because the process does not rely on cognitive learning alone, but rather seeks to uncover repressed or unconscious materials, the presence of a therapist is crucial. The infinite richness of complexity, which is an advantage of affective bibliotherapy, may be overwhelming, threatening, and anxiety provoking. Moreover, books may also model undesirable behavior. Finally, the information conveyed to the reader may be misunderstood, misinterpreted, and even distorted, particularly when children and adolescents and other high-risk populations are involved.

For example, we read a poem to groups of children who have suffered loss. In this poem, the character deals with the dilemma of being happy when she is expected to be sad. She feels guilty and ashamed for forgetting her father. This is a powerful poem, which presents the emotional dilemmas of mourning and also allows for a cathartic experience around the sense of loss. However, some children may identify with the literary character and conclude that they should literally not forget and never be happy. This is not the conclusion we want them to reach. Rather, we want to tell them that, at the initial stage of mourning, people feel that they will never be able to get back to normal life. This is a normal feeling that fades with time. We also want them to know that it is alright to feel happy sometimes, that having fun does not mean they have forgotten their loved one. Moreover, when it is a parent who died, we may want to tell the child that he or she would have liked to see the child happy. We also want to clarify to the children that people around them do not expect them to be sad all the time, and even if they do (as is the norm in some cultures), they can choose to reject this norm.

> We once read this poem to a group of adolescent girls, one of whom was an Ethiopian immigrant to Israel. Mira's mother had died while giving birth to her on the long journey to Israel; hence, her birthday was also her mother's memorial day. The group was talking about birthday parties when Mira mentioned that she has never celebrated her birthday. She didn't think it was appropriate; her father was so sad on that day that she felt it was only expected of her to join him in mourning. Following the discussion of this poem, a psychodrama was played out with another girl playing her mom. In her talk with Mira, her mom told her how proud she is of her, begged her to be happy in her life, and promised to continue watching her. In the next session, Mira reported to the group that she had celebrated her birthday with a few close friends and that it was the happiest day in her life. She also brought a cake to celebrate her birthday with the group. Without the therapist's intervention, a poem like this might have reinforced Mira's sadness despite the cathartic experience that she might have had as a result of identification with the literary figure.

It is the therapist's role to encourage the identification process, to alleviate emotions and express them, and to help the clients discuss and understand these emotions in a nonjudgmental way. An accepting attitude toward a literary figure conveys an important message to the client—namely, that emotions are accepted and understood. This in itself is therapeutic, as at the same time it legitimizes the client's feelings. When the discussion becomes more personal, the therapist also sends a direct message of acceptance to the client. These processes lead to a corrective emotional experience that allows for cathartic experiences and reflection on these experiences.

> In a group of teacher trainees we read a poem about an indecisive person who finds himself in a dead-end situation. The group brought up feelings of confusion,

frustration, and helplessness on the part of the literary character, and discussed reasons that led him to this situation. Issues such as a high sense of responsibility, the need to be compliant, and fear of being judged or rejected came up.

Sarah was particularly active in this discussion, providing insight into the situation, and later admitted that she identifies with the person in the poem. She then disclosed that she has a hard time in her practicum experience; she does not get along with her supervising teacher, who is extremely judgmental and belittling. This had been going on for 6 months.

I was quite surprised to hear this from a relatively older student, one of the best students in class. As I was also in charge of the program, I asked her "Why haven't you said anything for such a long time?" Her reaction was "I was ashamed that I can't get along with an authority figure. But when you expressed understanding and acceptance of that person in the story, I felt you would understand me, too." In this case, it was clearly the literature that brought up the emotions and the understanding, but the therapist was also an agent in this triangle of client, literature, and therapist, helping the client through acceptance of the literary figure.

The therapist's intervention in the interaction between participant and literature is particularly important when working with children and adolescents. The counselor is responsible for the safe climate of the bibliotherapy process, as in any other therapy, and must ensure that the literature is well understood and not distorted through the young reader's private experiences. The therapist must also sustain the reader's curiosity in the complexity of life and encourage participants to encounter and challenge life events. Therefore, I recommend using bibliotherapy as an adjunct to therapy, in which a triadic connection is fostered between the literature, participants, and counselor. The distance between the client and his or her problem created by the literature helps the therapist to guide the child to deal with troubling issues with more safety and less defensiveness and resistance.

Levels of Projection and Forms of Bibliotherapy Materials

The literature produces projection of thoughts and feelings by participants, but there are differences in the level of projection, depending on the materials involved. The story form is a powerful structure used to organize experiences. The sequence of events generally includes a beginning that sets out what is happening and what has led to the events. The middle of the story often adds complexities in the relationships among the characters, raising thoughts and feelings, while the ending ties up the feelings and events of the story (Teglasi & Rothman, 2001). Stories, therefore, are quite directive in channeling the client to a specific theme and set of emotions.

A story of an abusive father was read to a group of elementary-school children. Roger seemed to be extremely hyperactive and was acting out, and at a certain point rushed out of class angrily. He then came back to the counselor during the break, pleading to remain in the group. He apologized to her for his disrupting behavior and explained that the story brought up emotions that he could not handle in the group without crying, which he did not want. Roger disclosed his horrible secret of being abused by his father, following which the counselor took legal action. In this situation it is clearly the story itself that brought up all those strong emotions. It was good that a therapist was there to provide a holding environment for the child, as well as to offer instrumental help.

Poetry therapy is another method to help people deal with their emotions and conflicts. "It has the kind of variety and indeterminacy, richness, and flexibility that could make it privileged ground for experiencing with human potentialities and responses, redeeming the past, assimilating the present, and projecting the future" (Mazza, 2003, p. 3). In contrast to stories, poems are more ambiguous, and therefore less directive, making it is easier to project different thoughts and feelings on them.

A poem was read to a group of children who had each suffered the loss of parent. One of the lines in the poem was: "As long as I live, I will never forget and I will never forgive." Some children interpreted it as anger expressed toward God, while others understood it as anger expressed to the deceased person. Both interpretations are, of course, correct, depending on the child's particular experiences.

Finally, pictures tell a story without words. The more abstract or ambiguous pictures are, the less directive they are, and hence the less restrictive to projection. Thus, not only do they allow for individual reactions, but they are also highly effective in analyzing a child's problem.

> I often use a picture of a child lying in bed with a grownup standing next to her. I once used it in a group of elementary-school girls from a very disadvantaged background. Several children thought that it was the mother standing at the bed, saying goodnight to her daughter. But Kathy insisted that the girl is in the hospital and it is the nurse who is coming to give her a shot. She then explained that she was recently hospitalized and that her mom never came to visit or tuck her in; only a nurse stayed by her side. It is obvious that Kathy projected her experiences on the picture, but she also increased her experience through the reactions of the other girls in her group.

Included in the category of pictures are therapeutic cards. Therapeutic cards are a special genre of games based on association and communication. "They serve as a springboard into imagination and creativity, a tool for learning and a catalyst with potential for directing its players into intense communication about themselves" (Kirschke, 1998, p. 11). This is an interactive game between the player and his or her cards, in which the individual associates with or projects onto the cards. These cards do not have an objective meaning; whatever each player sees in them is valid and should not be interpreted by others.

> In the first session of a group of adolescent at-risk girls, participants played with therapeutic cards. Carol selected a card with a forest on it, while Beth selected a card with a boat on a stormy sea. Carol elaborated on her choice, saying that the girl on her card feels quite confused and disturbed. She also shared her feelings of being unclear about her own goals. Beth felt that the girl in her picture has a difficult life and that she

does not believe she will make it to shore. She also shared with the group that the picture reminds her of how shaky her own life is. The two girls, as well as others in the group, projected their difficulties in life on the chosen pictures and started communicating about their problems.

In short, in affective bibliotherapy the therapist has the same role as in any other affective therapy; first and foremost, he or she is responsible for the therapeutic alliance and emotional bonding created with the client (Hill, 2005; Horvath, 2005; Prochaska, 1999). The therapist must lead the client to positive and corrective experiences in the therapy process. However, in bibliotherapy, the literature itself may provide opportunities for corrective positive experiences, through the identification process with characters in the literature. The combination of the literature and the therapist's responses turns the experience into a powerful one.

Research Supporting the Contribution of Affective Bibliotherapy

Compared to cognitive bibliotherapy, affective bibliotherapy has been less rigorously investigated, as are, in general, humanistic therapies compared to cognitive-behavioral therapies. In the case of bibliotherapy, research is especially problematic, because the literature is used as an adjunct to therapy. Researchers argue that it is hard, perhaps impossible, to separate the unique contribution of the particular bibliotherapy intervention from the effect of therapy in general (Reynolds, Nabors, & Quinlan, 2000).

The reviews that do exist show mixed results regarding the effectiveness of affective bibliotherapy. Pardeck and Pardeck (1984), in their literature review, found 24 studies supporting the positive use of fiction books in changing attitudes of clients, increasing client assertiveness, and changing behavior of clients. In another review, Riordan and Wilson (1989) point to inconsistent results, concluding that "Fiction, poetry and inspirational sources for bibliotherapy remain essentially unvalidated" (p. 507). A more recent review (Heath, Sheen, Leavy, Young, & Money, 2005), based on unpublished dissertations, also reports mixed results. They conclude that affective bibliotherapy is helpful when working with children and families dealing with loss and transition, in helping adopted children to adjust to their new families, and in enhancing interpersonal relationships, but it is not effective in improving social skills, in changing attitudes toward individuals with mental disabilities, or in decreasing test anxiety. Most of the studies that showed nonpositive results used bibliotherapy as a single method, rather than as an adjunct to therapy.

As an adjunctive method to treatment, two studies using bibliotherapy were performed by Hedy Teglasi. She used a classroom-based program called STORIES, targeting children with social skill deficits and a tendency to act aggressively. The focus of the intervention was on social problem-solving skills and social information processing. Stories such as "Secret of the Peaceful Warrior"

(Millman, 1984) were used to discuss children's behavior in situations of social conflict. In the first study (Teglasi & Rothman, 2001), fourth- and fifth-graders were divided into 12 small groups, and the story form was used as a vehicle to discuss issues of aggression, bullying, victims, and bystanders. The researchers found, based on teacher reports of externalizing behavior, a decrease in externalized and antisocial behavior only for the children not identified as aggressive. Although, when compared to a wait-list group of children, those identified as highly aggressive showed significantly more favorable scores, their scores on aggression nevertheless *increased* following the classroom intervention. Thus, it cannot be concluded from this study that bibliotherapy has a positive impact on aggressive children.

In the second study (Rahill & Teglasi, 2003), processes and outcomes of STORIES (bibliotherapy) were compared with a skills-training program called Skillstreaming (McGinnis & Goldstein, 1997). The advantage of this study is that it compares bibliotherapy to another treatment that does not use books and so can shed light on the unique contribution of literature in the therapy process. Results indicated more favorable outcomes for STORIES and higher-cognitive levels and changes across sessions, compared to the Skillstreaming program, but not differences in behavioral responses. In other words, the children gathered information and cognitive understanding when books were used, but they were unable to apply the gathered knowledge to real-life situations.

Taken together, the outcomes of these two studies provide only partial support of bibliotherapy. However, one should note that the STORIES intervention is largely based on cognitive therapy. The stories used included content that sets models and standards for appropriate behavior, which the children could use for their increased understanding of social situations. Much less of this program has been devoted to the internal world of the children, the emotional struggles, the frustrations, and the fears.

In my own work with aggressive children and adolescents, I have used an affective focus in work with books, with a great portion of the intervention devoted to the exploration of feelings, the development of insight, and action taken to change behavior. Results of outcome studies with this method will be presented in the next chapter, when I discuss the method of treatment. For now, I will provide results of the three studies aimed to evaluate the unique contribution of bibliotherapy to treatment outcomes. To achieve this goal, I compared treatments of the same theoretical orientation, where the only difference between experimental and control groups was the use of bibliotherapy as an adjunctive method. The three studies vary in terms of population, but most of the measures were identical, thus allowing for some generalization of results. I used the process of change (Prochaska, 1999) to track the stages of progress clients made, as well as the Client Behavior System (Hill & O'Brien, 1999) to evaluate clients' functioning in the therapeutic process. While both are considered process measures, they are also indicative of the progress clients make in the therapy process. These measures are of special value considering the difficult population involved in my three studies. For such clients, children and adults alike, questionnaires may be a less reliable method of measuring progress than process measures based on observational data.

Of Prochaska's (1999) six stages of change—precontemplation, contemplation, preparation, action, maintenance, and termination—the first two are indicative of no progress, the next two do point to progress, and the last two could not be measured in this short-term treatment. Clients who have reached the stage of preparation are motivated to change, which I consider a key factor in improvement, and those who have reached the stage of action have made actual attempts to alter their behavior. Even though these attempts do not always sustain with time, clients are considered in a more progressive stage of change when they are at least considering change, or make efforts to change, as compared to a state of a lack of awareness or of awareness with no motivation to take action.

The Client Behavior System (Hill & O'Brien, 1999) includes four behaviors indicative of less productive functioning in therapy (resistance, agreement, simple request, and recounting) and four behaviors that point to more productive functioning (cognitive exploration, affective exploration, insight, and therapeutic change). According to Hill (2005), in order for the therapy process to be effective, the client must go through cognitive and affective exploration, following which insight might develop, and therapeutic change eventually takes place. The last behavior, based on the client's report of change in behavior, is particularly important, as it is more than a process variable; it actually points to outcomes based on the client's perceptions.

In the first of the three studies (Shechtman, 2006a), 61 aggressive adolescents were randomly assigned to three conditions: bibliotherapy ($n = 24$), helping sessions ($n = 24$), and control-no treatment ($n = 13$). The two individual treatments were identical in respect to the theory orientation; their only difference was the addition of bibliotherapy as an adjunct to therapy. Results pointed to more favorable outcomes for bibliotherapy in terms of outcome and process measures alike. Both treatment groups had increased scores on empathy and decreased scores on aggression, as measured by self-reports and teacher reports, compared to the children who received no treatment, but those boys in bibliotherapy showed more favorable outcomes on empathy than those receiving helping sessions alone. Moreover, counselors who worked with bibliotherapy reported higher satisfaction with the process than counselors who employed the helping-session method. In terms of Prochaska's Change Process measure (Prochaska, 1999), more boys in the bibliotherapy treatment reached the more advanced stages of change—preparation and action—than did their peers in the helping sessions. Finally, boys in bibliotherapy had higher frequencies of insight and therapeutic change, as measured through the Client Behavior System (Hill & O'Brien, 1999). The use of multiple measures, some based on observation, adds validity to these results, which, taken as a whole, suggest that bibliotherapy makes a unique contribution to the therapy success.

The finding that therapists feel more satisfied with bibliotherapy treatment is interesting. I attribute this result to the written materials used, which provided a framework for discussion, thus helping children to express themselves and therapists to navigate the discussion. When para-professionals or less trained professionals are involved in the therapy (e.g., teachers), this is a particularly meaningful advantage.

The second, more recent study (Shechtman & Effrati, 2008) provides support for the higher client functioning in bibliotherapy conditions. Whereas in the earlier study, the population was randomly divided into treatment conditions (a routine procedure in experimental research), in this study I compared the two similar treatments, within the same population and with the same therapists, thus controlling for both client and therapist variables. Children were treated in both methods—bibliotherapy and helping skills—on a rotational basis; that is, bibliotherapy was employed every other session, out of a total of eight sessions. The study included 20 boys, within the age-group of 11–16 years. We measured differences between every two sessions (e.g., session 1 vs. session 2, session 3 vs. session 4), as well as differences across the four sessions of each treatment. We also accumulated scores for the four less productive client responses versus the four more productive ones. Results indicated that, overall, the less productive responses were more frequent in the helping sessions, while the more productive responses were more frequent in bibliotherapy. These differences were found between sessions 1 and 2, and between sessions 7 and 8. More specifically, of the less productive responses, only one difference was found on recounting, while of the productive responses, differences were found in cognitive exploration and therapeutic change. Thus, it appears that clients worked more effectively in bibliotherapy treatment, as they were engaged more in cognitive exploration and reported more therapeutic changes. This last finding is particularly important, as it points to behavior change as perceived by the children.

As in the earlier study, here, too, I compared the stages of change the children underwent. Although no significant difference was found between the two types of treatment sessions, the evidence suggests that boys remained in the precontemplation and contemplation stages during the helping sessions (10 children vs. 5 in helping sessions and bibliotherapy, respectively), while more children in bibliotherapy were at the preparation and action stages (8 children vs. 4 in bibliotherapy compared to helping sessions, respectively). The lack of significant differences may be attributed to the small sample size. The fact that more children in bibliotherapy reached the two higher stages in the change process points to the unique contribution of bibliotherapy. For, other than the use of bibliotherapy as an adjunctive method, the process was based on the same theory, employed the same therapists and was provided to the same clients.

Finally, the third study (Shechtman & Nir-Shafrir, 2007) was conducted with an adult inpatient population. The effect of affective group bibliotherapy was compared to affective group therapy, in three groups of about 10 members each. Each client from all three groups participated in both treatment types, undergoing three sessions in each of the two conditions. Functioning in therapy was assessed through Hill's and O'Brien's (1999) Client Behavior System. Results indicated that clients in the bibliotherapy condition were less resistant, used simple responses less frequently, and exhibited affective exploration more frequently than in the group therapy condition. In fact, resistance and simple response were twice as high in group therapy than in treatment by bibliotherapy. However, the greatest difference was found in affective exploration: In the first stage of treatment, clients in bibliotherapy responded with affective exploration 28% of the time, as opposed to 13% in group therapy, while in the last stage, the figures rose to 57% and 27%. These differences are highly impressive, particularly if we consider that about half of clients' responses were directed to the literature in the bibliotherapy sessions, and therefore not counted in the comparison. In other words, in bibliotherapy, affective exploration was twice as frequent in half the time.

In sum, whether in the treatment of individuals or groups, children or adults, clients in bibliotherapy seem to be more productive than in other comparable treatments. These results point to the contribution of bibliotherapy to the therapeutic process outcomes. I realize that process outcomes are not sufficient to rest the case in favor of bibliotherapy; however, as stipulated by Chambless and Cris-Christoph (2006), "Treatment methods are not where all the action is in relation to outcomes, but they are the logical place to intervene to improve care" (p. 200). Ogles, Anderson, and Lunnen (1999) conclude their review of methods with the recommendation to study the contribution of methods through process-oriented session-by-session evaluations, because they seem to provide a unique perspective for their usefulness. Outcome research follows in the next chapter.

Summary

Reading books to children and by children is a common practice that has intellectual, emotional, and social benefits. Kilpatrick and colleagues (1994) mention several reasons for using bibliotherapy for character education:

> First, because stories can create an emotional attachment to goodness, a desire to do the right thing. Second, because stories provide a wealth of good examples—the kind of examples that are often missing from a child's day-to-day environment. Third, because stories familiarize youngsters with the codes of conduct they need to know. Finally, because stories help to make sense of life, help us cast our own lives as stories. And unless this sense of meaning is acquired at an early age and reinforced as we grow older, there simply is no moral growth. (p. 18)

However, bibliotherapy goes beyond character education. Children and adolescents are vulnerable young people who often have no one to turn to for help with their everyday difficulties or more serious crisis situations. The richness of literature may be an important source to help them understand human interactions, increase their sensitivity, and enhance their empathy. In reading literature, children identify with the character. They create an emotional bond with them and see them from the inside; they live with them, hurt with them, and learn a new respect for people. Books broaden children's minds and give them a larger picture of the world and its habitants (Kilpatrick et al., 1994). Through the imaginative process that reading involves, children have the opportunity to do what they often cannot do in real life—become thoroughly involved in the inner lives of others, better understand them, and eventually become more aware of themselves. Indeed, in their work with children and adolescents, psychologists, social workers, school counselors, and teachers all use books and films to further their well-being and improve therapeutic outcomes.

In the past, children's books were mostly of a didactic type, which made them appropriate for cognitive bibliotherapy. But modern books are different; they are complex, rich in feelings, beliefs, and values. The advantage of such literature is that it can address the various difficulties children currently face. The disadvantage is that overly rich literature may add to the confusion that children experience. To address properly the emotional complexity of the literary figures, children need assistance, supervision, and guidance. Therefore, I suggest affective bibliotherapy as an adjunct to integrative therapy. Based on my studies, there is merit to affective bibliotherapy, although further research is needed to turn this into a scientific conclusion. Such research will be further provided in the next chapter, in which the connection between bibliotherapy and treatment of aggression is discussed. The effect of bibliotherapy on aggressive behavior has not been investigated in the past. This is my own creative attempt, and that of my colleagues, to address childhood and adolescent aggression.

Chapter 3
Bibliotherapy and Treatment of Aggression

The Rationale for Using Bibliotherapy with Aggressive Children

Aggressive children and adolescents all seem to be struggling with a range of internal and external conflicts. Some are conscious of the reasons for their aggression and its consequences, while others are not. Bullies do tend to be conscious of their behavior and its repercussions, yet get gratification from inflicting harm on others (Olweus, 1993). Proactive aggressors are directed toward achieving certain goals, but are not always conscious of the possible consequences of their actions, or are unwilling to restrain themselves. Reactive aggressors respond impulsively and often are unaware of what caused their aggression or what the consequences might be (Dodge & Schwartz, 1997).

Whether the aggressive children are conscious of their aggressive behavior or not, they do not intend to give it up easily, each type for their own reasons. For the bullies, ceasing their aggression means relinquishing secondary gratifications, such as excitement, fun, and power. If we also consider that they have an obvious deficit in perspective-taking skills and empathy, and that their moral level of reasoning (Horne, Stoddard, & Bell, 2008) is quite low, it is clear that they have little motivation to change their behavior.

Proactive aggressors also have many secondary gratifications. Their use of force enables them to achieve their designated goal, thus reinforcing their aggression. Reinforcements and rewards are also achieved through the powerful status such aggressors hold. As they are hostile and threatening, even dangerous, few people are willing to take the risk of standing in their way. Many of them are also angry and rebellious individuals, resisting authority. With the absence of moral values, this group of aggressors is difficult to change (Gurian, 1997). Aggression works well for them; why give it up?

Finally, reactive aggressors often use moral reasoning and express remorse after their aggressive act. Their main problem is that they do not foresee their violent reaction, as their level of awareness is low. They act from the defensive standpoint of a victim, interpreting their response as self-defense. Unable to control their impulses, they often feel shame and guilt following an aggressive act, and regret their negative behavior. But for the moment, aggression serves as

Z. Shechtman, *Treating Child and Adolescent Aggression Through Bibliotherapy*,
The Springer Series on Human Exceptionality, DOI 10.1007/978-0-387-09745-9_3,
© Springer Science+Business Media, LLC 2009

a cathartic experience, so they cannot inhibit their urge to act aggressively. They often feel weak and helpless, and find it difficult to change their already established pattern of response.

It appears that all types of aggressors receive some gratification from their aggressive behavior; however, their aggression also exacts a price. Although many of their peers do not object to their behavior and even support it directly or indirectly, others criticize, and even reject it. Adults tend to be angry at them for their lack of concern for others and their poor moral judgment, and often end up punishing them. While bullies spawn mostly anger in others, proactive aggressors create fear in peers and adults alike, and reactive aggressors arouse dislike. Rejection seems to be what they all receive from normative society.

Yet, boys and girls—and this includes aggressive adolescents—need to belong socially. Gurian (1997), in his famous book, *The Wonder of Boys*, suggests that boys need a tribe to grow up with, but nowadays, as we have only nuclear families, a group is needed to teach boys to reach manhood. Aggressive boys, out of their deep sense of loneliness and rejection, usually hook up with a deviant group that holds similar values of power endorsement. Nevertheless, they do not remain blind to social rejection. Finally, reactive aggressors pay a double price: They are aware of the rejection of their peers, who consider them unpredictable and sometimes "crazy" people, but they also suffer from internal conflicts as a result of the shame, guilt, and anxiety that they experience.

Despite the social and emotional prices that aggressive children pay, they are usually less conscious of the costs and more conscious of the benefits, or they act based on patterns of behavior they have internalized. No wonder, then, that the literature considers aggressive behavior as persistent and resistant to change (Huesmann & Reynolds, 2001). Nevertheless, the price they pay to society always remains in the back of their minds. Hence, although aggressive children and youth appear strong, confrontational, and threatening, they are actually confused, anxious, lonely, and rejected, sometimes helpless. They are constantly on guard, feeling that they need to protect themselves from criticism and blame, and they do not trust others, or even themselves. The aim of treatment, therefore, is first and foremost to overcome such defensiveness, raise their motivation to change, and help them become cooperative in the change process. Bibliotherapy serves just this goal.

As described in Chapter 2, bibliotherapy is an indirect method that can be helpful in the treatment of child and adolescent aggression. Looking at life's circumstances from a distance may help individuals to deal with the complexity of the situation with less defensiveness, allowing understanding, and insight to grow. We have also seen that literature nurtures constructive thinking and is a basis for creative problem solving (Gladding, 2005). With children, bibliotherapy is even a better match than with adults. Children, in general, and aggressive children in particular, do not love therapy, but they do love stories, songs, and films. Gurian (1997) argues further that all children love and need stories, but boys are desperate for them:

Boys, as they get older, feel less and less able to compete in the emotional arena. They feel less and less emotionally astute and mature compared to the girls around them. Boys need stories and archetypes to give them an internal, reflective language for their feeling experiences. They need help from stories in accessing their feeling. Often a boy won't be able to talk about his feelings unless he has analogs, metaphors, and stories through which he can say, "I feel like the young man in the story." (p. 207)

Similarly, Pollack (1998, 2000) and Garbarino (1999) argue that boys feel incompetent emotionally, and need stories to give them an internal, reflective language for their feeling experiences. Aggressive boys, in particular, need stories because of their deficiencies in verbal expressiveness and their low empathy (Moeller, 2001).

Preaching to an aggressive boy that he must change rarely changes him. Even reinforcing a violent child for change in behavior seldom has long-term effects. I learned this from a group of delinquent teenagers in a corrections home for violent offenders, where they used behavioral modification as the main method of treatment. These teenagers indeed tried to behave according to expectations, so that they could earn some rewards. But when praised for their efforts, they responded that they will act this way only so long as they are in the corrections facility. "Once we get out, we will resume our normal behavior," they said. It seems that a more rigorous change is required—change in values, behavior, and even personality.

Although I agree that much of the aggression has been transmitted through the particular culture the child grew up in, and that scripts from past experiences govern present behavior (Eron, 1997; Huesmann & Reynolds, 2001; Dodge & Schwartz, 1997), I also believe that additional variables play a role. Cognitive theories fall short in explaining the anger, hatred, and hostility that characterize much of the aggressive behavior. There is a whole world of emotions that affects the aggressor's reactions. Experiences of neglect and abuse by one's own parents or other significant persons in one's environment raise a wealth of disturbing emotions, including fear, shame, guilt, and mistrust. These emotions must be addressed, yet they are usually deeply repressed and hence not easy to talk about. To be able to connect to those feelings, express them, and explore them, one needs a good literary piece and an excellent therapist.

As discussed earlier, aggressive young people are not motivated to give up their powerful position, often do not see their behavior as a problem, and, even when they do recognize the problem, they cannot control themselves. Such children cannot walk away with a book they are supposed to read, draw the expected conclusion from the story, and take action to change their behavior. I suspect that in self-help therapy, they are doomed to drop out of the program and fail, as many do (see review in Pardeck, 1998). To overcome these difficulties, a theory of change is needed, as well as a trained therapist, one who is skilled in following the integrative change model. I will discuss first the theory of change I offer, then the therapist's skills.

The Theoretical Foundation

Aggressive behavior is a complex phenomenon, which a single theory cannot explain or provide guidelines for treatment. I therefore employ an integrative theory of change that considers humanistic, psychodynamic, and cognitive-behavioral principles, adjusting to the change process of the individual. As the model of treatment is similar to Prochaska's (1999) change process, his six-stage model will serve as a frame of reference (see also Chapter 2). To illustrate the process of change, I will use the case of Joey, a highly aggressive boy.

Joey, aged 12, is chronically angry and often lashes out aggressively at anyone and everyone. His parents are divorced and his father has been highly abusive to his mother and to Joey. At one point, his mother even sought safety in a shelter for abused women, but went back home after a while. Joey's teacher has assessed him as the most aggressive student in the class, and referred him to the school counseling center where a small group for aggressive boys was established. There is one other aggressive classmate in this group, as well as three boys who were not considered aggressive and were invited into the group to serve as role models for the two aggressive group members. This is a routine policy in my group work with aggressive boys. I prefer heterogeneous groups, because it helps balance the level of aggression in the group process and upgrades the group discussion (Shechtman, 2007).

At the first session, during the getting acquainted activity, Joey expresses his great need to protect himself. When the children are asked to select one of the objects displayed in the room that is meaningful to them, he picks a rock, explaining: "I need to be ready for any incident." This is the philosophy, the world view, of this young man. He has learned that life is dangerous and that no one else will come to his defense unless he protects himself. The threat is constantly present in his life; he is alone and anxious, but pretends to be strong. Because he pretends to be strong, he is a threat to others, who, out of their own fear, dislike him, reject him, or even punish him. Such reactions only enhance the sense of isolation he experiences, confirming his philosophy of life that "people are out there to get you!"

In Prochaska's first stage of *precontemplation*, aggressive children are unaware of their aggression, mostly because they perceive it as common, acceptable behavior and even endorse it. "If someone attacks you, you must defend yourself" tends to be the line of thought. This is what they have experienced throughout their lives, and it is rationalized and supported by thoughts such as "If you don't hit back, you will become a target for further attacks"; "They will not appreciate you anymore"; "You will lose your powerful status"; "They will consider you a sissy"; "You will not be considered a man." It is obvious that, in terms of Prochaska's change process, Joey is at the precontemplation stage. He does not consider himself as an aggressor, but rather as a victim who needs to protect himself.

The next stage is *contemplation*. At this stage, children are aware of their aggression, but nevertheless continue to defend it. Such awareness may be a natural process, particularly for reactive children, whose behavior may be a hot-blooded, impulsive response to a threat that they subsequently regret. It may also be achieved through therapy if the first stage has been treated properly. At this early contemplation stage, aggressive children are not convinced yet that it is worth taking a step toward changing a pattern they are so familiar with.

Joey, in a later session at the contemplation stage, admits that he was wrong to explain his behavior as a defensive reaction:

> It is true that sometimes I hit when I get angry. For instance, when the gym teacher stopped our game a minute before it ended, I was so furious; you know, we could win this game, but he didn't care. I wanted to show him that he was not fair, so I kicked the ball right in his face, I was so angry.

At this stage, Joey knows that he is aggressive, but finds it legitimate to express his anger in an aggressive way. As he cannot communicate his anger verbally, he does so through aggression. This was a cathartic experience for Joey, which actually helped him to relax. At this stage, Joey has progressed to some awareness of his behavior, yet he still cannot see the problem.

The third stage is *preparation*, where a shift occurs in the motivation of aggressors to make a change. This progress may occur in a natural process of self-growth. For instance, young children use impulsive automatic response quite often, but when they grow older, they become aware of the negative consequences of their aggression and look for replacements. Indeed, although aggression is a relatively stable pattern of behavior, only a third of the aggressors at a young age remain aggressive as adults (Connor, 2002). Sometimes, a therapeutic intervention helps them to arrive at this stage.

At one of Joey's sessions, the boys listened to a story of an abusive father. They were very angry at this man, who had such unrealistic expectations of his 4-year-old son, and hit him when he failed. Joey was particularly angry:

> This child will grow up to be a criminal because of the stupidity of his father. He will learn nothing in life because he will be focused on his fears. ...I am also afraid of my father. He attacks me with his belt whenever he is upset. It has nothing to do with me, and I can't defend myself, because he is very big. I really want to hit him back but I can't, so I go out and hit whoever I can, you know, just to get rid of the anger.

At this stage, Joey understands what causes his aggression and that he replaces his anger to his father with anger to other targets that are more easily available. Understanding that innocent people suffer because he cannot face his father is an important insight. Comprehending that this is not fair may help develop a different line of values and enhance empathy, which is a key to raising motivation to change behavior.

At the *action* stage, children start making efforts to reduce their level of aggression. Again, some children can arrive at this stage with the help of a grownup who serves as a role model and establishes a corrective emotional relationship. I know of a distinguished social psychologist who grew up in a violent neighborhood in the United States with his immigrant parents. He used to take part in street fights, belonged to gangs, and was wounded more than once. It was his eighth-grade teacher who realized his intellectual potential and, through a close bond that he established with his young student, managed to redirect the youngster to a different avenue of growth. Another example was told by a professor during a professional interview, who explained that his alcoholic father was abusive to his mother. His fantasy as a child was to rescue his mother. One night, when his father came back drunk, he decided to set the house on fire, rescue his mother, and run away. He was all prepared to start the fire, he only needed to light the match, and for some reason, he got frightened and ran away without his mother. He was 16 and never came back home. An Indian farmer took him in, raised him as his son, and directed him to go to college. A college professor took over from there and made it possible for him to complete a PhD. He later became a distinguished professor himself.

Other children, who are not that lucky or do not have a significant other to support them, need therapy. As a result of therapy, Joey went through a cathartic experience and developed insight into the roots of his behavior. He was particularly moved by his understanding that innocent victims suffer as a result, and started exhibiting efforts to change. He would come in every session, reporting on his progress:

> - Today we lost the game. Usually I would pick on a member of the competing team, but today I just walked away.
>
>   -My teacher picks on me whenever someone misbehaves. Normally I would get angry, but this time I just let it go. I understood that she may not know yet that I have changed.

Occasionally, he could not control himself and regressed to an earlier stage. He also shared these incidents of failure with the group:

> - Yesterday my brother ruined my homework. I got so angry that, although I thought about you, I could not hold myself back.

Such regressions are common, which is why a maintenance stage is so important. However, being able to talk openly about one's negative behavior and own this part of oneself, rather than deny it, is very helpful.

Maintenance is the stage in which the child works to sustain his or her achievements. Relapse is one of the great dangers in the change process, as it is easy to regress to earlier stages without the support needed (Prochaska, 1999). Maintenance usually occurs after the therapy sessions have terminated. Counselors should keep some form of contact with the treatment person; this can take the form of occasional brief meetings, phone calls, and the like. In Joey's case, his therapist is also his school counselor, so she is able to maintain continuous contact with him. He comes to see her whenever he faces a difficult situation in school or at home. She comforts him and encourages him to continue with his progress.

A formal *termination* of treatment is recommended 6 months after the client shows the expected behavioral change (Prochaska, 1999). Joey never had a formal termination, because treatment is provided as a school service. He can always turn to the school counselor in times of need. The change that has occurred and is sustained in Joey's life has been confirmed by his teachers, his academic achievement, and the reduction in aggressive behavior to a minimum.

More specifically, the group in which Joey participated was evaluated for reduction of aggression through a short form (15 items representing aggressive behavior) of the Achenbach (1991a, 1991b) adjustment scale. The evaluation, which is based both on self-reports and on teacher reports, is made on a 3-point scale: never (0), sometimes (1) and most frequently (2), with higher scores indicating greater aggression. On the self-report, Joey started with a score of 11 (out of 30) and ended with a score of 6, while on the teacher's report, Joey started with a score of 20 (out of 30) and ended with a score of 10. Lower scores on self-report compared to teacher report may be expected; what is important is that scores were reduced following treatment. Moreover, his matched control participant in the study showed no change in behavior over the same time period (a self-report pre-score of 10 and a 9 on posttreatment, and a teacher report pre- and postscore of 15). The mean score on aggression for the experimental group decreased, while no change was observed in the control group (see Shechtman, 1999).

My students and I followed the children's functioning in the therapy process in this group, so as to shed light on the variables that made the change possible. Thus, using session transcripts, we counted the number of verbal behaviors that fell in the following five categories: self-disclosure, responsiveness, empathy, insight, and aggression (Shechtman, 1999). Results showed that self-disclosure increased with time; in the last four sessions (out of 10), it had the highest frequency. The progress made in responsiveness was even more impressive. It rose in every session, and in the last sessions, the children actually doubled the number of responses to other group members. Empathy also increased with time; its frequency in the last two sessions was double the number in the first two sessions. Statements indicating insight moved from 13 to 15 in the first three sessions to 27 and 28 in the last two sessions. Finally, endorsement of aggression was high at the beginning of the therapy (17 instances in the second session) and was reduced to a minimum at termination (5 statements in the last session). These results suggest that the whole group was effective in achieving important goals, including Joey.

In an interview following treatment, Joey was able to verbalize what helped him change:

> When I talk about things that bother me and people listen to me, I am open to listen to others. When they yell, I yell back. . . .This group was special because everyone listened to each other. I could tell them about the worst things I did and they did not blame me . . . they really liked me; they understood and tried to help.

This brief feedback tells us that it is not enough to understand the stages of change. The therapist needs to recognize each stage and match the treatment to that particular stage. Prochaska suggests an integrative theory, in which principles of several major theories are brought together as long as they match the stage of change. For example, children who function in the initial stages of precontemplation and contemplation would not make much use of a requirement to change their behavior, as they are unaware at this point of *what* needs to be changed. Since this lack of understanding is a defensive reaction, we need to first establish a therapeutic relationship. We particularly want these children to talk about their experiences of frustration, fear, shame, and abuse— those emotions that block their feelings toward self and others.

Humanistic theory is most helpful at this stage. Using skills of active listening encourages children to share their narratives, express some of their emotions, and release some of their tension. But most importantly, they must sense that their experience with the therapist is going to be different from their accumulated destructive experiences. They must feel secure in the knowledge that the therapist will listen and care. The literature helps bring up first experiences of victimization to convey that we are not blaming, just trying to explore their difficulties together. Stories, poems, and films that show the vulnerability of the characters serve the children best at this stage. The story of the abusive father is perfect for this purpose, but there are also many other stories that focus on the victim's experiences rather than those of the perpetrators. It is this type of literature that is needed at this initial stage.

When children reach the preparation stage, they have already admitted to their aggression, and now must deal with understanding the causes and consequences of their behavior. Some of the causes are more hidden (repressed) and require more time to unearth, and some children go through a slower process than others. Thus, the major questions at this stage are: *Why* does this happen to me and *why* is it important to make a change? Although this is a difficult time of confusion and inner struggle, children may be curious to understand what makes them behave the way they do. The development of insight into one's behavior is not an easy process. At this stage, psychodynamic principles are most appropriate. Drawing out repressed emotions and experiences helps to understand the dynamics of aggressive behavior as they apply to the individual in treatment. Stories, poems, and films that deal with issues related to the dynamics of aggression provide the material for such discussion. Through identification with the aggressive character, children learn how anger, frustration, a sense of unfairness, shame, fear, and guilt lead to aggression. They can then apply this understanding to their own lives and identify those dynamics that best fit their own situation. At this stage, it is also important to recognize the consequences of aggressive behavior: what the victims go through, and what price the aggressors pay for their impulsive or distorted behavior.

For example, at this stage, we air the movie *Madi*. In this film, the perpetrator pushes his victim, Madi, down a two-story building at a construction site, causing paralysis. The film shows the reasons for the aggressive act—frustration, anger, jealousy, loss of control—and the critical outcomes of the aggression—serious injury from which the victim may never recover. Watching this helps the children understand some of the motives that lead to aggression, which they may be able to apply to their own unique situations. The next step is to help the children evaluate the pros and cons of their own aggression. They each share a situation when they were involved in aggressive behavior, and we try to evaluate the positive and negative aspects. This is a clarifying process in which the children assess their feelings, thoughts, and behavior during and after an act of aggression. During this process, some children realize that their reaction is inappropriate to the stimulus, or too extreme. They explore their feelings of satisfaction or regret following their aggressive behavior, and they evaluate the price they pay. This clarifying process is the beginning of the use of cognitive therapy, in which the focus is on information processes (Dodge & Schwartz, 1997). The situation is explored in terms of cues that they see in a social conflict situation, their thoughts when evaluating the intentions of the others involved in the conflict, the level of aggression endorsement, and possible alternatives to their aggressive behavior.

In the action stage, aggressive children experience many ups and downs. It is not easy to change aggressive patterns of behavior that have been long learned and practiced. They do want to become better after exploring their behavior, and they also want to meet the therapist's expectations, so they are willing to try out new behaviors. But old patterns are stronger sometimes, and so are the circumstances in their lives that made them aggressive in the first place. Their behavior at this stage tends to be inconsistent. They require a lot of reinforcements and rewards for their attempts to give up aggression, which they don't always receive. Parents, teachers, and peers are not always able to notice the change or the efforts the child invests, and do not necessarily provide the deeply needed support, as is evident in the next case.

> We once worked with an extremely aggressive boy, Daniel, who made real efforts to change. One day, toward the end of his treatment, his class went on a field trip. While waiting for the bus to arrive, another classmate pushed him towards the teacher, causing Daniel to bump into her. She angrily turned to him, saying "What a waste of time it is to treat you; you have learned nothing." This statement discouraged the boy to such an extent that he refused to continue therapy.

In the action stage, children are vulnerable because they do not trust their own ability to change. The teacher's comment was so devastating to Daniel not only because he was frustrated that she did not see his progress, but also because he did not trust himself to succeed. Thus, at the action stage, the main question is *How* one overcomes all the obstacles to making the desired change in behavior. Behavioral principles are appropriate at this stage. Rewards, reinforcement of positive behavior, and sometimes ignoring negative slips of behavior are all important at this stage. They continue to play a central role in the maintenance stage until termination.

Studies Validating the Change Process

Two studies undertaken by my students and me validated the change process in our work with children, both indicating that, as treatment progresses, children move to a higher stage of change. The first study (Shechtman & Ben-David,

1999) showed that, in individual treatment, almost 70% of the aggressive boys expressed statements indicating lack of awareness of their aggression in the first session. These scores decreased gradually, and in the *eighth* and *ninth* *sessions*, only 7% of the children were still unaware. Awareness with no intention to change decreased from about 60% in the first three sessions to 30% in the tenth session. In contrast, in the initial sessions, preparation was low (around 25%), but in the last session it reached 60%. Finally, attempts to change were totally absent in the first five sessions, but reached almost 30% at termination. A similar pattern was observed in group processes (Shechtman & Ben-David, 1999, Table 3). This pattern of change was also tested in a correlation analysis between session number and the percentage of state-ments at each stage of change. Results indicated a significant relationship between the stage of change and the course of treatment, suggesting that, as the treatment progressed, the children moved to more advanced stages of change.

The results of the second study (Shechtman, 2003a) indicated that, at the onset of therapy, only a few children (10%) had reached the preparation or action stage. In contrast, at termination, most children (close to 80%) had reached one of the two advanced stages. Results were similar for individual and group treat-ment. A regression analysis showed that the probability of reaching a higher stage of change increases significantly as treatment progresses.

It is clear that most children were unaware of their problem behavior when the counselors first met them. Any attempt to teach them skills at this stage was doomed to fail. Thus, a therapeutic process was needed, based on establishing a therapist–client alliance and the development of self-awareness before trying to modify behavior. As we have seen, bibliotherapy is implemented in accordance with the child's stage of change. At the initial stages, they need to express their stress by identifying with victimized characters and they need to be acknowl-edged for the difficulties in their life. This conveys the message that they are accepted and understood, no matter how they behave. This is the basis needed to help children with difficulties in information processing. However, as sug-gested by Pepler and colleagues (Pepler, King, Craig, Byrd, & Bream, 1995), we should not overlook the emotional and personal experiences in this process of change. In fact, in our work (and supported by Prochaska), emotional and personal experiences precede the cognitive processes necessary for change. Bibliotherapy helps us to achieve these processes, but the therapist plays a central role in them.

Therapist Skills

The therapist has a central role in navigating the bibliotherapy process, starting even before the sessions, with the selection of the literature itself. The story, film, or poem has to be adjusted to the child's intellectual ability, identity, and problem. A boy should read about the life of another boy of a similar age and in a similar situation. The literature has to be of high quality so that an emotional identification process is permitted and models of constructive problem solving are presented. All these are necessary, but insufficient conditions for effective work in bibliotherapy. Children don't always understand the story and its meaning and do not necessarily see the richness of the solutions offered. Like any therapeutic process, whether with adults or with children, the therapist must help the clients explore their problems, develop insight to the cause of the problem, and eventually take action (Hill, 2005).

The therapist accomplishes these tasks through a set of skills that he or she uses in accordance with the stage the clients are in. In Hill's model, the therapist uses mostly encouragement, paraphrases, and questions at the initial stage of change. As the process evolves, more rigorous skills are used, including therapist self-disclosure, interpretation, and challenges. At the final stage, when a client is ready to take action, the therapist uses guidance and information provision (Hill & O'Brien, 1999). These skills have been found to be applicable to many theoretical therapies and thus are considered a-theoretical.

In child and adolescent therapy, however, the helping process works a bit differently. In our observation of aggressive children's processes in bibliotherapy treatment, we noticed that therapists ask a lot of questions. In individual therapy, questions accounted for over 70% of therapist responses, and in groups they accounted for 64%, according to one study (Shechtman & Ben-David, 1999). In a later study, questions accounted for 67% in individual treatment and 57% in group treatment (Shechtman, 2004a). The results are quite consistent, indicating that child therapists use more questions than do other therapists. As these two studies involved many therapists, the conclusion must be that questions are important in counseling young aggressive clients. In fact, in another study (Leichtentritt & Shechtman, 1998) that tried to trace children's reactions to the therapist's use of skills, we found questions to be one of the two most important skills (the other being structured activities) in producing children's self-disclosure, which is the basis for self-exploration. Moreover, questions were the only therapist skill that was significantly related to the responses of aggressive children in the therapy process (Shechtman, 2004b).

Questions in bibliotherapy sessions vary: sometimes they relate to the content of the literature discussed; other times they relate to the child's experiences that are raised by the literature. Questions that relate to the literature are aimed to assist children in understanding the dynamics underlying the behavior of the character, while questions addressing their personal experiences are aimed to assist them in exploring the unique issues they face, and to lead the children toward self-understanding.

It is reasonable to expect many therapist questions in children's therapy in general, and with aggressive boys in particular. These boys find it very difficult to respond spontaneously to a story/poem read to them, because their level of self-expressiveness is usually low. They must be guided to understand the characters and themselves, and questions are central in this process. In fact, when we traced the frequency of questions throughout the process, we found that not only were they much more frequent than other helping skills, but that they remained high throughout the process, in individual and group treatment alike (Shechtman, 2004a). Note, however, that the type of questions we refer to and prefer are open-ended (rather than close-ended) ones that encourage children to reflect on the literature and on their own experiences.

After questions, the next most frequent group of helping skills was guidance, which accounted for over 30% of the therapist skills (Shechtman, 2004a). Although guidance and information provision were much less frequent than questions, they were still more frequent when working with children, according to our studies (Shechtman, 2004a, 2004b), than with adults, as reported by Hill and O'Brien (1999). Child and adolescent therapists guide their clients in understanding the content of the literature and drawing the right conclusions from it. Guidance also helps children plan and make changes in their behavior. The high frequency of guidance found in our studies is understandable, considering that we are dealing with aggressive children and adolescents whose ego and superego are not fully developed. Although we believe that young clients can develop and grow, we do not expect them to automatically transform their insight into action, and so we feel the need to provide them with instrumental help, which is represented by guidance. Hence, whereas in adult therapy, guidance is mostly used at the final stage of treatment (Hill, 2005; Prochaska, 1999), in child therapy, it remains relatively salient throughout the process.

After guidance, the next most frequent group of helping skills were facilitative skills, including approval and reassurance, reflection of feelings, reassurance, and encouragement, which accounted for about 15% of the helping skills (Shechtman 2004a; Shechtman & Ben-David, 1999). Another study with nonaggressive children (Shechtman & Gat, 2008) replicated this result. In my opinion, these important skills are not used frequently enough. Their lack of usage even among nonaggressive children raises serious concerns regarding the skillfulness of the therapists. These skills must be developed so that they can be used with aggressive young clients, who have a particular need for encouragement and help in expressing feelings, for which reflection of feelings is the most appropriate helping skill.

In contrast to adult therapy, in which interpretation and challenges play a large role, these two skills accounted for about 1% of therapist helping skills in my frequency study (Shechtman, 2004a). Interpretation in individual child therapy reached a peak in the middle of the process (fourth or fifth session), while challenges reached a peak toward the end of treatment (seventh or eighth session). This is in keeping with the theoretical claim that interpretation and challenges help to develop insight and are therefore used more often at the middle and later stages (Hill, 2005; Prochaska, 1999). Challenges in the treatment of aggressive children serve to help them make a decision to take action. They help explore the pros and cons of their aggressive behavior, which eventually leads to behavioral change.

It should be reiterated that the frequency of both these skills is quite low, certainly lower than in therapy with adults. This can be attributed to the unique characteristics of aggressive children, whose intellect and personality are still underdeveloped. Their ego tends to be quite weak, and they are immature, resistant, and antisocial. Interpretations and challenges may frighten them. Because they attribute hostile intentions to other people, one has to be cautious about using these skills with them. Indeed, empirical evidence suggests that interpretation and challenges have a negative effect on children's behavior in therapy, in general, particularly when provided in a nonconstructive manner (Shechtman & Yanuv, 2001). One can only imagine how difficult it must be for aggressive children to cope with challenges and interpretations. Moreover, when we correlated therapist and client behavior in therapy, challenges was the only skill negatively related to children's behavior; that is, the more challenges that were used, the less the decrease in aggressive behavior following treatment.

In summary, the therapist has a central role in integrative bibliotherapy and must be trained in the abovementioned skills. However, the development of therapist skills in itself is not sufficient. Aggressive children need to work on some special contents in which they particularly show deficits.

The Content of Intervention

In Chapter 1, I outlined several main characteristics of the behavior of highly aggressive children. They include difficulties in dealing with emotions, a deficit in empathy, endorsement of power, and lack of control. These themes are addressed in our program.

Anger

Most aggressive children and adolescents are "chronically" angry (Potter-Efron, 2005). Deffenbacher, who has investigated anger for many years, suggests that highly angry people not only experience intense anger in their daily lives, but also express that anger in more outward, negative, less controlled ways, engage in more physical and verbal antagonism, and experience more frequent and severe anger consequences. They also experience more general anxiety, depression, and lower self-esteem (Deffenbacher et al., 2002). Michael Gurian (1997) argues that anger is actually the only emotion that boys are comfortable expressing.

There are many reasons for the aggressive children and adolescents we treat to be angry: disappointment, frustration, failure, jealousy, loneliness, fear, and helplessness. As the children can neither identify those feelings nor express them openly and directly, they express them through externalizing behavior, aggression, and violence. The reason they cannot identify such feelings lies in their tendency to repress negative emotions, so they won't have to deal with them. These feelings are not pleasant for aggressive children because they make them feel weak and powerless.

Being angry feels safer than feeling helpless, and expressing anger restores their sense of power. Therefore, in our bibliotherapy treatment, we address anger as a frequent and legitimate emotion, and help the children understand what makes them angry. We want to convey to them the message that anger is a normal human reaction when mild and expressed in a constructive, nonhostile manner (Deffenbacher et al., 2002). Moreover, we want to show them that out-of-control anger may have serious consequences.

One example of literature that delivers this message is Molly Bang's (1999) book for young children, *When Sophie Gets Angry—Really, Really Angry*. The book tells of a little girl who refuses to share the family dog with her younger sister. When her mother tells her it's her sister's turn now, her sister snatches the dog away, causing Sophie to fall down. Now she is even angrier, so she screams and kicks, becoming a volcano about to explode. But, instead of exploding, she runs to the woods, where she calms down. When she comes back home, it is to an accepting family. In this short book, children identify a common antecedent to anger—namely, frustration. They also learn how anger grows inside themselves until it reaches a boiling point, where there is lack of control and a sense of helplessness. They also learn about sublimation as one mechanism for self-relaxation.

> Amy, age nine, is rejected by her classmates. One reason for the rejection is that she is overweight, so the other kids make all kinds of nasty remarks about her. She responds with verbal and physical aggression. In one session, she shared with her counselor that her biggest problem is her mother. Her mom is constantly watching everything Amy puts into her mouth. She particularly hates it when her mom picks on her in front of other people, family, or friends. When that happens, she feels she is about to explode; and when she does, it is an extremely unpleasant scene, after which she feels shame and remorse. After reading *When Sophie Gets Angry* (Bang, 1999), Amy could clearly see what makes her so angry. She understood that her mom is trying to help her solve a difficult problem, and yet felt that she should go about it in a different way. Amy agreed to have a consultation session with her mother and the counselor, and to express to her mom her true feelings—her understanding of her mom's good intentions and her desire for her mom to help her in a more private manner.

Empathy

Empathy is considered the flip side of aggression. Research suggests that aggressive boys have a serious deficit in empathy skills. Many argue that angry children who are detached from their inner self and do not accept themselves cannot connect to feelings of others (Garbarino, 1999; Moeller, 2001; Pollack, 1998, 2000). It is reasonable that one cannot hurt another person and remain empathic to him/her at the same time, as it creates cognitive dissonance. If you hit or insult someone, you have to justify it to yourself. Aggressive children rationalize their actions in different ways, so that they can feel some self-integrity. Findings suggesting that increased empathy reduces aggression (Feshbach, 1997; Shechtman, 2006a) make sense. One can recognize and feel another's pain, you will not want to hurt them. Therefore, developing empathy is a major goal in any intervention with aggressive youth, whether primary (Horne et al., 2007) or secondary (Garbarino, 1999; Gurian, 1997) preventions.

Literature can help increase empathy through the aggressive child's identification with the literary victims. As long as they are not involved directly in the conflict, there is no need to defend themselves and there is no cognitive dissonance. Looking at the victim from the distance of a story, poem, or film and analyzing the behavior of another aggressor (someone who is not them) helps to increase perspective-taking and empathy skills, considerably reducing their skill deficits.

But empathy is more than a skill; it involves motivation to care about someone. In a study on group conflict (Shechtman & Bashir, 2005), the authors found that the same Arab children showed more empathy to suffering children from their own identity group than to Jewish children in the same situation. Motivation for empathy can be increased through psychological interventions. In an intervention program to increase the empathy of Arab adolescents toward Jews, the counselors showed the participants a film of the Holocaust, and read to them the letter of a mourning Jewish mother whose son was killed in one of the battles in the Arab-Jewish conflict. This had great impact on the Arab children's empathy toward Jewish people (Shechtman & Tanus, 2006).

To increase the motivation to feel for another person, learning from the indirect process of bibliotherapy must be applied to the aggressive children's own experiencing. First, the children develop empathy toward the literary character. It is relatively easier to feel for an imaginary figure than for a real child because this does not demand action. This in itself is an important step in developing feelings of compassion and empathy. If the therapist models acceptance and understanding of the literary character, the aggressive child may develop hope that the therapist will accept and understand him or her as well. Such corrective experiences open the way for self-acceptance and insight into their own aggression, raising motivation to give greater consideration to the suffering victim.

For example, for young children we use the poem, "Eitan" (Rabikovitz, 1981), in which a group of older children hit a younger boy, Eitan, because he broke the rules of the game. The older kids feel cheated and do not understand that Eitan's behavior was the result of a misunderstanding. After reading of the poem, during the treatment process, we discuss the dynamics of the aggressors' behavior, focusing on their feelings of mistrust and unfairness, which led to their reaction. We also address the dynamics underlying the victim's behavior: His young age, his lack of knowledge of the rules, his sadness and sense of loneliness following the incident. Most children understand the situation, feel sorry for the little boy, and are angry at the older perpetrators who took advantage of the victim's weakness. When they later apply their understanding to their own experiences, they admit many times to taking advantage of weak victims and often express remorse for what they have done.

> A counselor read "Eitan" to a group of third graders: Dan, Gary and Martin. It was easy for the boys to identify with the situation, as it happens to them often when first graders join them in a game during recess. Dan, the most aggressive member of the group, stubbornly insisted that the older children had to teach Eitan a lesson, just like his father punishes him when he does something wrong. Gary and Martin were more empathic to the young child, admitting that, although they sometimes behave like the older boys in the story, they cannot justify it now that they see why Eitan cheated. Gary added that he is aware that he is sometimes impatient, but also expressed remorse. The main point that convinced them was the focus on the misuse of power against a helpless victim. Eventually, even Dan agreed that if the child is really young, then it may indeed be unfair.

Power Use and Misuse

Even when we manage to increase empathy, aggressive children still lack the necessary social skills to resolve a conflict. They still don't know how to read social cues and often use an automatic response of aggression. Feeling rejected and under attack, they tend to attribute hostile behavior to others, endorse the use of force, and believe that aggression is the proper reaction.

Observing aggressive children, I have come to the conclusion that their need to use power is more than just a response that they have learned from their environment, as suggested by cognitive and behavioral psychology. It seems to originate from a deep sense of inferiority and shame, as a result of rejection and neglect. Therefore, it is more than just a defensive reaction; it is a matter of dignity and of survival.

One cannot speak of the misuse of power without referring to Alfred Adler. In his discussion of the obstacles to psychological growth, he names a state of inferiority and neglect as major causes. These experiences result in a lack of social interest, isolation, and the development of a noncooperative lifestyle. Most aggressive children grow up in conditions of neglect, rejection, poverty, and failure (Loeber & Farrington, 2000). A neglected or an unwanted child who has never known love and cooperation at home, therefore finds it extremely difficult to develop these capacities. Such children have no confidence in their ability to be useful and to gain affection and esteem from others. They tend to become cold and hard when they grow up. A sense of neglect coupled with a sense of inferiority and shame puts them in an unfair competition in life. Thus, in their striving for superiority and with their lack of feelings for others, they cannot help but become individuals who use their power to dominate, threaten, and abuse. Here is Adler's observation in generalized terms:

> The traits of unloved children in their most developed form can be observed by studying the biographies of all the great enemies of humanity. Here the one thing that stands

out is that as a child they were badly treated. Thus they develop hardness of character, envy and hatred; they could not bear to see others happy. (Adler, 1956, p. 371)

Other psychologists also point to the deep wounds caused by parental neglect and abuse. Children are born to be loved for who they are, and if a parent behaves inappropriately rather than disciplining the child, the child feels like "an object of the parent's distress" (Gurian, 1997, p. 94). The more that children are abused, the more that they learn to hide their wounds, but they continue building up resentment and hatred, and, in extreme cases, they act out in self-defense. Hence, the use of force serves the child's pride. They will not admit they are wounded, as this means loss of dignity. They are also unaware that they use replacement as a defense mechanism.

Therapy should help these children realize that they are not bad, but rather wounded. They have to learn that they are using their power to hurt others in reaction to their own pain, and they need to learn to forgive and ask for forgiveness. Forgiveness is especially helpful emotionally, because it helps people let go of hurt and bitterness, and promotes positive regard, compassion, and sympathy (Wade & Worthington, 2005). Applied research seems to agree that forgiveness is a useful method of coping with hurt or offenses through a reorientation of thoughts, emotions, and action toward the offenders (Wade, Worthington, & Meyer, 2005).

For aggressive individuals, forgiveness is a sign of weakness. They confuse it with submission, with giving in to the offender, and so are resistant. The truth is, however, that forgiveness is an act of courage, a sign of strength, and positive self-esteem (Potter-Efron, 2005), which opens up a path to assertiveness. This message must be conveyed to the children, and we achieve this goal through several literature pieces.

When we focus on the replacement of anger as a defense mechanism, one story we often use is "He Did Not Come" (Tester, 1970; see Appendix B). This short story tells of a neglected child following the divorce of his parents. He is waiting for his father, who promised to come, but, as in the past, he does not show up. The boy convinces himself that he does not care whether his father comes or not, and so he goes out to play, but on his way he expresses his resentment against objects he finds on the street, against a friend he sees passing by, and against his mother. The children understand his replacement of anger, and start talking about the real source of his behavior and his true feelings—his disappointment and anger, but also his longing for his father.

Sam, age 11, is highly aggressive, particularly to girls. His mother left him with his father and went off with another man. She tries to keep in touch with Sam, but he becomes extremely abusive whenever she calls, screaming, cursing, and hanging up on her. When the counselor read "He Did Not Come" to Sam's group, he got very angry at the father in the story, and suggested that the child should punish his father and never see him again. "Why does he need a lousy father like him? Let him die lonely as a dog, I don't need anyone to take care of me." Other children in the group, however, under-stood that the little boy in the story is very hurt and that his aggression is a replacement defense. Following this discussion, Sam admitted that whenever he thinks about his mom, he wants to kill someone. In his eyes, her biggest offense is that she didn't even fight over him, and simply left him behind. This is the first time that Sam has come close to expressing his true feelings. The group members, all from families of divorce, were extremely empathic with him, and some even shared similar feelings, but Dora suggested that Sam is like the boy in the story: he expresses his anger towards weak victims because he cannot do so directly at his mom. The group reached a consensus regarding a possible solution for him. "You should talk to your mom and tell her how angry and hurt you are, and you have every right to be angry," they added. Armed with group support and his own insight, Sam eventually did talk to his mom, their relationship improved, and he calmed down.

To help children with forgiving, we often use a poem called "Forgiveness" (Nir, 2000). In this poem, the character goes through an internal struggle, recognizing the benefits of forgiving, but feeling inhibited from doing so. Following are sample lines from the poem.

> It is hard, very hard
> Anger leaves a trail
> . . .
> No doubt, an apology is embarrassing
> But in the end brings comfort
> . . .
> It is hard, very hard
> The taste of tears lingers in one's mouth.

The pain, the shame, and the sense of helplessness are easily identifiable in the poem. The children not only identify with these feelings, they also learn that it is not easy to forgive because it may be interpreted as a weakness. They come to understand that, in fact, you need to be strong and brave in order to forgive. They bring up their own experiences of lack of forgiveness and usually find someone who they would like to forgive and restore relationships with.

Ken listened to this poem with two other aggressive classmates, one of whom used to be a good friend, but a year before an unresolved conflict had broken up the friendship. Following the discussion of the difficulties in forgiving, Ken brought up the incident, admitting that he had been wanting to renew his friendship with Carl for a while, but didn't know how his gesture would be accepted. He was mainly afraid of being rejected. Carl was very happy that Ken had brought this up, saying: "I never apologize, but I don't even remember what it was about." The two boys left the session as good friends again.

Lack of Self-control

One does not have to be a Freudian psychoanalyst to understand that when instincts and impulses govern personality, individuals suffer a loss of self-control. How do children develop self-control? Most theories suggest that it is parent–child relationship that has the most influence on the child's development of emotional regulation (Cassidy, 1994; Dodge, 2002; Pettit, Laird, Dodge, Bates, & Criss, 2001). A relation has been found between parental reactions to their child's expressiveness and the child's socioemotional development. Studies show that parental acceptance is related to the development of positive social skills and peer relations, while parental restriction and punishment of expressiveness is related to emotional suppression, avoidance coping, and anxiety (Denham, 1997; Fabes, Leonard, Kupanoff, & Martin, 2001).

Gilliom and colleagues (2002) suggest that the child's negative emotionality and the parents' reaction to it is relevant to how children learn to handle frustrating situations. Angry children who are highly irritable become too disorganized when frustrated, to self-regulate effectively, and this is exacerbated by harsh, restrictive parenting or, conversely, attenuated by supportive parenting. Available, sensitive, and responsive parents raise children who are confident in their ability to cope with most stressful situations. In contrast, unresponsive and harsh parenting does not help children deal with stress, but it also actually accelerates the conflict and increases the anxiety, which in turn leads to a rigid and ineffective response to stress. It appears that the parent–child attachment style lays the foundation for those parenting behaviors that increase loss of self-control in the children: Lack of warmth, harsh control, physical punishment, and abuse. Such parents not only serve as models, reinforcements, and accelerators of aggressive behavior; they never prepare their children to organize themselves when faced with a stressful event.

Once aggression becomes a pattern of life, it is difficult to change. Very often we take aggressive children and adolescents successfully through the stages of exploration and insight, but get stuck at the stage of self-control. Even when they understand their difficulties and make a commitment to change, habits seem to control them.

In our work, it is the therapist–client alliance that begins the habitual change. Essentially, the therapist has to redo the child's socialization process, by providing positive interpersonal re-experiences. Children need to feel that the therapist is trustworthy and that he or she will not let them down in a stressful situation, as their parents did. After establishing rapport, we introduce literature in which characters take charge of their lives and made a change despite the difficulties. For example, we use the poem, "I am My Own Commander" (Bokek, 1980), in which a boy who used to lose control quite often decides that he is going to be his own commander and his hands will take orders only from his own mind.

> Once if someone touched me
> Even by accident...
>
> I would immediately get mad and "heated"
> Immediately react...
>
> Then one day I said to myself:
> Wait a minute, wait a minute
> No one is going to tell me how to react
> From today on,
> I am in charge
> Period
> From today on
> Only I give the orders
> From today on I decide how to react...

The major dynamic in this poem is that a person is autonomous only when acting on free will. Children, particularly adolescents, love this poem because they struggle for independence and a sense of autonomy. Realizing that they are giving in to an external or internal force without controlling it, they sense their own loss of power. That is when they realize how important self-control is, and they become ready to try it out.

> George, a highly aggressive boy, was participating in a group of four adolescents that also comprised two mildly aggressive boys and Judy, a non-aggressive girl. The counselor read "I am My Own Commander" (Bokek, 1980) to them towards termina- tion. Judy tried to explain to the other group members that it is all in our minds, and we can actually control aggression if we choose to. "The mind gives the person an order to pick up his hand or not," she explained. George had a hard time understanding the concept, because he felt that his hands move automatically. To this, Judy responded: "It is only a matter of will. If you are strong enough, and decide not to hit, you will succeed." George responded, "So are you saying I'm not strong enough? I guess I need to work on controlling my hands."

High-quality literature, an effective therapist, and a reliable program are all important ingredients of a treatment program for childhood aggression. However, the validity of the program will be proven only if we can show that the treat- ment help children reduce their level of antisocial behavior and increase proso- cial behavior. Outcomes of the suggested treatment are therefore discussed next.

Research Supporting Outcomes

The research carried out by myself and my students involves mostly boys, as they make up the majority of aggressors in the school. Several studies involving hundreds of aggressive boys, from regular and special-education settings, mea- sured the change in these children's level of aggression following treatment. These studies employed a quasiexperimental design, mostly using Achenbach's (1991a, 1991b) self and teacher reports, in their long- or short-form. In some of the studies, additional measures were employed. Each of these studies will be further discussed to provide the evidence base for the method of the treatment I suggest in this book.

The first study (Shechtman & Nachshol, 1996) was of adolescents, aged 13–16 enrolled in three special-education vocational schools for maladapted students. These children were all drop-outs of the regular educational system; they were treated in special vocational facilities, in one last attempt to prepare them for constructive citizenship. The schools are characterized by high rates of aggression and victimization, and the teachers in these schools pleaded for help in their attempt to cope with the aggression. The population of these particular schools included emotionally disturbed, behaviorally disordered, and socially malad- justed youth. Most of the students were inner-city youth from disadvanta- ged neighborhoods, disturbed families, and communities with high-delinquency rates.

In all, we treated 85 adolescents in small groups of 6–8 (based on their homeroom class). Treatment was provided in the context of a language class as part of the school curriculum, to minimize the impression of psychological therapy—very important when treating antisocial and resistant youth. The school counselors, who were trained in the program, conducted the intervention in each class along with the language teacher.

Behavior problems, including aggression, were measured by the Walker Problem Identification Checklist (Walker, 1976), completed by the homeroom teacher, who knows the students well. In addition, aggressive behavior was measured through peer assessment, as recommended in the literature (Pepler & Rubin, 1991). Finally, attitudes endorsing aggression were measured through the Direct Situation Test (Goldstein & Glick, 1987).

Using a prepost experimental and control design (with groups randomly assigned to one of the conditions), results of the statistical analyses indicated a significant difference between the experimental and control groups following treatment, on attitudes endorsing aggression, on aggressive behavior as reported by peers, and on two subscales of teacher evaluations: withdrawal and disturbed peer relations. Further analyses indicated that, while attitudes of aggression endorsement were not reduced in the experimental group, they significantly increased in the control group. This last outcome suggests that, without treatment, endorsement of aggression increases in adolescents, and that treatment actually was able to stop such an increase. The positive results for aggressive behavior were even more salient: Aggression significantly decreased in the experimental group and significantly increased in the control group at the end of the treatment period. Finally, acting out of behavior, withdrawal, distractability, and disturbed peer relations decreased in the treatment group, while no change in these variables was reported for the nontreated children.

An additional interesting comparison was conducted for one group that was initially on the waiting list (control) and then became an experimental group upon receiving treatment. Except for attitudes endorsing aggression, for these same adolescents, the level of aggression increased while under the condition of control and decreased under the condition of treatment. The difference in scores between the two conditions was significant on all the variables measured. Although random assignment to experimental and control conditions is "state of the art" in experimental psychology, I find the last results particularly intriguing, because these were the same aggressive adolescents compared under the two conditions.

Moreover, the participants liked the sessions, often expressing curiosity about the story being told and sometimes bringing in stories of relevance to the topic discussed. Their satisfaction with the program supported our argument that an indirect method is needed for these difficult youngsters. The favorable outcomes for such youth encouraged us to continue testing our program with a larger variety of children and therapists.

The second study (Shechtman, 2000) included students from 10 special education schools. The same treatment program outlined above was conducted by

10 graduate students trained in a 56-hour seminar. The 70 adolescents in the study (ages 10–15) were identified by teachers via a 10-item questionnaire on verbal and physical aggression. Items included, for example, "name students who often get into fights" and "name students who tend to bully others." Therapists could work with one child, a pair, or a very small group. They chose the format of treatment based on the number of aggressive children in the class. As a result, there were five small groups, four pairs, and three individual treatments, with a total of 34 treatment children (29 boys and 5 girls). The control children were matched to the experimental children. That is, for each treated child, a classmate with a similar score in aggressive behavior served as control. When two students from the same class were treated together, two other students served as control, also from the same class; when a small group was used, another peer group served as a control. Treatment was provided outside the classroom, in a separate room, in 10 weekly 45-minute sessions.

The uniformity and validity of the intervention was ensured in several ways. First, treatment materials and activities were provided to the therapists. Second, they received supervision throughout the treatment process. Finally, all sessions were recorded and transcribed, and the lead investigator read the transcripts to ensure the validity of treatment. Nonetheless, a certain amount of flexibility was permitted in the choice of materials to ensure suitability for each age, in keeping with recommendations of Kendall and Morris (1991).

To measure change following treatment, scores on the complete scale of Achenbach's (1991a, 1991b) self-reports and teacher reports were compared in a prepost experimental-control design. The scales include eight specific measures: withdrawal, somatic complaints, anxiety/depression, social problems, thought problems, delinquent behavior, attention problems, and aggressive behavior. Statistical analyses on the self-report measure indicated significantly more favorable scores for the experimental group than the control for withdrawal, anxiety/depression, social problems, and aggressive behavior. In the teacher report measure, more favorable scores were given to the experimental group for anxiety/depression, thought problems, attention problems, and aggression. Interestingly, self-report and teacher-report gains matched with respect to anxiety/depression and aggression.

It may be concluded from the above that aggression was reduced following treatment. As no prescore differences were observed between the groups, the results may be attributed to the intervention. These results support the findings discussed earlier, hence strengthening the validity of the intervention. Moreover, the reduction in anxiety/depression supports my argument that aggressive children are actually children who have been hurt, are vulnerable, and are anxious. Such findings suggest that aggression and anxiety are indeed related factors, and that aggressive children are frightened and anxious young human beings.

The results on a process measure used in this study add to the validity of the program. Process variables were gleaned from discussion in the last session in response to a question focusing on termination: "How do you summarize your experience and the impact of the treatment on you?" The session was recorded and transcribed, and the content was analyzed in terms of three categories. The first pertains to the goals of the intervention: nonaggressive skills involving empathy, insight, and self-control. The second category pertains to the therapeutic factors that permitted the change, based on Yalom's (Yalom & Leszcz, 2005) factors, for example, catharsis, interpersonal learning, and cohesiveness. The third category involved the appeal of the methods used: films, stories, games, and discussion.

Content was analyzed by two independent raters, whose agreement ranged from 90 to 100%. With respect to nonaggressive skills, 62% of the treated students mentioned insight, 56% mentioned self-control, and 29% referred to empathy. Of the therapeutic factors, children mentioned catharsis the most (53%), followed by interpersonal learning (38%) and problem solving (26%). All other factors were rarely mentioned. Participants liked films the most (44%), then stories (26%) and games (21%), while discussions were least appealing (9%).

These results shed light on the unique features of the program. The intervention provided experiential learning, offering opportunities for emotional relief, the development of self-awareness, and the enhancement of social skills. Indeed, the decrease in withdrawal, in anxious and depressed behavior, in social problems, and in attention problems confirms that the program achieved its goals. Actual responses by the adolescents reinforce this conclusion:

> During the sessions I felt OK. I felt comfortable telling things about myself that I had never shared, even with parents or friends. I especially appreciate the support and care. . . .I have learned that by using words I can reduce tension. I now am aware of my own behavior, and I also consider feelings of other people, which inhibits me from using force. I loved the poetry and sometimes felt that I was part of the poem.

The indications of the importance of catharsis and insight in the change process resemble results reported by Prochaska (1995). These factors have the power to generate motivation to change. Only after the decision is made is the introduction of skills training appropriate, he claims. A similar rationale worked for our program. First, feelings are released and insight into one's behavior is increased in an accepting and supportive climate; only thereafter are ways to achieve change introduced, selected, and practiced.

In summary, this study again confirmed the short-term effectiveness of our intervention. Unfortunately, we could not conduct a follow-up measurement on these children. Therefore, the conclusion is limited to short-term outcomes only.

In the next two studies, we investigated the effect of this program on children from first to ninth grade, comparing individual and group treatment. While the comparison of these two formats of treatment are discussed in Chapters 5 and 6, here I would like to focus on the outcomes of the intervention following treatment, regardless of its format. One variation from the earlier studies is that we used a short version of the Achenbach scales (1991a, 1991b), including only the externalized behavior subscale. Thus, 18 items of the aggression and delinquent subscales made up our measure.

The first of these two studies (Shechtman & Ben-David, 1999) involved 101 students, 90% of whom were boys treatment of a vast majority of boys is in keeping with the literature. A comparison of pre- and postscores for experimental and control conditions indicated that treated children achieved greater reduction in aggression over time than did control children. Moreover, results indicated that the experimental children actually reduced their level of aggression, while there was no change in the control group. For example, children in individual treatment reduced their average score on aggression from 0.93 to 0.64 (self-report), while the control group kept the same scores (0.88 and 0.82). Similar results were obtained from teacher ratings: 1.01 and 0.80 for experimental prepost scores, and 0.95 and 0.91 for the control group. Results were similar for group treatment children.

The second study (Shechtman, 2003a) included younger children, from elementary school only. Treatment was administered in 51 different settings by 51 graduate students in counseling. Outcomes strongly resemble those of the previous study, providing a replication of results. For example, experimental children in individual treatment scored 0.81 and 0.65 on pre- and postmeasures (indicating a decrease in aggression), while the control wait-list children scored 0.81 and 0.83. In group treatment, the scores of experimental children were 0.79 and 0.61, respectively, while those of the control children were 0.60 on both pre- and postmeasurements. Similar results were found for teacher reports.

Due to the relatively large number of groups included in the study, we were able to employ a hierarchical linear model to test the efficacy of treatment. Hierarchical models take in account the dependency of scores in each particular group, so that children's scores are nested within the scores of their small group. Such models are particularly suitable for research on groups because of the different processes of each group, which, in turn, may influence outcomes. Results again pointed to more favorable outcomes for the treatment children than control children, with no difference between individual and group formats of treatment (Shechtman, 2003a).

In these two studies (as in the earlier ones), no follow-up measurement was possible, limiting the conclusion to short-term outcomes. However, in a more recent study (Shechtman & Birani-Nasaraladin, 2006), we were able to follow up gains after 3 months. After teachers in four schools identified 75 fifth and sixth graders (58 boys and 17 girls) as highly aggressive, the children were randomly and equally assigned to one of three conditions (25 per condition): children-only treatment, mother + child treatment, and no treatment (control). As the effects of treatment on mothers is discussed in a Chapter 8, here I will discuss the gains for the children. In this study, in addition to child and teacher reports (Achenbach, 1991a, 1991b), we also had parent reports of their children's level of aggression (Achenbach, 1991c). Results indicated that children in the two treatment conditions (with or without mothers) showed a significantly greater decrease in aggression scores than those in the control condition on all three sources of report: self, teacher, and parents. Moreover, children whose mothers were also treated showed more favorable gains than did children whose mothers were not treated, although this effect was apparent only in the self-reports. The unique contribution of this study to earlier results is that gains following treatment were maintained on all three measures after 3 months' time.

So far, all the reported studies compared treatment conditions with no treatment, the conclusion being that the suggested treatment is more effective than no treatment at all. A more sophisticated approach, however, is to compare this treatment to another type of intervention (Deffenbacher et al., 2002). A comparison of this sort can shed light on the unique contribution of the proposed treatment of bibliotherapy.

Such research was recently conducted (Shechtman, 2006a) with 61 aggressive boys from 24 classrooms (and schools). Ages ranged from 8 to 16 years ($M =$ 12.07, SD = 1.69). The treatment children ($n = 48$) were assigned to one of two conditions—bibliotherapy and helping sessions—with 24 children in each group. An additional 13 aggressive children were on a wait-list for treatment, hence serving as control for the two experimental groups (for details, see Chapter 2). Significant differences between the three conditions were found on aggression and empathy (both self and teacher reports). Simple contrasts indicated significant differences between the two treatment groups, on the one hand, and the control group, on the other, but only on empathy were gains higher in the bibliotherapy condition.

While this provides only partial support for the unique contribution of bibliotherapy, it does support the long list of earlier findings suggesting that the program we offer is effective in reducing aggression. We attributed the noneffect of bibliotherapy on aggression to the similarity of theoretical principles used in the two comparison conditions, as both were based on the change process suggested by Prochaska. The only difference between the treatments was the use of stories and poems. This may be insufficient to differentiate between treatments. Yet, despite the similarities in treatments, empathy increased significantly more in bibliotherapy, pointing to literature as a promising method. This is an important finding not only because empathy is essential for constructive interpersonal relationships, but also because it has an adverse relationship with aggression. In other words, empathy is an effective path to reducing aggression. Future studies should compare this affect-oriented treatment with the prevailing cognitive-behavioral treatment.

Summary

This chapter provides a bridge between Chapters 1 and 2. Whereas the former described aggression as a unique behavior, the latter described bibliotherapy as a therapeutic mechanism. The present chapter has provided the rationale for using bibliotherapy in the treatment of aggressive children and adolescents. My main point is that the indirect form of treatment provided by bibliotherapy best suits the defensive nature of such young people.

In the treatment of aggression, bibliotherapy is employed within a theoretical framework based on Prochaska's theory of change. The principal concept underlying Prochaska's theory is that clients change in a six-stage process, starting from lack of awareness and ending when they have full control over their behavior. Thus, the literature used in bibliotherapy is applied in keeping with the stage at which children are situated at a given point of time. It is the therapist's role to identify the stage of change and adjust the literature and the use of helping skills to the needs of the treatment children at the particular stage they are in. I have presented research supporting the theoretical model, showing that aggressive children indeed progress in stages of change. This is an important contribution to our understanding of psychotherapy, which has been rarely investigated, according to Deffenbacher and colleagues' (2002) comprehensive summary of the principles of anger management.

This chapter has also outlined the content of our intervention. Assuming that the major issues of aggressive youth are a difficulty in self-expressiveness (e.g., of anger and fear), lack of empathy, misconception of power and force, and lack of self-control, we use stories, poems, and films to develop these four areas. Finally, support for the effectiveness of the suggested intervention has been provided in a series of research projects.

Deffenbacher makes the distinction between the absolute and relative effectiveness of a program. Absolute effectiveness is determined by comparing results of treatment to no treatment, whereas relative effectiveness is based on comparison with another type of treatment. He also criticizes the field for being dependent on very small sample sizes ($N = 10$–20) and self-report data. In this chapter, I reviewed absolute effectiveness studies where treatment children were compared to control children (no treatment), under random conditions, with relatively large samples, and with teacher, parent, and peer reports in addition to self-reports. I have also reported relative effectiveness studies: one such study, described in the current chapter (Shechtman, 2006a), indicated that bibliotherapy was more effective than another treatment in increasing empathy; two others, discussed in Chapter 2 (Shechtman & Effrati, 2008; Shechtman & Nir Shafrir, 2007), both indicated that children worked more effectively in bibliotherapy treatment. All this research points to the unique contribution of bibliotherapy to the treatment of aggressive children.

The consistency of results is striking. In all studies, treatment children showed more favorable outcomes than no-treatment children, based on self, teacher, parent, and peer measures. Moreover, if one adds to the outcome studies the result of our process measures discussed earlier, it is quite clear that treatment children not only reduce their level of aggression, reduce endorsement for aggressive response, and increase empathy, but they also go through a cognitive change. Based on these cumulative results, it seems safe to conclude that our intervention is effective in reducing aggression, at least for the short-term, with indications that gains are sustained at least after 3 months. More research attempting to follow up such gains at longer periods of time is still needed.

In an era in which most of the treatment of angry and aggressive children is cognitive behavioral (Deffenbacher et al., 2002), evidence of the effectiveness of affective bibliotherapy as a method of treatment is important. However, the effectiveness of the intervention is highly dependent on the skillful application of bibliotherapy with children and adolescents. Chapter 4 outlines various ways to apply literature in the treatment of these difficult youngsters.

Chapter 4
The Application of Affective Bibliotherapy

The application of affective bibliotherapy starts with the selection of the literature and includes the therapeutic process based on the selected literature. The criteria for selecting literature include its quality, the themes it discusses, its suitability to the change process, and its appropriateness for the child's developmental level. The therapeutic process includes the following four stages: (1) Reading the literature/watching the film, (2) Identifying feelings, (3) Understanding human dynamics, and (4) Self-exploration. It is the therapist's role to navigate the therapeutic discussion of the literature, help the children make the connection between the literature and their personal experiences, and help them explore those experiences, gain insight, and make the necessary changes in behavior.

Selecting the Literature: Literary Quality

The most important characteristic of the literature is its literary quality. Whether a story, film, poem, or picture, it has to be complex; that is, it should include emotions, an internal or interpersonal conflict, a dilemma, or a debate. It should enable children to recognize and discuss emotions, struggles, and conflicts with which they can identify, and it should allow them to explore their own issues before a solution is offered.

Perhaps it is easier to explain what such literature should not be: It should not be simplistic, didactic, or provide simple solutions to a complex problem. Our intention in using such literature is not moralizing, preaching, or even character education. Therefore, merely presenting good models for identification—a method that many psychoeducational programs employ—is insufficient.

My general assumption is that aggressive children are filled with anger that has to be released before any change can be achieved. Thus, we want them to go through a cathartic experience, to explore their issues on emotional and cognitive levels, and to arrive at the motivation to take some action in the direction needed to change their behavior. Although vicarious learning or modeling of

Z. Shechtman, *Treating Child and Adolescent Aggression Through Bibliotherapy*,
The Springer Series on Human Exceptionality, DOI 10.1007/978-0-387-09745-9_4,
© Springer Science+Business Media, LLC 2009

proper behavior is an important component in affective bibliotherapy, it is not the main one. In accordance with our integrative model of change, self-exploration should precede cognitive learning, and only later should guidance and instrumental help be provided. Let me illustrate this point through an example of selected literature.

How to Take the Grrrr out of Anger, by Elizabeth Verdick and Marjorie Lisovskis (2003), is a very cute book on anger management that cognitive bibliotherapists might find useful in the treatment of aggression. The book starts by identifying the feelings of anger ("I want to take it out on somebody"), then discusses the reasons for being angry ("if somebody gets a better grade than you"), and then moves immediately to "quick ways to get your Grrrrr out" ("get physical", "talk smart to yourself", "relax in 10 easy ways," etc.). The book is rich in ideas to control anger, and I would be happy to use it with angry children, but only at the last stage of our intervention. The reason is that the book teaches a lesson and skills, but misses the cathartic experience, the self-exploration and the insight—all that affective bibliotherapy argues for. The assumption of cognitive bibliotherapy is that the angry child is willing to change, which may be true for some mild cases. However, the children and adolescents we work with are not prepared for change at the initial stage of therapy (see research results in Chap. 2). Indeed, some openly reject change and wish to hold on to their aggression:

> Michelle, a second grader, comes from an abusive family. She is highly rejected by her classmates. After hearing the story of a fight between two brothers, Michelle places herself on 10 (the highest score) on a continuum of aggression, explaining: "my brother always hits me; if I don't hit him back, I get very edgy. I need to get it out so I won't be taken advantage of and I do want to remain on 10, because I want everyone to be afraid of me, and to know that I can win. And my mother thinks so, too, she says that once people sense your weakness, they will step on you.

Michelle is aggressive because she comes from an abusive family. She has learned from her own experience that she must be strong, so that people do not take advantage of her as her father did to her mother and her brother does to her. The need to be threatening is reinforced by her mother's set of values, which derive from her own personal experiences. Armed with such perceptions of social situations, Michelle automatically uses aggression when she is rejected by her classmates. However, her aggression is not only learned, but it is also an expression of her frustration from her present situation of being so lonely and rejected. It is too early to provide her with alternative actions. She first needs to be heard, she needs a positive re-experience with a significant other that is not violent, and she needs to explore her feelings and understand how she arrived at such perceptions and behavior. I suspect that offering Michelle a book which includes a "lesson" to control anger would be of little use until she wants to make a change. It takes a whole process to get to the point where a child such as Michelle is willing to do that.

The type of literature that we seek for affective bibliotherapy has the power to bring out feelings that permit cathartic experiences, is rich in conflicts, and

does not explicitly say what should be changed. The poem "Joey," by Shel
Silverstein (1974), is one such example.

> Joey Joey took a stone
> And knocked
> Down
> The
> Sun!
> And whoosh! It swizzled
> Down so hard,
> And bloomp! It bounced
> In his backyard,
> And glunk! It landed
> On his toe!
> And the world was dark,
> And the corn wouldn't glow,
> And the wind wouldn't blow
> And the cock wouldn't crow,
> And it always was night,
> Night,
> Night.
>
> All because
> Of a stone
> And Joey.

Although short and simple, I consider this poem to be of high quality for
affective bibliotherapy. It presents a child who simply throws a stone, but the
consequences are dramatic. We don't know why Joey did it, and this ambiguity
is good, because it allows children to project on the situation reasons they have
to be aggressive. The poem does not judge Joey, which helps aggressive children
to identify with him, his pain (as the stone fell on his toe), and his sadness,
sorrow, and regret in facing the outcome of his deed. The children can identify
with those impulsive acts that they have done and the consequences that
followed. They can try to understand how such behavior happens to them,
because the conditions created by the poem are of acceptance, without judgment or blame. It is these processes that are essential in affective bibliotherapy,
especially in the initial stages; we are not interested in providing alternatives to
aggressive behavior at this point of therapy.

For example, *Is it Right to Fight?* (Thomas, 2003) might theoretically be
considered a suitable option for discussing anger. This book focuses on the
proper dynamics of aggressive behavior, conveying to the children the message
that anger is a legitimate, almost inevitable emotion. Moreover, feeling angry is
sometimes good, because it gives you the courage to speak up and the motivation to resolve a conflict. The book discusses the many things in our daily lives
that can make a child angry and the importance of understanding the causes of
our anger. Finally, it distinguishes angry feelings and thoughts from action
based on anger, such as aggression and fighting, arguing for promoting social
skills. Although all these dynamics are in place when providing counseling
to aggressive children, there is a major drawback to the book— namely, its

immediate move to suggestions for prosocial behavior. For instance, the first page focuses on the legitimization of anger, but on the very next page, the message is that fights arc no good and that talking is preferable. Moreover, at the end of page 2, there is a direct question to the reader: "What about you?" Such organization of content does not permit the exploration of a situation or oneself, because the "right way" immediately follows the dynamics. The moral lesson comes too soon in relation to the stage of change.

There are many children's books that deal with the dynamics of aggression without moralizing or teaching, although it is not easy to handle aggression in a nonjudgmental manner. For instance, one of the problems with anger is that it tends to grow until it gets out of control. Children are afraid of their growing anger; it seems like a balloon about to burst. The state of losing control is very unpleasant, and makes them feel rather helpless. Adults are usually extremely judgmental in such situations, and do not understand how fearful young children get because of their own aggression. Many of the children deal with such situations by using an avoidance mechanism—they run away or at least want to. The next two stories deal with this theme in an effective way and are suitable for affective bibliotherapy.

In the book *When Sophie gets Angry—Really, Really Angry* (Bang, 1999), Sophie's anger results from frustration and an escalation of the situation (see Chapter 3 for details). When that anger accumulates to the point where she is about to explode, she runs to the woods nearby and finds comfort in nature. After she calms down, she comes back home. This book is important not only to normalize and understand anger, but also mainly to identify with it and own it. The content, and particularly the illustrations, make it easier for the children to identify with Sophie and connect to their own experiences of anger. In this story, the identification of feelings is its biggest advantage. But it is also important to identify the pattern of coping. Stepping away from the situation, finding ways to relax but remaining close to home, are important messages. Thus, although a solution is offered, it is not presented in a "should do" manner, but rather as a model for vicarious learning. Children who identify with and accept Sophie's emotions will also learn that leaving the scene for a while is not a bad idea; it is not running away from home, just cooling down.

In *Alexander and his Terrible, Horrible, No Good, Very Bad Day* (Viorst, 1972), Alexander has a terrible day. Everything that happens to him that day is bad. These negative experiences accumulate to the point where he cannot deal with them, so he decides to run off to Australia, very far from home. The book suggests many difficult situations with which children can identify. However, the interesting concept this book introduces is that of self-fulfilled expectations. Once Alexander faces a challenge, everything irritates him. His initial difficult situation then colors his subsequent experiences, and as he expects bad things to happen, they do. Self-fulfilling prophecies is an important issue to discuss with children. Moreover, as with the case of Sophie, avoiding the conflict is only a partial solution and not the most effective one. We need to stress that it was only a wish to run away, not a real runaway situation. This distinction is important to avoid having the children jump to the wrong conclusions. Most understand it on their own, but sometimes monitoring a child's understanding of the book is highly important. Without such monitoring (such as in self-help bibliotherapy), reading such a book could have severe consequences.

Themes for Discussion

The literature we select for affective bibliotherapy should be within the realm of the children's problems and represent the difficulties they experience and the dynamics of their behavior. When working with children from divorced families, we want the literature to present the complexity of divorce; when working with children who have experienced loss, we want the literature to present the difficulties of grief; when working on issues of social inclusion in school, we want it to present characters who suffer social rejection. Generally speaking, the children should be able to identify with the characters, so that they can understand the feelings and behavior underlying the situation and perhaps also learn from their experience.

However, you need to be cautious about presenting characters and situations that are too close to the child's actual problem, because it may be too threatening and inhibit responses. For example, presenting a child character, who is highly rejected by his or her classmates may be too threatening for a rejected child to cope with, whereas presenting the issue in the form of a poor duckling or elephant may be helpful to young children. Another option is to present a closely related problem, which is less anxiety provoking. For instance, I once worked with a teenager in crisis who was the victim of bullying in school. Although he was small for his age and physically weak, I selected for him a poem about a child who didn't like his glasses and felt intimidated by that. The discussion of the literary character with a focus on glasses permitted us to deal with the relevant feelings and dynamics of being rejected without focusing on the real issue and threatening the teenager.

At the same time, it is clear that we need to focus on literature that is relevant to the problem. In the case of the treatment of aggression, the literature selected should address four themes, in accordance with the deficits that aggressive children present: improve their handling of emotions, increase empathy, decrease endorsement of power, and enhance self-control. These four components are interrelated. Aggressive children hide their real emotions to defend themselves, and as they try to avoid feeling the pain of neglect, they are unable to feel the pain of others. They endorse power to avoid feelings of helplessness and to cover up their difficulties in controlling impulsive behavior. Hence, the topics for discussion that are relevant are anger and anger management, empathy to other's pain, misuse of power, and self-control. Although most of the texts we use present combinations of these four components, each topic is discussed here separately for the sake of clarity.

Anger and Anger Management

In dealing with anger, children need to understand what makes them angry, what their typical reactions are when angry, how anger escalates into aggression, some consequences of impulsive or planned aggression, and how to sublimate aggression. For young children, the book *When I Feel Angry* (Spelman, 2000) is suitable. It outlines the many reasons that children become angry, such as dealing with put-downs ("when someone makes fun of me"), frustration ("when I have to stop the game to clean my room"), and when it's not fair ("the teacher says I was talking and I wasn't"); it talks about reactions to such situations ("I want to say something mean," to kick, to hit); and it provides ways to sublimate the anger. In short, children can identify their anger, their spontaneous reaction to it, and self-control mechanisms, such as using sublimations.

The poem "Joey" by Silverstein, mentioned earlier in this chapter, presents similar dynamics for discussion: Joey throws a stone and shuts down the sun. No matter what his anger was about, he did not foresee the harsh consequences of his behavior. The group can talk about his unintentional or impulsive behavior, his possible feelings of remorse, and his sense of helplessness in facing the outcome of his actions.

Competition and jealousy are themes that come up often in discussions with aggressive children. A text we frequently use with young children is a poem which describes a poor little boy with few toys at home. He is watching his close friend playing with a new toy that he refuses to share. Feeling jealous, insulted and betrayed, the boy picks up a rock and, without really meaning to, hits his friend, who is badly injured and has to be hospitalized. Adults get involved, and everyone blames the little boy for the incident. But the aggressor only feels anger and a deep sense of insult. In this short poem, the dynamics of anger as a result of insult and frustration is clear. Young children can easily identify these feelings, understand how anger can induce lack of self-control, grasp how lack of control can lead to serious unexpected outcomes, and find parallels in their own experiences.

For older children, we use a story with a similar theme, named "The Bully" (Tester, 1974; see Appendix B). Here, academic failure is the cause of aggression. A highly aggressive child attacks a weaker classmate because he is excelling in school. This hostile bullying is meant to inflict harm on a helpless victim. Classmates and the teacher see the bully picking on his victim, but are unable to help. The story ends with the victim getting beat up by the bully on his way home from school. The children in our groups recognize the sense of failure, the jealousy, and the need to show off. They also identify with the victim's helplessness, which usually raises feelings of empathy. Finally, they understand how frustration leads to aggression and is transferred to a victim on hand.

Another suitable poem for older children is "The Evil Palm" (Rabikovitz, 1995), which relates the story of a teenage girl who suffered from an abusive father when she was young. Although the poem is written many years after the abuse took place, that girl still feels intimidated, ashamed, angry, and fearful.

She wants people to hear her, believe her, and understand her suffering. Following is one verse of the poem:

> Streaks of smoke swayed aside
> Father stopped hitting me
> The evil hand spouted fingers
> And all its actions are valid and alive

Adolescent girls are able to identify with her feelings, understand her deep emotions, and really feel for her. Hence, empathy is increased toward the character, and later to people in their surroundings, as illustrated in the following case.

Stephanie, a highly aggressive teenager, was placed with Patricia, her victim, in the same group. The two were classmates, and in their interactions inside and outside the class, Patricia suffered consistently. Their unhealthy relationship came up after reading this poem, when Patricia gained the courage to share her being bullied with the group. At first, Stephanie just felt attacked and refused to participate, but after the group discussed the suffering of the victim in the poem, she admitted to her bullying. She rationalized her aggressive behavior as a response to Patricia's lack of assertiveness; she directly attacked her for not responding to attacks and not defending herself. But eventually, Stephanie admitted that she used to be a victim in class herself for many years. Ever since she took upon the role of the aggressor, she cannot stand weak people, "they remind me of where I used to be, and I never want to go back to that place." Following this interaction in the group, the bullying stopped and Stephanie actually became Patricia's major protector in and out of class.

I believe that Stephanie respected Patricia's attempt to defend herself by bringing this up in the group. The change in this aggressive girl occurred, however, only once she got in touch with her true feelings, and from there she could also see Patricia's pain. Moreover, being more truthful to herself, she could develop insight into the causes of her aggression.

Increasing Empathy

A second goal of our intervention is to increase empathy to the suffering of victims. Empathy is an effective protector against aggression, as you cannot hurt someone and recognize his or her pain at the same time. Indeed, aggression and empathy are reversely correlated in research (Feshbach, 1997), and most treatment programs for bullies and aggressors include a component of empathy in their training, such as in the *Bully Buster* program (Horne et al., 2007), and many others. The problem with empathy, however, is that it is not only a trait or skill. One needs motivation to apply empathy in certain situations. In many cases, aggressive boys choose to appear nonempathic in order to retain the mask of masculinity.

Literature, due to its distance from real life, permits empathic reaction more often than real situations do. In fact, we see this very often in our treatments.

John, a highly aggressive boy, listened to the poem about jealousy mentioned earlier. He identified with both characters; he understood why the aggressor hit his victim, but he also recognized the latter's pain. He went on in length talking about the sad consequences and how terrible the victim must feel. He then shared with the group an incident in which he was betrayed by a close friend who didn't want to share his new bicycle. Insulted and furious, he lost control, hit the friend, and broke his arm. When the counselor asked, "How do you feel about this incident?" he surprisingly answered "I feel good, very good, he should have learned his lesson!" The counselor continued probing: "What about his pain and suffering?", and John replied; "I don't care." The counselor went on questioning: "What about the victim in the poem? You seemed to understand and sense his pain well." To this, John responded: "Yes, I know he was suffering. Everyone was mad at me. I guess I could wait until he got used to his bike, then he would probably have shared it with me." It was the poem that was more powerful in arousing empathy, but the counselor managed to transfer this empathy to the real-life situation.

In order to arouse empathy in aggressive children, the literature has to be particularly emotional. Most of the stories and poems mentioned above have the potential to raise an empathic reaction: *Dumbo the Elephant*, *The Ugly Duckling*, *When Sophie Gets Angry—Really Really Angry*, "The Evil Palm." For adolescents, I find *The Outsiders* (Hinton, 1995) to be particularly helpful in enhancing empathy. The book talks about a fight between gangs, a topic that is familiar in adolescents' life. Here I quote a paragraph that illustrates the pain of a victim:

> One of them laughed, then cussed me out in a low voice. I couldn't think of anything to say. There just isn't a whole lot you can say while waiting to get mugged, so I kept my mouth shut. "Need a haircut, greaser?" the medium-sized blond pulled a knife out of his back pocket and flipped the blade open. I finally thought of something to say. "No." I was backing up, away from the knife. Of course I backed right into one of them. They had me down in a second. They had my arms and legs pinned down and one of them was sitting on my chest with his knees on my elbows. . . .a blade was held against my throat. "How'd you like that haircut to begin just below the chin"? (p. 5)

Often, aggressive teenagers cannot see the pain they are inflicting on others, but when they see it from the distance of the literature, it is easier to recognize, allowing them to connect to their feelings of empathy for the victim's suffering.

There are two pieces of literature that in our experience draw out empathy the best way in aggressive kids. One is the story, "The Present" (Sade, 1990; see Appendix A), and the other one is the film, *Madi* (1987). When we ask children for feedback on the treatment program, these are the two literary pieces that they mention most frequently. "The Present" has been mentioned several times: the story is of a father who hits his 4-year-old son for not being able to tell time adequately. The story creates empathy for the young victim, who did no harm and seems so helpless against his powerful father. *Madi* is about the impulsive reaction of a boy who caused another child to become paralyzed. The power of the film is its focus on the pain of the victim and his family and the remorse that the aggressor feels. Watching the rehabilitation efforts that the victim goes through is so powerful that even the most aggressive boy can identify with his pain.

A group of second graders is watching *Madi*, and their reactions to the victim are very warm and spontaneous. Kevin, one of the more aggressive kids, reacts with surprising empathy. Before Madi has his tragic fall, Kevin says in horror: "Wow, he is going to hurt him, this will be tragic, he will kill him." After Madi falls, Kevin, in tears, says, "He may be dead. . . .he must be in so much pain." Later, when the perpetrator tries to visit Madi in the hospital, Kevin comments: "Of course he should ask for forgiveness and help him until he is well." When the children see Madi in a wheelchair, someone notes that people will now make fun of him, but Kevin intervenes: "What's funny about it? No one should laugh at him, they should help him." In the clubhouse, when people make fun of Madi, Kevin responds: "Poor thing, he must feel terrible."

All these reactions came from an extremely aggressive boy, who is badly abused by his parents and three older brothers. Kevin had been complaining throughout the program about the abuse in his home and seemed quite helpless. He might have strongly identified himself with the victim, which raised empathy toward the victim's suffering, but at no time beforehand did he show such empathy to victims in other stories. For him, it seems, the content and medium of the film were powerful, as it was for many other treatment children.

The Misuse of Power

In Chapter 1, I discussed at length the reasons for aggressive children to endorse power. Some are related to their personal experiences of abuse, where misuse of power did work for the aggressors. Children who grew up in an abusive environment or violent community learned that the person who uses force against others is the winner. The clear conclusion of these experiences must be that power and strength keep you safe. I once worked with an adolescent boy at a foster home who said to me: "How do you expect me to change in this violent place? Do you know what would happen to me once I gave up my power?" Yes, I did understand that in a place like this, the strong survive and the weak become victims. However, many other aggressive children, particularly boys, misuse power to avoid a sense of neglect and helplessness. These boys need to get in touch with their feelings and develop insight into the causes of their behavior. We use stories, poems, films, and pictures for all types of power misuse: for the bully, the proactive aggressor, and the reactive aggressor.

Kevin, as you may recall, is extremely aggressive in class and comes from a very abusive family. For him, aggression is a way of life and the only way he knows to resolve a conflict. In one session, Kevin came to understand the cycle of his violence: his brothers call him names; this makes him extremely angry, so he curses back; his older brother then starts a fight; his mother is helpless; and when his father is around, he gets wild and hits Kevin with anything he can get his hands on. Kevin showed the group a scar on his face that was the result of one such incident. He feels helpless at home, and wanders the streets most of the time in an effort to avoid such conflicts, but cannot stop them. In class, he feels strong. He is a year older than his classmates, and the others fear him. Kevin brings his frustrations and patterns of violent communication from home to school. For him, school is a safe place where he can feel forceful and strong. His verbal participation in this activity reflects a lot of the power issues that many aggressive children present.

After Kevin saw the film, *Madi*, he participated in an activity in which he was asked to place himself on a continuum from 1 to 10 in terms of his impulsiveness. He gave himself a 10, explaining that what makes him impulsively angry is when he is grounded and can't go out with his friends, when he is locked in the bathroom, and when he is hit by his siblings and parents. When these things happen, he goes wild or cries in bed, because he feels the punishment is unfair and that his family is using unjustified power against him only because he is the youngest and weakest. To the counselor's query of how he feels when he gets hit and abused, he responds, "very sad, and I think then that I am quite lonely; I am like the ugly duckling that no one wants." The counselor assures him several times in the course of the conversation that she enjoys talking with him, which makes him look very happy. Establishing a good rapport with Kevin, she can now go back to the cycle of violence in his life, which she wants him to understand.

Counselor: Have you realized that insults do evoke a verbal violent response from you, which triggers the fight? Is there a way to stop the cycle?

Kevin: Yes, if I don't respond to the insult. But that's hard, because I feel hurt. I try not to react, but I'm not always successful, because I feel they are taking advantage of me and I have to be strong. . . .in class I do not have such problems because I am one of the strongest boys, and I am not afraid of anyone here.

Counselor: Does it feel good to be the strongest?

Kevin: Yes.

Counselor: And how do you feel when children are afraid of you?

Kevin: I feel good, but also not very pleasant; it is just like me and my brothers.

Counselor: Where do you want to be on the continuum?

Kevin: On 5, because I don't like violence, I don't like to hit, but sometimes they don't leave me any choice.

Kevin, like many other aggressive children, holds on to the perceptions that being strong and frightening others is a desired status. This is not surprising, as he comes from a family that reinforces those values. However, it seems that the movie *Madi* aroused some empathy, enabling him to recognize the connection between his situation at home and his behavior in school and to realize that he does not particularly like his behavior. There is still a long way to go with Kevin until behavioral change occurs, but something in his attitude of endorsing violence seems to have changed, and motivation to make a change has been raised. It was the story of aggression among brothers and the movie, as well as the therapeutic session, that probably had a positive impact on Kevin.

A related issue of the endorsement of power is the difficulty to forgive or ask for forgiveness, as these are perceived as signs of weakness. Forgiving means admitting that you are wrong, and asking for forgiveness is even worse in the eyes of those who admire force. Yet, forgiveness is crucial for helping children let go of their anger and free their energy for more constructive behaviors. We use the poem, "Forgiveness" (Nir, 2000), in which someone struggles with the will to forgive when asked for forgiveness, and admits that asking for forgiveness is difficult, too. The children identify the sense of weakness, which they erroneously attribute to the act of forgiveness, discuss the dynamics underlying forgiveness, and come to the realization that forgiveness is actually an act of strength. They usually also reach a decision to forgive someone specific that they identify, or to be more forgiving in socially conflicting situations in general. As Tommy claimed, "When the opposing team would win a soccer game, I used to be outrageous, looking for a victim to take immediate revenge. This helped me accept our loss. I don't do it anymore. I forgive them and hope that next time we will be the winners."

Self-control

Chapter 3 discusses the difficulties of developing self-control in length. Lack of self-control is reflected in impulsive behavior, in external locus of control, and in lack of responsibility. This is probably the most difficult of the four goals to achieve, because patterns of behavior are sometimes stronger than self-understanding and insight. This is the stage when many kids get stuck and become quite frustrated. They may have developed insight into their own behavior, made a commitment to change, and even gained some conflict resolution skills, but, as with many other addictions, they often return to their former, more familiar patterns of behavior. They often desperately ask us to help them control themselves. Meaningful people in their social environment—teachers, parents, peers, and certainly the therapist—must be very patient at this stage, encourage the attempts, and enhance their sense of success.

At this stage, literature should focus on the undesirable consequences of impulsive behavior and the effect of loss of control on a person's self-concept. It should instill hope in children's ability to change their aggression, and empower them in order to prevent relapse. "The King and his Hawk," retold by James Baldwin (Bennett, 1998), is one such story about impulsive aggression and lack of self-control. This is a tale about Genghis Khan, the great king and warrior. One morning, when he was home from war, he was riding in the woods with his pet hawk. In the evening, when he was really thirsty, he tried to drink some water from a stream. The cup filled up very slowly, but each time it was almost full, the hawk came and knocked it from his hands. After the third time, the king got so mad that he killed the hawk. Only later did he find out that there was a dead snake in the stream and the water was poisonous. He then understood that the hawk had saved his life and that he had actually killed his best friend. The story ends with the words, "I have learned a sad lesson today, and that is: never do anything in anger."

A poem we often use at this stage with younger children is called "The Disastrous Monster" (Shilon, 1981). In this short poem, a child discovers that it is his monster, which governs his behavior rather than himself. He wishes to get rid of the monster but has a hard time doing so. Treatment children quickly connect to the metaphor of the monster; they tell us in words or drawings what it looks like, and they discuss the difficulties of getting rid of it, but consider an alternative behavior. This poem clearly acknowledges the children's difficulties in controlling their behavior and does so in an accepting, nonjudgmental, even amusing manner.

Finally, we use the poem, "I am My Own Commander" (Bokek, 1980), which focuses on a child's decision to take charge of his behavior. The character in the poem comes to the conclusion that it is all up to his wish to command himself, rather than give into impulsive behavior, and that he can do it. Again, the metaphor of the commander and the perception that you can take charge of your life is very appealing to youngsters.

Adjusting the Literature to the Change Process

As discussed in Chapter 3, the concept of the change process is composed of several stages (Prochaska, 1999). We need to select and use the literature to suit the stage of change the child presents.

The Initial Stage

At the beginning stages, when treatment children are still unaware they have a behavior problem, or are aware but do not want to change it, we need literature that focuses mainly on children's victimization. Whether victimized in the past or present (and many of them are) or not, dealing with victimization suggests that we are interested in them as a person rather than only in behavior change. It gives the children the attention they need, the sense that they are listened to, and accepted for who they are, regardless of what they do—all necessary conditions for establishing rapport and reducing their defensiveness. Aggressive children have difficulties trusting others, and this includes the counselor or therapist. It is a time when these children test us to see if we really care about them, or are just another agent of change.

> Myra is a clear case in point. This second-grade girl was acting out in a group of four treatment children. She was particularly picking on one group member, even as she knew she was breaking the group rules. Every time she did this, she immediately asked

the counselor "Are you going to ask me to leave the room like my teacher does?" Only after the counselor reassured her several times that she is an important group member and is welcome in the group did she stop this behavior.

Focusing on victimization also helps the children to identify and express feelings and to develop empathy—two major goals in our intervention. This is the stage they can talk about fears, anxiety, pain, sorrow, helplessness, and hopelessness. Not only do they learn to identify themselves in the victimized characters, but also can allow themselves to feel for them. Kevin, mentioned earlier in this chapter, illustrates this instance well. He felt sorry for Madi, the victimized child, and also for himself.

Another story for young children at this stage is *The Ugly Duckling* (Anderson, 1843). This poor soul is humiliated and rejected by his fellow ducklings only because he was born different. Michelle, a highly rejected girl, strongly identifies with him: "He is so lonely, and he can do nothing because they are all against him, and he is ugly and different, poor thing. ... Only his mother is protecting him." Finally, she says, "why do they care so much about his appearance? After all, what is important is what he is like on the inside, like for me, I am a good person, but kids don't see it." Through this identification process, Michelle, who was rated extremely high on the aggression scale by her teacher, is able to identify emotions, feel empathy, and start exploring her own issues.

Dealing with victimization helps children start examining some of the reasons that lead to their aggressiveness. Looking at the background of the poor victimized characters and identifying with certain situations helps them begin to look into their own background in a more realistic way.

Mark, a teenager from a foster home, used to tell us fantasy stories about his weekends every time he came back from home visits. In his stories, his parents were together, prepared the food he likes best, and took him to the movies. But, whenever he returned from such visits, he was extremely violent. It turned out that his mother, a prostitute, would kick him out whenever it interfered with her "clientele" and he actually spent his time wandering the streets and hungry. "The Present," a story about an abusive father, which we use early in our program, helped him share with the therapist his real experiences on these visits at home, and helped him understand why he is so angry when he comes back. This poor youngster could not face such a painful and hopeless reality. He was also ashamed of the situation, so he used a simple defense mechanism, of reaction formation, which helped him survive and not lose face in front of the other kids.

There are plenty of stories in which the characters—animals or children—are victimized and may serve as references for the initial stages of change. There is a very expressional picture in the Teaching Pictures series (Tester, 1974) in which a grown man hits a child. The adult appears strong and mean and the boy seems to be extremely frightened.

Andy, a highly aggressive boy who comes from an abusive home, had several emotional and empathic responses to the picture: "I feel sad because the child is hurting so much; you can see how frightened he is, he does not deserve to be spanked." Later, in response to the question, "What would you do in such a situation?", he says, "I would definitely run away from home. ...I would ask my mom to leave, just the two of us ... She tries to protect me, but she is not strong enough." When asked "How do you feel when he hits you?" Andy says: "I wish I was never born."

For older children we use the movie *Life is Beautiful* (Benini & Cerami, 1997), which tells the story of a father and his small son in a concentration camp during the Holocaust. To reduce the child's fear, his father pretends that it is all a game. However, the fear and horror of the place is clear, and can elicit intense emotions and strong empathy toward the victims. We use this film to help Arab adolescents better understand the Jewish narrative (Shechtman & Tanus, 2006). Despite the intergroup conflict between the two rival groups, many of the Arab adolescents responded with empathy to Jewish suffering after viewing it. "Children shouldn't go through such agony, no matter where they belong," Martha said. "I can now understand why having a land for the Jews is so important for them," said Janice.

The Working Stage

At the working stage, the main task is to help children explore their anger, understand what triggers it, understand how anger escalates into aggression, and see the consequences of their behavior. The literature selected for this stage should focus on the dynamics of anger and aggression, including power struggles, misuse of force, and the consequences of impulsive behavior. Whereas in the initial stage the focus was on victimization, it now shifts to the perpetrator, his or her behavior, and the consequences of such behavior. The literature should thus present characters who for various reasons, become violent. Through an identification process, the treatment children can begin understanding how they, too, get violent.

Most of the literature presented earlier (see "Themes for Discussion")—on anger and anger management, empathy, power issues, and self-control—is relevant at this stage, but the therapeutic process that the counselor conducts now becomes particularly important. Whereas in the initial stage of treatment, the therapist listens carefully, assesses the situation, and establishes safety in the relationship, at this stage he or she must more actively guide the children through the exploration stage and lead them toward insight, using a more probing intervention.

The film *Madi* is an excellent choice for the working stage. It presents possible causes of aggression, the escalation of a conflict, the harsh consequences of impulsive behavior, the suffering of the victim, and the remorse and suffering of the aggressor. Both aggressor and victim are excellent characters for identification. Moreover, being a film makes it a powerful medium to influence children and adolescents; it is convincing and interesting. The following illustrates how a counselor uses this movie to initiate an exploration process with a young boy in a group setting.

Eight-year-old Alan comes from a dysfunctional family; his father has disappeared and his mother is a drug user. An older sister is taking care of the family, in which Alan is the youngest. He is called "the terrorist" at school because of the hard time he gives other children. He is absolutely unaware of his problematic behavior and constantly complains that other children and adult are giving him a hard time.

The film *Madi* was presented to the treatment group in which Alan was a member in the eleventh session. By that time, bonding with the therapist and group was strong, permitting a sound therapeutic conversation. After watching the movie, the counselor asked the children to place themselves on a continuum from 1 to 10 in response to the question: "How impulsive are you in your reaction to a conflict situation?" First, the counselor helped Alan to explore what makes him angry. He mentioned the following: when they insult me, curse, hit, and take things away. Alan then assigned himself a 10, because he reacts by cursing, fighting, and hitting, in order to "teach them a lesson, so they never start up with me again. . . . I want them to be afraid of me."

Counselor:	How do you feel about others fearing you?
Alan:	Excellent! Is it better to be afraid of them?
Counselor:	What do they feel when you hit them?
Alan (after a long silence, in which he seems to be uncomfortable):	What did you ask?
Counselor:	What do they feel when you hit them?
Alan:	They are frightened, afraid.
Counselor:	Is it pleasant for you?
Alan:	Not so much.
Counselor:	You said earlier that you like others to be fearful of you.
Alan:	That is not entirely true.
Counselor:	What is true?
Alan:	I really want them to be more my friends.
Counselor:	So you frighten the children to make them be your friend?
Alan:	Yes, and it helps, because they let me join them whenever I want, which they don't do with anyone else. That feels good.
Counselor:	So you want to be different from other kids? Or you want to be like them?
Alan:	Yes and no, because they don't invite me to parties, the teacher doesn't like me as she likes them, she is always angry, yelling at me, always blaming me, I want her to like me.
Counselor:	Why do you think she is angry at you?
Alan:	Because I come to school late, I run around in class, and when I come in hungry, I fight with the kids, it drives her crazy.

Counselor:	So what do you think about your behavior?
Alan (after a long silence):	I cannot help it. Mom doesn't wake me up, I am tired and restless. I look at her [the teacher], but I don't listen, because I can't sit that long, and I don't understand a lot of what is going on, anyway. .... I wish I could get out for a while, get some air and come back, then I will probably be more relaxed.
Counselor:	Would you like to talk to the teacher? Perhaps we can help you understand each other.
Alan:	Only if you come with me.

Besides coming from a background of neglect and abuse, Alan also suffers from learning disabilities, perhaps also from attention deficit disorder. During the conversation with the counselor, he came to understand what makes him so restless and nervous, and admitted for the first time that it is not that much fun to be aggressive. He could have been influenced by the film and the hard consequences of impulsive behavior that it depicts, but the counselor led him to explore his own behavior and to start looking at his true feelings. He does not really want to be aggressive, and is now able to see the social price he pays for being violent. This is a starting point to raise motivation for change, and a beginning of an action change.

The working stage constitutes the greatest bulk of the treatment time. Very often the therapist moves to action—that is, guidance and instrumental assistance—already, as in the case of Alan. However, most of the guidance and training occurs at the final stage of treatment.

The Action Stage

Our task at the action stage is to highlight the gains in self-understanding and insight and assist children in achieving the desired change. At this point, we want to strengthen their motivation to reduce aggression, provide them with effective tools for resolving conflicts, and help prevent their relapse to earlier stages of change. The literature for this stage should present characters who can be role models, who can serve as a viable source of vicarious learning. Also useful is literature that presents alternative behaviors, thus expanding the limited repertoire of responses of aggressive children.

A book that we particularly like to use at this stage is *A Fence, a Sheep, and a Man With a Problem* (Biran, 1994). It tells of a man who had trouble falling asleep, and so he counted sheep trying to get through a fence. He noticed that each sheep had its own style of passing through one went around the fence, another crawled under it, one cooperated with another sheep, while yet another went headlong into the fence. In short, each sheep represents a way of coping with conflict. The children are asked to identify the style that suits them best, discuss the pros and cons of their coping style, choose a sheep whose style they would like to adopt, and discuss how they can succeed in achieving their goal.

> In a group of teenagers, several boys selected the sheep that goes headlong into the fence. Alex said, "For years I have behaved this way, I get into trouble at school and at home, but I never thought there are so many different styles of coping. My friends usually act like I do. . .I wish I could let go sometimes, and act like the sheep that stands aside and looks away . . . life could be so much easier."

In each of the themes we cover are stories that offer some guidance and resolution. When focusing on anger management, I mentioned many books, most of which also discuss ways to deal with anger, such as *When Sophie Gets Angry, Really Really Angry* (Bang, 1999). To understand power struggles, we often use the story, "The Smiley Face" (Noy, 1995; see Appendix A), to show how being modest and refraining from the use of force actually gives one real power. When dealing with lack of control, the poem "I am My Own Commander" (Bokek, 1980) presents a model of a boy who decided to take charge of his life.

Developmental Considerations

In selecting the literature, the therapist must consider the age of the treatment children and their cognitive and emotional development. The content of the story must be clear, so that the child can easily identify with the situation. Sometimes we prefer to tell a story rather than read it to the children in order to ease their understanding and accelerate the identification process. In other cases, we break a story or poem into segments and deal with each piece at a time, in order to get the most out of the text.

Vocabulary, especially words related to emotions, can be a hurdle, which inhibits the child's ability to connect with the imaginary component of the literature as well as his or her self-expressiveness. Sometimes we have to develop a language of feelings deliberately before we even start, in order to smooth the therapy process.

Empathy is a skill that develops with age. Older children are more capable of perspective taking and of understanding the psychological situation. Thus, the complexity of the situation in the text must be adjusted to the child's age and ability.

The type of problems that lead to aggressive response also differs with age. Young children are more concerned with concrete situations, such as sharing objects, learning difficulties, parental punishment, and abuse by siblings, while adolescents are more concerned with social issues, such as fairness, respect, justice, friendships, and relationships with the opposite sex. Thus, the situation presented in the story should be relevant to the issues of concern for the age level of participants.

Gender is another related issue; boys and girls have different interests even at the same age. Boys are more instrumental and power seeking, while girls are more intimate. The literature should be adjusted to the different interests of boys and girls, and the characters presented to each should be of their own gender, in order to ease the identification process.

The Bibliotherapy Session: Process and Format

There are many ways to apply bibliotherapy, and there is no one right way. For instance, the session can start by identifying emotions and then move to the content, or vice versa. No matter how a session is arranged, what is of utmost importance is that *the literature serves as a vehicle* to help the children partici-pate in the therapeutic process. A therapeutic process takes place in all types of sessions, and the merit of the literature and the effectiveness of the therapist are both responsible for the change in children's behavior.

A Recommended Bibliotherapy Format

The format that we have found to work best is comprised of four steps. The first three steps are structured to follow the literature, while the last one constitutes a direct therapeutic process with the children. Our observations suggest that about two thirds of the session is devoted to the discussion related to the literature and one third to the direct intervention (Shechtman & Nir Shafrir, 2007).

We start the session by *reading aloud* to the children, usually without handing out the text. There are several reasons for such a practice: the simplest one is, of course, the difficulties some children face in reading a text; some children have attention problems, others have language difficulties. If a child has to struggle while reading, much of the excitement and enthusiasm is gone. As we work with many young children, reading to them is a necessity. Yet, many teenagers that we work with have reading difficulties too. To them, reading aloud in the right tone and voice helps them capture the imagina-tive level of the story. Images are mental pictures and such images have a way of sticking in our memory much longer than words, argues Kilpatrick (Kilpatrick et al., 1994). Shared reading is actually a practice that professors use with adult students. I had a professor who read Shakespeare to us. It was a very different experience to listen to him than to read it on our own. Shared reading works, says Kilpatrick, because "the right book, read in the right way, brings a thrill of excitement and enchantment" (p. 26).

However, from a therapeutic point of view, the even more important aspect of reading aloud is the messages it conveys to the children that the counselor cares about them by taking the time to provide some enjoyment in their lives. Listening to an adult reading is a luxury, which is why many children like their parents to read to them long after they have mastered reading—a luxury that most aggressive children are deprived of in their everyday life. Shared reading helps to create an emotional bond not only to the story, but also with the person doing the reading, that is, the counselor. Related to this is the emotional climate we want to establish in our sessions. We certainly want the sessions to look different than a regular classroom lesson, which commonly bears a negative connotation for the treatment children because of their frequent sense of failure. Thus, we want our sessions to be free of functional difficulties (e.g., reading), and we want them to be enjoyable and fun. After all, our treatment children are not a captive audience, and we do want them to come back.

Another reason to avoid showing the text to the children is to prevent them from getting engrossed in the details. We want to keep the content as ambiguous as possible, so that they can identify with or project onto the characters. Therefore, we prefer reading a text just once, and usually do not go back to the same one at a later session unless the children request it. The listeners need to capture the spirit of the story and the central emotions of the character. Going into detail inhibits their emotional involvement in the literature.

The next step is *identifying emotions*. After reading the story/poem or watching the film, we identify the main characters and ask, "How does he or she feel?" Many counselors and therapists are tempted to ask, "What do you think?" which prevents us from dealing with emotions. When we ask about the characters' feelings, we achieve several goals. First, we send a message that we are focusing on emotions. This is not the focus that children know from school; we want to establish the norm of speaking about emotions in our treatment. Second, by relating to the characters' emotions, we develop the children's vocabulary of feelings and assist them in identifying and exploring their feelings. I believe that self-exploration leads to catharsis and insight—two of our aims in therapy. Finally, the focus on feelings of the characters enhances empathy, another major goal of our intervention.

Let's take, for example, the poem "Joey." Asking a question about Joey's feelings brings up emotions such as anger, sadness, pain, frustration, fear, and anxiety. For some children, this list expands the vocabulary of emotions. For all of them, it is an opportunity to relate to these emotions from their own experiences and develop empathy to the pain and suffering of the child. Moreover, by starting with feelings, we eliminate the critical tone attached to wrong or deviant behavior. We also convey a message that all feelings are accepted, that none are right or wrong.

The third step involves *exploring the dynamics of the character's behavior*. A good text usually reflects the dynamics of human behavior accurately. Some feelings may lead to certain behaviors. For example, frustration and unfairness may lead to anger and aggression. Loneliness, helplessness, and fear may lead to aggression or conversely to withdrawal. Such behaviors also have consequences that may further lead to a certain set of emotions.

Going back to the same poem, "Joey," after we explore Joey's feelings, we may want to explore three dynamics of behavior: reasons that lead to aggression, the consequences of aggression, and the price the aggressor pays. Thus, we can ask about possible causes of Joey's behavior. As these are not mentioned in the text, the children will project on the poem their own causes of behavior. This is important diagnostic information for the therapist. Some children may talk about their parents, others may speak of a sibling or teacher, and many talk about friends—all of whom treated them unfairly, with force, or with neglect, or rejection. It is not clear from the poem whether Joey's behavior is intentional, but we discuss unintentional behavior because it is less threatening and try to understand how an unintentional act can cause so much harm. We then explore anger, impulsiveness, and the inability to foresee the consequences of one's actions. Finally, we talk about the way aggression inflicts harm back to the aggressor. This is an important point because of the attitudes of endorsing aggression that many aggressive children and youth hold. They need to understand how their own aggression reflects back on them. Kubovi (1993), one of the early bibliotherapists, refers to this as a "mini-psychology lesson" for young people, in which they can learn the principles of human behavior.

The fourth step is *self-exploration*. We leave self-exploration for the end of the session for several reasons. First, we want the children to take advantage of the indirect method of affective bibliotherapy, going through the identification process with the literary characters, the identification and expansion of feelings, and the understanding of their behavior from a distance. Such a process is nonthreatening, because it is not directly related to the treatment children; the literature is used as a protective shield. Second, the all-accepting climate that the counselor establishes assures the children that, no matter what they say, their feelings will be acknowledged and accepted and their behavior will be understood.

We open the self-exploration stage of treatment with the question: "Can you share your own experiences that are related to this poem?" Most of the time, the children are able to do so. This is when self-exploration takes place more directly, including reflection on their behavior. Such reflection often leads to insight into their behavior, after which children start developing motivation to make a change.

A very important strategy at the exploration stage is the clarifying process. This process helps children evaluate their own level of aggression, make a decision regarding the change they want to see in their behavior, and see how they can arrive at the desired result. A clarifying process can be achieved by selecting a response from several given options, choosing between extreme situations, or placement on a continuum (with younger children, drawing may replace a verbal response, and self-exploration is then carried out based on the drawing).

The last strategy is the one we use most often. We ask the children to place themselves on a continuum from 1 to 10 on aggression. They mark the place, explain why they placed themselves there, and discuss their feelings, thoughts, and behavior in this place. Then we ask them to put themselves on the continuum in the place they wish to be. We then work on the gap between the real and ideal behavior. This is a powerful technique, based on an integrative theory, treating the child as a whole.

For example, in a group of 9-year-old boys, the counselor read the poem, "Yaron is Angry" (Omer, 1978; see Appendix A). Following a discussion of the dynamics of anger and aggression—in this case, Yaron's frustration with himself that led him to destroy his own drawing—the counselor moved on to a clarifying process. She asked the boys to place themselves on a continuum from 1 to 10, expressing how angry they get when frustrated, and to list their typical behaviors in response to the frustration. They were asked to mark the continuum in blue on the place they are in the present and in yellow on the place they want to be.

Jeremy, a highly aggressive boy with ADHD, but smart and popular, gave himself a blue 9 and spelled out his own typical behaviors: fighting, cursing, and door slamming.

Counselor:	How do you feel about your behavior?
Jeremy:	Sometimes I feel ashamed.
Counselor:	What makes you feel ashamed?
Jeremy:	I am different than the other kids.
Counselor:	Well, people are different from each other.
Jeremy:	Yes, but I am different in a negative way. Sometimes my friends wonder about my behavior; some of them would actually like me more if I didn't behave in such an impulsive way.
Counselor:	It seems to bother you enough for you to look for some change.
Jeremy:	Yes, and I placed myself in yellow on number 3. I would like to be less aggressive, to be able to ignore some things that trigger me, to relax, to communicate when there's a conflict, to take out my anger on something without hurting anyone, just like Yaron did in the poem.
Counselor:	Any idea how you are going to achieve the desired change?
Jeremy:	Maybe take out my anger on something rather than hurt someone, like Yaron did in the poem.

As this was only the third session, the counselor refrained from proceeding to the action stage. She felt that Jeremy had done enough work for this stage in the change process. He does not like his behavior and can even identify the desired alternative behavior. The motivation is there, and any attempt to push further at this point may frustrate him. He needs to continue with such clarifying processes until he is confident that it his own choice to make a change. This, in turn, will increase the efforts he makes to create change and sustain the newly acquired behavior.

It is not always necessary, though, to go through the whole clarifying process, working our way from thoughts to feelings to behavior. Children are in different stages of change when we meet them, and sometimes they are already aware of the negative aspects of their behavior. In such cases, we need to adjust the process to them. Let's say we are working on anger management, and as soon as the therapist finishes reading the poem, "My Monster," Dina says, "I can show you my monster," and draws an ugly screaming creature. "I hate my monster," she says," but I can't get rid of it." Dina seems to be aware of her verbal aggression; she has already admitted that she does not like her behavior, but has difficulties controlling it. There is no point in insisting on the discussion of dynamics in an indirect way with her. We may go on and discuss the dynamics of her own monster and concentrate on ways to get rid of it. The process is most effective when it is adjusted to the unique situation of each child. Nonetheless, for those who are still highly self-defensive, it is better to follow the sequence of steps described above, so as to ready them for the stage of self-exploration.

Sometimes we add a fifth step, which is *skills training*. However, we refrain from doing this at the initial stages of the change process. Rather, this additional step is most appropriate when we reach the insight and action stages of treatment. We then use a lot of role-playing, letter writing, play writing, psychodrama, and therapeutic cards—all important to increase skills of prosocial behavior. All these methods will be illustrated in detail in later chapters.

The Role and Skills of the Therapist

The role the therapist takes in the treatment process is immanent to its success. The literature provides the structure, the content, and models of desired behavior, but, after all, it is the therapist who navigates the process toward self-exploration, insight, and action. I once walked into a class of bibliotherapists and asked them what a therapeutic process is, and they didn't know how to respond. So I went on, asking what behaviors the therapist expects of the client. What would be considered constructive work? Finally, I asked them what skills does a therapist need to be efficient in his or her work? They didn't know how to answer these questions either, because they had only been trained to use the text. That is, they were trained in the "biblio" aspect of the process but not the therapy aspect. I ended up teaching helping skills to this group.

Therapists in affective bibliotherapy use the skills that therapists are normally familiar with. They ask questions, use encourages, paraphrases, summarizing statements, reflection of feelings, interpretations, challenges, guidance, and self-disclosure. These skills have been widely discussed and researched, as noted in Chapter 3. However, in using literature, the therapist has three additional roles: a preparation role that is related to the content of the text; identification of legitimizing messages in the text that are important to enhance the children's well-being; and conducting the clarifying process to increase self-exploration and change.

It is not enough to select a good piece of literature. The therapist needs to identify the major theme of the text that could help children change, and *identify the dynamics* that he or she can use to lead children effectively in the process of change. An unprepared therapist may get lost in the text because the children may lead the discussion to entirely different directions. Therapists must not be rigid about this, but must know in advance how they want to utilize the text.

Take, for example, a poem I have often referred to: "The Angry Heart." Its major theme is impulsive behavior. This is important to identify, because it also dictates the theme for the clarifying process that should be conducted at the end of the session (see below). In this case, the dynamics of such behavior would be:

- Envy, insult, and a sense of betrayal lead to anger, which may in turn lead to impulsive behavior.
- It is often impossible to foresee the consequences of impulsive behavior.
- After facing the consequences, people may feel shame, sorrow, and remorse.

These dynamics are typical of human behavior, and becoming aware of them means understanding others' behavior as well as your own.

Therapists use *legitimizing statements* to convey a message of understanding and acceptance. Normally, when children misbehave, they are judged, criticized, or subjected to moralization about their behavior. In contrast, we want to provide a new interpersonal experience for these children. We use statements relevant to the text that show we understand, that it does happen to others. We try to normalize the feelings and behavior in order to reduce resistance and self-defense.

Continuing with the example of "The Angry Heart," we can say

- Children hurt each other, sometimes without being aware of the consequences.
- It is quite painful and lonely to be betrayed by a friend; we expect friends to share stuff, and when it does not happen, we get very frustrated.
- Sometimes we lose control and feel badly afterwards; when we are very angry, it is difficult for us to verbalize our feelings.
- Sometimes we cannot foresee the consequences of our impulsive behavior, even though they may be very bad.
- Seeing a person in pain because of you makes you feel guilty, ashamed, frightened, and sad.
- Explaining yourself, expressing remorse, and asking for forgiveness can help you feel better following a bad incident.

These are therapeutic statements, unique to bibliotherapy, which help people grow emotionally and change. One of the advantages of using literature is to convey to children the message that things that they feel or do are universal, that they are not the only "bad guys," that we are not mad at them, that we are not shocked, and that in the current session they are accepted. In my experience, the more the therapist uses such statements, the better the therapeutic climate and the client's compliance with the process.

The session ends with a *clarifying process*. As mentioned, the theme of the text is also the clarifying question. In the case of the above poem, it is impulsiveness, and the question would be "To what extent do you react impulsively?" The question may be limited to friends or family and can take the form of a continuum, extremes, or levels. The therapists needs to lead the children using questions, so that they understand what they think about their behavior, how they feel about it, how they currently act, and how they wish to act in the future. The goal is to make children aware of their thought process, feelings, and action, and to identify the discrepancies among them. For some children, there is no discrepancy. Usually aggressive children endorse aggression and feel good about their strength and power. Yet, many children, if not at the beginning stage, then along the process, are ready to admit that they don't always like what they do, but cannot control themselves. It is the role of the therapist to help them look at the pros and cons of their behavior. Once they identify the price they pay, the children are more ready to take action. If the therapist is equipped with techniques to work with children, the clarifying process can take the form of a game.

One counselor worked with a group of three mildly retarded children, two boys and a girl. With each of them, she did a clarifying process. They first drew a picture of the sun, in which they wrote the words "what makes me angry." They then added arrows around the sun and wrote along those arrows things that cause them to react impulsively. The things they wrote included: when someone draws them into a fight, when someone puts them down, when they face difficulties in schooling, when the teacher yells at them, and when they are punished or abused by parents or older siblings. Then each child was asked to state the most frequent cause of his/her aggression and the typical reaction to it. Next, each received a thermometer and was asked to show how high (hot) he or she gets when this happens. Finally, each went through a short clarifying process regarding the behavior he/she wants to reduce. For example, Jimmy wanted to stop screaming in class.

Counselor: Why is it important to you? [thinking level]
Jimmy: Because children and the teacher get mad at me.
Counselor: How do you feel when you scream in class?
Jimmy: I am ashamed, it is a bit childish. [feeling level]
Counselor: How will you lower the "heat" on your "thermometer"?
Jimmy: I will draw on my paper until I destroy it; this will help me get out the anger [he took the idea from a poem he heard in class].
Counselor: That could be one way, as it doesn't hurt anyone.

In this case the counselor used additional techniques to adjust the process to the level of the children, and make it more enjoyable for them, but she used the same method of clarifying processes.

Summary

This chapter has discussed the application of affective bibliotherapy, first addressing the selection of literature, then outlining the process of therapy. The selection of literature depends on several criteria. First, it should be high-quality fiction books, poems, movies, or pictures. By high quality, I mean nonsimplistic content, presenting human conflict that reflects the dynamics of human behavior accurately, a story that is well-built and has balanced characters.

Second, the content of the selected literature needs to fit the problem being treated and the goals of the intervention. In our intervention, we included four goals in accordance with the deficits common to aggressive children: dealing with emotions, increasing empathy, understanding the issue of power struggles and abuse, and increasing self-control. The literature that we use has all these elements, often combined, as the four are highly related. Nevertheless, some literature fits a certain deficit better than another.

Third, the literature has to be applied in accordance with the level of change the child experiences. Some texts are more appropriate at the initial stage, particularly those relating to victimization, while others suit the working stage better, because they focus on the precedents and consequences of aggressive behavior. Literature that centers on problem resolution best fits the last stage of action, in which we help children find alternatives to aggression.

Finally, the selection of literature needs to take into consideration the developmental abilities—cognitive and affective—of the treatment children, as well as their gender.

The second part of the chapter has discussed the way we employ affective bibliotherapy, and the therapeutic discussion that follows. The format that we use most often is comprised of four steps. We first read the literature aloud, then discuss the feelings of the character, next discuss the dynamics of the behavior presented in the literature, and end with self-exploration. This structure fits our assumption that most of the intervention with aggressive children should be indirect; this is why bibliotherapy was selected as a method of intervention in the first place. Nonetheless, the described four-step format is flexible. Often, children invite us to work with them directly much earlier. If the child or the group seems ready, we may skip steps, go back to earlier steps, or even ignore them.

Therapists play an important role in the therapy process. Not only do they have to be able to use the necessary helping skills that any therapists needs, they also need to possess skills to use the selected literature effectively. They need to identify the major theme of the text, be able to use legitimizing statements to increase the well-being of their clients, and to conduct clarifying processes that will accelerate change. As in any therapy with children, using methods and techniques that make the experience more enjoyable and ease the learning process is of utmost importance. The next chapters will guide the reader in mastering such methods and skills.

Chapter 5
Groups for Aggressive Children

Introduction

The effectiveness of groups for aggressive children and adolescents is still under debate. Although many clinicians do work in groups with such children, some researchers caution that aggressive children may have a negative impact on each other in a group setting. Dishion and colleagues (Dishion, McCord, & Poulin, 1999), published a well-known study on violent adolescents treated in groups in a summer camp, which showed that violence among treatment youth increased. However, in the same article they also refer to other studies, where aggression decreased among aggressive children following group inter-vention. Several factors in their study might have affected the results: the age of the participants, the initial level of their violence, and the setting in which treatment was provided. Perhaps placing violent youth together in a camp situation, in which participants are removed from mainstream norms, and putting them in intensive relationships with each other for many hours is not a promising setting for changing aggressive behavior. Nonetheless, it makes sense to be concerned about negative mutual impact in a group comprised entirely of aggressive children, particularly in adolescence, when group pres-sure becomes particularly strong.

Aggressive children are more difficult to control in a group situation because they trigger destructive responses among each other, thus creating major discipline problems. Moreover, aggressive children usually come from a difficult family background and may be inhibited from sharing their troubles in a group setting:

> Take the case of Andy, a ten-year-old boy from a family of neglect and abuse. Until his recent disappearance, his father used to hit him with a belt. Andy was placed in a group with four other aggressive children of his age. Though restless all the time, he did cooperate—until the fifth session, when the story, "The Bully," was read to them. In this story, a bully abuses another classmate because of a history of abuse by his father. At that point, Andy became wild, and when the story mentioned that the perpetrator had been hit by his father, he made the comment: "all fathers are alike." At the end of the story, when the perpetrator attacks his victim, Andy said: "He is just

Z. Shechtman, *Treating Child and Adolescent Aggression Through Bibliotherapy*,
The Springer Series on Human Exceptionality, DOI 10.1007/978-0-387-09745-9_5,
© Springer Science+Business Media, LLC 2009

like his father. . .he wants to imitate his father . . . there is no way out." Following that interaction, Andy became very destructive in the group, picked a fight with another boy, and hit him. It was impossible to calm him down, and the counselor eventually asked him to leave the room. He did, but continued to disturb the process until the end of the session, then dropped out of the program altogether.

It seems that Andy was threatened by the story. He strongly identified himself with the boy, was angry at his father, and felt hopeless about himself. But he couldn't handle this in a group situation at such an early stage of the treatment. In an individual session, Andy might have been able to share his story with the counselor. In a group setting, where it was so simple to trigger another boy into a fight, denial seemed like an easier path. Discipline problems are very frequent in groups with aggressive children because such behavior is contagious, most kids are intolerant and easily irritated, and they too have internalized patterns of aggressive responses.

Taking into consideration the difficulties of group work with aggressive children, we take certain precautions to prevent negative mutual impact and, in fact, increase positive effects by securing a better working climate. First, we strive for a heterogeneous group composition; that is, we include a few non-aggressive children in each group of aggressors. These nonaggressive children are an important addition to balance attitudes endorsing aggression with attitudes opposing aggression. These kids strive for a positive climate in the group and help maintain it by modeling, providing support, and insisting on sticking to group rules. Moreover, as they are known to be nonproblem children, they increase the value of the group; after all, who wants to belong to a group of troublemakers? They also help to diminish labeling, an important component in treatment of aggressive kids. A group comprised solely of aggressive kids may decide that, since they are already labeled as such, they might as well live up to expectations. In addition, we work with very small groups (3–6) in order to handle discipline problems effectively. Finally, adding girls to groups of aggressive boys is another strategy we have found helpful in maintaining positive group interactions.

Despite the difficulties involved, I see many advantages in group work with aggressive children once the above precautionary measures are in place. Indeed, in the two studies (Shechtman, 2004a; Shechtman & Ben-David, 1999) in which I compared individual and group treatment of aggressive children, no differences were found in children's progress. In both studies, children reduced scores on aggression following treatment compared to a control group, regardless of the treatment format.

Advantages of the Group Setting

The group is a natural setting for children. In groups, children learn about other human beings, about their thoughts and feelings. This, in turn, enriches their own lives, as they learn social skills and develop social competence. The difficult situations that arise in a group of aggressive kids may actually become a laboratory for learning prosocial behavior.

For example, after Andy dropped out of his treatment group, the rest of the children were quite unsettled by it. When a group member leaves, this can be devastating for a cohesive group (Yalom & Leszcz, 2005), and in this case they were in their fifth session, after some cohesion had been developed. At the beginning of the next session, the counselor asked about the children's feelings following the incident. Some felt relieved, but Dennis said, "I feel sorry for him because he misses a lot. We are here talking about special things in our lives, not like in any other place in the school, we talk about personal things, and that is a nice feeling." Andy's dropping out also became an opportunity for an activity focusing on group rules. The children were asked what would make the place more comfortable for them. They mentioned behaviors like listening to each us, respecting each other, keeping secrets, and cooperating. These four became the ground rules for the group and, whenever there was an interruption, the counselor referred them to the rules they had all agreed upon.

A group setting provides many opportunities to develop attitudes and values. The variety of thoughts, opinions, and attitudes that come up may help children rethink their initial thoughts. This is particularly important in the case of aggressive children, whose thought process is biased toward endorsement of aggression. Hearing others' opinions can be an eye opener. For instance, while watching the movie *Madi*, this same group had the following spontaneous discussion as to whether Madi should forgive his aggressor:

Sandy: I don't really understand how Madi forgave him and became friends with him. I would never forgive him.
Howie: I would report him to the police.
Adrian: He didn't know the harsh consequences of his behavior. He didn't really mean it. Don't you see how unhappy he is? Don't you recognize his efforts to make up for it?
Sandy: I agree. He must be terribly scared now and does make efforts to help Madi.

Later on, when they discussed Madi's medical situation, Sandy mentions that it is scary. Howie says it would be better to die than live such a life, but Sandy argues with him that handicapped people learn to live with their disability. "My mom is disabled and she gets on well, and I certainly wouldn't want her to die," he says. Hearing such a different opinion, particularly when expressed in such a personal manner, has a strong effect on others.

Group members' feedback is an important avenue for learning. Children use their common background to provide feedback, and sometimes here-and-now situations provide opportunities for feedback as well.

The group described above is talking about how to control anger. Howie turns to Dennis and cites his screaming in class as an example of losing control. Dennis seems indifferent. Howie goes on, using an "I statement": "When you yelled at me in front of the class, I was really embarrassed." After initially responding "so what?" Dennis looks at Howie and admits, "Yeah, sometimes I can't control my anger, I break things, I also hit kids, especially my little brother."

A group also becomes a source of support. Toward termination of the above group, the discussion focused on self-control.

Dennis summarizes his achievements in the group: "I am much less involved in fights nowadays. And I don't involve my older brother that much anymore, so I can prevent him from being aggressive, because he gets really wild. Instead, I talk to my mom. But I can't promise I will have full control. I don't know if I will always remember, and besides they all expect me to help in a fight because I am the strongest guy in class."

To this monologue, Howie responds: "But you also promised here to control yourself, so maybe we can remind you." Sandy adds: "I'll help you. I will remind you of your decision. I'll pull you away from the scene of a fight, and you can help me."

Interpersonal interactions and feedback are unique to group situations, Burlingame and Fuhriman (1990) argued during a debate on the similarity of individual and group treatment. Holmes and Kivlighan (2000) found that group clients differ from individual treatment clients in the therapeutic factors they value in treatment: group clients mentioned group climate and vicarious learning as the most important mechanisms of change, whereas clients in individual treatment appreciate more catharsis/insight and problem identification. Burlingame, Fuhriman, and Johnson (2004) identified interpersonal feedback and alliance with the group as the most promising mechanisms of change in any group. Such unique mechanisms of change also work in groups of aggressive children and probably compensate for the lack of other therapeutic factors that do exist in individual therapy.

The combination of a group format with bibliotherapy is particularly effective. Many suggest that bibliotherapy should be provided in groups: Mazza (2003) has found that poetry adds to group cohesion; Gersie (1997) suggests that the engagement of group members in a story helps explore the richness of the literature; and Klee (2000) points to the enrichment of attitudes and values in a group setting. I would add to these advantages the frame or the structure that the text provides, which eases the process in the group work. In one study, I measured therapist satisfaction when using bibliotherapy compared to therapy without literature. The level of satisfaction was significantly higher in the group of therapists who employed bibliotherapy (Shechtman, 2006a).

Two group processes will now be presented in detail to further explicate the bibliotherapy process in a group format. I begin by relating the process of a group of elementary-school children, and then follow this with a description of the process in a junior high school group of adolescents. Some of the literature texts are identical, while others are adjusted to the participants' age and developmental needs. Mechanisms unique to the group format are highlighted in each group.

Demonstration: A Group of Young Children

Introduction

The group was comprised of three 10-year-old children from a special class for children with learning difficulties and disabilities. The three aggressive boys were identified by their classmates as being highly aggressive, and then was randomly divided into experimental group and control conditions group. Thus, the two of the aggressive boys, Jacob and Eliot, were placed in the experimental group, together with Susie, a less aggressive girl. (Recall that we work with heterogeneous groups in terms of level of aggression and gender, in order to limit negative influences of aggressive children on each other.) The third aggressive boy served as a control group.

> Jacob was adopted. He is restless and verbally and physically aggressive. He uses abusive language towards peers and teachers, threatens younger children, screams in class, and frequently gets involved in fistfights. He perceives himself as a victim, complains that no one loves him, and threatens to kill himself.
>
> Eliot comes from a poor family of divorce in which his mother is psychologically dysfunctional. He has a hard time complying with rules, is resistant, and gets easily out of control, particularly when frustrated.
>
> Susie comes from a family in conflict; her father has been unemployed for years, and the family is poor. She is restless, tends to bother her classmates, and associates mainly with younger kids. She was advised to be treated with Ritalin, but her parents refused.

Because these three children were reactively aggressive, their major problem was lack of self-control. The goal of the intervention was, therefore, to help them deal with anger and increase self-control.

The Group Process

In the *first session*, the counselor introduces a poem that discusses emotions, such as envy, betrayal, and unfairness, as the cause of an aggressive act and points to the unexpected consequences of lack of control. The children first identify the emotions of the aggressor: his disappointment with his friend, who he always treated so well; his sadness for not having toys that his friend has; and his anger for being rejected. They also identify his concern and fear of the consequences of his behavior. "I'm afraid he killed his friend," says Eliot, and Susie adds, "His friend is badly injured and needs to be hospitalized." But Jacob, still identifying with the perpetrator's anger, insists: "He really insulted him! ... He made him so angry ... He does want him to die."

The counselor uses several responses to convey the message that the act was accidental, such as, "He was very, very angry, but he didn't mean to hurt anybody." She avoids being judgmental, so that the children can eventually own up to their own lack of control. Indeed, when she asks them about their experiences with uncontrolled anger, Jacob admits that he hits his little sister when she messes with his stuff, and Eliot admits that when his teacher screamed at him in front of his classmates, he was so furious that he hit her hard and injured her. "How did you feel following this incident?" the counselor asks. "I was very frightened, because I knew my parents would be called in and would punish me by spanking me and locking me in the bathroom." It is very difficult to raise Eliot's empathy to the teacher's pain; at this point, he can only talk about his anger. When asked about possible alternative behaviors, he can't think of any. Nor can he accept the feedback of his friends or any of the alternatives they offer. Jacob says that if he didn't hit the teacher she would love him, and Susie suggests writing her a letter, but all Eliot can say is: "She is a bad teacher."

This is only the first session, yet Eliot's strong identification with the character in the text is evident. At this very early stage of change, he is unaware of his behavior and is governed by an external locus of control. The counselor makes a summary statement suggesting that a large amount of anger may lead to unexpected results and that alternative ways need to be sought. She does not discuss alternative behaviors unless suggested by peers, and rightly so. At this point, they need to establish trust with the counselor and the group, rather than be pushed toward solutions.

In *second session*, the counselor introduces the poem, "My Monster," to the children. The poem tells about a monster that controls the character's behavior and makes him do a lot of bad things. The children identify with his fear and the shame he feels about his deeds. The discussion focuses on the difficulties of controlling our behavior. The children do not wait to move to the personal reflection stage; they immediately connect to the sense of lack of control through personal stories.

Susie: When somebody hits me, I hit them back. I am no pushover.
Eliot: When Joseph [a classmate] hits me, I immediately hit him back.
Jacob: When I am edgy, I hit but then I cry.

None of the children are thinking of the victim at this point. They all feel that they need to defend their power and prestige, and therefore do not see a need to change. The counselor asks how they feel.

Jacob: I like the poem. Sometimes I feel like that boy.
Counselor: How do you feel like him?
Jacob: I don't always succeed in class.
Counselor: How does it make you feel when you don't succeed?
Jacob: I'm sad and angry at everyone … then I cry and my mother forgives me.
Counselor: Do you think you can manage your monster?
Jacob: I have to control myself, to stop throwing things, and stop yelling at the teacher.

Here we notice the beginning of a reconnection to his true feelings and a motivation to change.

Eliot also confesses that he hits others, but he seems helpless because older kids take advantage of him. He feels sad, and the group members try to help.

Susie: You can play with our classmates rather than the older kids.
Jacob: You can be my friend and we won't fight.

These reactions indicate that a positive group climate has been established. Indeed, the counselor notices it and reinforces the trend, saying, "I feel that a pleasant climate has been established here. Thanks for cooperating so well."

The *third session* is very similar to the previous one, except that they work with another poem. Thus, the discussion continues on how frustration leads to anger and aggression, and the children share examples from their lives. But now the children identify the triggers to their aggression more specifically. Whereas Jacob talked at the previous session about being unsuccessful, he now identifies that it is particularly in math class; Susie identifies chores at home as a cause of her negative behavior; and Eliot is frustrated when his father skips a visit. They also become critical about negative behavior: "It is not nice to behave like that," says Jacob. In their attempt to fight the bad guy that is controlling their lives, new alternatives come up, particularly direct communication, which is probably one of the best strategies in resolving a conflict. They mention the option of talking to an adult, sharing concerns verbally, expressing their feelings, and, in Jacob's words, "fantasizing that the bad guy went away."

The *fourth session* to address the children's sense of victimization, is devoted to the poem, "A Fight in the Garden," in which an older boy picks a fight with a younger boy, only because he wants to win, but unexpectedly the younger one hits back and wins the fight. The children identify the need to show strength and power, but they also criticize the perpetrator for selecting someone weak to fight with. They identify with the young boy because they are often abused by older and stronger children and feel good about the victory of the younger child.

When they discuss the issue from their own experiences, they recall that they, too, sometimes behave like the perpetrator in this poem. Susie shares with the group that when her mom is angry with her, she takes out her anger on her little brother, but he hits back and it hurts. Susie's remark teaches the others the principle of transference, thus creating an opportunity for them to look at their own behavior. Indeed, Jacob confesses that there is a classmate he hits only because he is quiet and doesn't react. Eliot shares that he cannot resist the provocations of a classroom bully. Focusing first on the victim rather than the perpetrator seems to be an effective strategy to reduce self-defense and increase the children's willingness to admit to their own wrong behavior.

The counselor then asks them if they want to change their behavior, and what is it that they want to change. Jacob says he wants to stop being aggressive and he'd actually like to be like the quiet boy he bullies. Eliot says he wants to improve his relationship with his teacher and stop cursing her. Susie wants to stop hitting her little brother. They all have identified goals for change. At this stage, ways to achieve change are discussed, including involving an adult or communicating verbally: "Tell the teacher that she is making you irritable, but do it during recess so she is not hurt," Susie advises Eliot. As a girl, Susie is more attuned to interpersonal relationships, and her contribution to Eliot, who can't see the other party's point of view yet, is invaluable. "I will try to control myself, and not react to her," he responds.

In *fifth session*, they discuss a story about a group that bullies a victim, which raises a lot of empathy for the victim. The discussion focuses on group pressure, direct and indirect support of aggression, and possible ways to cope. Jacob and Susie suggest involving an adult. Only Eliot still holds on to attitudes endorsing aggression. "I would get help from another classmate and hit back," he says. Next, when they discuss their own experiences, they mention a victim in their class, a new immigrant, whom they all bully. Now it becomes clear to them that they don't like their own aggression. Susie suggests helping the new immigrant, Jacob says he can teach him to play soccer, and Eliot wants to invite him home to play on his computer. We do not know whether all this will be put into practice, but their attitudes seem to be changing.

In the *sixth session*, the counselor reads the poem, "Yaron is Angry" (Omer, 1978; see Appendix A) to the children. This poem tells about a frustrated boy who doesn't like his own drawing. The children first identify the sense of helplessness when anger takes over, then the discussion moves to ways of handling it. The character in the text wants to do many aggressive things, but ends up throwing away the picture. The children understand that this is a way of getting relief without hurting others. They are now very open about their aggression and concentrate on behavior change. Eliot wants to stop the cycle of aggression-crying-sadness. He first reacts aggressively, then gets into trouble, starts crying, his mom calls him a baby for crying, then he gets depressed, "then I don't care about anything," he says. The clarifying process with him is interesting.

Eliot:	When I am attacked, I hit back to get even, I don't want to be a sap.
Counselor:	And afterwards, how do you feel?
Eliot:	Sometimes OK and sometimes not.
Counselor:	How is that?
Eliot:	I feel good that I did not lose, but then I get punished by teachers and my parents.
Counselor:	Do you want to prevent such fights?
Eliot:	Yes, but I don't know how.

Jacob suggests getting away from children that trigger fights. Susie suggests involving a teacher, but Jacob provides him with feedback: "But first you have to stop throwing stones, you are triggering their anger." Such feedback, provided in a safe climate, is invaluable. It helps the children reconstruct their perception of the situation.

Counselor:	Which of the ideas brought up appeal to you?
Eliot:	Not to play with violent children, and to talk to the teacher.

Similar clarifying processes are conducted with the other two children, reflecting the changes in their responses. Jacob has adopted the alternative presented in the poem and will take out his anger drawing on the paper. Susie, who has a problem with an abusive teacher, says at the end of the clarifying process, "I realize that it is not nice to talk back to a teacher. I will talk to her about our relationship." Clarifying processes are particularly helpful to look at the pros and cons of aggressive behavior, thus raising motivation to make a change in behavior.

The seventh session focuses on tolerance and forgiveness, some serious deficits in aggressive children. The text this time is a poem called "Eitan" (Rabikovitz, 1981), in which a group of older kids are intolerant of the mistake made by a younger child during a game. Suspecting that he was cheating, they hit him. The children in the treatment group are quite empathic to the child's pain. They can clearly see that the older boys should be more tolerant of him. The clarifying process is about "how forgiving I am about mistakes that others make." The counselor asks the children to place themselves on a continuum from 1 to 10, with the higher score being more forgiving. Eliot gives himself a 5, because he is forgiving when his father skips a visit, as he knows he works hard, but he does not forgive a classmate for his abuse, because it may end up in tragedy. Jacob says he forgives his sister, but doesn't forgive a classmate who always puts him down and calls him names. Susie forgives her grandma, but not the teacher who is getting her into trouble. It seems that it is easier to forgive family members than it is to forgive friends or teachers. They all want to improve their ability to forgive so they can reduce their aggression.

In the *eighth session*, the counselor introduces the story, "The Present" (Sade, 1990; see Appendix A). The text presents a young child who was spanked by his father because he couldn't tell time to his satisfaction. The story is appropriate because all these children have difficulties with schooling and with parental punishment and abuse.

When the counselor asks what might be some of the ways parents handle children's difficulties in school, the answers include getting hit with a shoe or other object, getting locked in the bathroom for the night, having food or other things withheld. To the question of what other behaviors make parents so angry that they become abusive, the children disclose quite intimate information. Eliot admits to taking money from his mom's purse; Jacob describes a horrible fight in which he badly injured a classmate, and Susie talks about her aggression to her little brother. They were all physically punished for their actions.

The children feel helpless to deal with their parents' aggression, and really don't seem to have much support from other adults. They are quite alone in their struggle. Why don't they involve other adults? Susie is afraid that her parents would get divorced, Eliot is afraid he will be sent to an institution (as his mother threatens), and Jacob feels that, although his mother disapproves of physical abuse, she cannot help him when his father gets angry. The counselor expresses her objection to any type of abuse and encourages them to look for support. She closes the session with the activity "My imaginary birthday." The children are asked to invite to their birthday party some people they can trust. They mention grandma, a neighbor, and an older brother. This is an important activity to help them feel less lonely.

Ninth Session is the action stage. The counselor airs the film *Madi*, focusing on the tragic consequences of heated aggression, where a meaningless conflict ends with a child their age becoming paralyzed. The strength of this movie is its effective demonstration of the agony, shame, fear, guilt, and remorse that the aggressor feels. The importance of taking control of one's impulsive behavior becomes very clear. The kids share more experiences of their own violence, and this time want to reduce their aggression to a minimum. Jacob again brings up his relationship with the new immigrant in class, saying: "He must be in pain when I hit him, he often cries. . ." and they all agree with this.

The *tenth session* deals with self-control through the poem "I am My Own Commander" (Bokek, 1980). It occurs to the children that it is possible to control their behavior once they make a decision to do so. Asked what they would like to command themselves to do at termination, they respond as follows:

Jacob: I know now that hitting is bad. I command myself to stop myself when triggered.

Eliot: I command myself to talk to a teacher or to my father before I get involved in a fight.

Susie: I command myself to avoid violent friends and spend time with good friends.

Evaluation

Evaluation of the children's progress was performed in comparison with two other children from the same class, but only one of the children in the control group was aggressive. The scores on aggression, measured by a short version of Achenbach's Adjustment Scale (CBCL), showed a reduction on both self-report and teacher report in the experimental group only. On self-report, on a scale from 0 to 35, Jacob moved from 18 to 10 following treatment, Eliot moved from 14 to 10, and Susie moved from 8 to 5. In the control group, scores for the aggressive boy did not change (remained with the same score of 13 in pre and post measure). Even more convincing is the reduction in scores based on teacher reports (again, a range of 0–35): Jacob decreased from 35 to 16, Eliot from 31 to 14 and Susie from 22 to 9. There was no change for the control boy (who remained 31).

Attitudes endorsing aggression were gleaned from a 10-item questionnaire developed for this group, based on Heusman's scale (Huesmann & Guerra, 1997). Sample items included, "It's OK to hit someone that started up with you"; "It's not too bad to take out your anger on close friends." Scores ranged from 0 to 10, where higher scores indicated greater endorsement of aggression. For Jacob, scores were reduced from 9 to 7, for Eliot from 8 to 2, and for Susie from 6 to 3. The control boy remained on a score of 10 before and after treatment.

Although attitudes do not guarantee change in behavior, attitudes endorsing aggression are part of the social information processing that characterize aggressive children. Therefore, change in this respect is an indication of possible change in actual aggression, as also evidenced in self-reports and teacher reports of adjustment problems. Although we didn't have a follow-up on this evaluation, the transcripts of the sessions clearly suggest that considerable progress was made.

Demonstration: A Group of Adolescents

Introduction

The group of participants was drawn from a special education class comprised of students with LD and hyperactivity disorders. This was a tenth-grade class, located in a regular high school, which included 14 students—ten boys and four girls. Such classes are meant for students with learning disabilities who fall within the normal range of intelligence; they are kept small and led by a special education teacher. For the intervention and the experiment, this class was divided into two equal groups, each comprised of seven participants, five boys, and two girls. In each group, four of the participants were identified as highly aggressive (three boys and a girl) and the other three were nonaggressive classmates (one girl and two boys). The experimental group was conducted by a school counseling graduate student, while the other group remained with the homeroom teacher to discuss social issues.

The class was split into half for two reasons. First, the groups we work with normally do not exceed eight students and, when treating aggressive children, we keep them even smaller. Second, we wanted to compare outcomes to a control group. This made for a strong design, as the children were matched by gender and level of aggression in the experimental and control conditions, and were drawn from the same class led by the same teacher, thus controlling important possible mediating variables.

As with the elementary school group, I will first illustrate the group process, then provide an evaluation of the treatment. In describing the group process, besides expanding on the practice of bibliotherapy, I will draw attention to the unique features of adolescents in group therapy.

The Group Process

The group was introduced to participants as one that focuses on social issues pertaining to youngsters of their age. The goal of reducing aggression was not mentioned in order to minimize defensive reactions. It also seemed appropriate because the group included nonaggressive students as well. The four aggressive youths in this group are Johnny, Natalie, Don, and Ron, and they are the focus of my illustration.

The *first session* is devoted to getting acquainted, breaking the ice, and establishing group rules, as in any other type of group. The counselor explains the importance of regular attendance, establishes procedures for absentees, explains the reason for videotaping the sessions, and asks for participants' permission. She presents herself as a graduate student who needs the tapes for her final project and they all agree to help her, but raise the issue of confidentiality. She promises to keep all information within the group and expands the discussion of confidentiality to all participants. Finally, she promises to listen to them and make efforts to help them with their struggles, and she assures them that they are going to have fun by listening to stories, watching movies, and playing games.

She starts the group with a card game which state words of emotions. Participants are invited to choose a card with an emotion most relevant to them and share it with the group. Ron, a hyperactive boy, tries to disturb in every possible way; he eats the leaves of a plant, takes several cards and creases them, wanders around. The group is getting irritated, and Shawn, a nonaggressive participant, says angrily, "Stop this nonsense! We want to start," but Ron does not pay much attention. The counselor then makes the following comment: "It is important that in the group we respect each other. We do not use put downs or insult each other, but we can help a group member who has difficulty complying with the group rules in a positive way."

It is quite clear that Ron is testing the limits in this group, as well as the counselor's authority, a typical behavior of teenagers. Although he is acting out throughout the session, the counselor ignores most of his destructive behavior and at the same time uses every opportunity to engage him in the discussion. She also lets the group put some pressure on him, yet makes sure that this is done in a constructive manner. The group tries to adjust to the newly established group rule of asking Ron to cooperate rather then getting irritated and putting him down. At a certain point, when he gets up and wanders around the room, some group members ask him to sit down "because we would like to start." He apologizes and joins the group.

Larry, one of the nonaggressive boys, shares his card that says "tired." He explains that he is particularly tired of school and often skips it because he cannot get up in the morning. It is not the amount of sleep, he argues, but rather his irritation at school; he is just burned out, he says. Several participants join him in this theme, talking about anger toward teachers and failure in schoolwork—topics that are common to students with LD.

Ron does not participate in this discussion. Actually, he is the best student in class and what keeps him in this special education class is his disturbed behavior. He seems indifferent regarding the discussion that goes on and continues eating the plant. The group members feel insulted and lose their patience. Natalie, an aggressive girl, gets really annoyed and shouts, "Who needs him here?" The less aggressive kids express different responses. "It is inhumane to eat the plant," says one, and "That is inappropriate here," says another. This feedback helps and Ron apologizes and stops disturbing the group for a while.

Ron takes a card with fear on it. He explains that he likes to see frightening movies, he hates violent neighborhoods, and he is extremely angry with policemen, but any further attempts to expand upon this topic are met with resistance. "I am afraid only of God. I am not afraid of anyone," he responds to the counselor's attempt to probe a bit further. The message he wants to convey to the group is typical of aggressive youth, that is, to be powerful. Fear must be quickly denied. Ron elicits several negative emotions, sometimes using harsh words, but the counselor demonstrates patience and respect for him, while establishing boundaries, and the group members seem to learn from her modeling and try to imitate her.

Second session starts with bibliotherapy. As we often start the intervention with a focus on victimization rather then aggression, the counselor introduces to the group the story, "The Present" (Sade, 1990; see Appendix A), which I have already referred to several times. The text deals with a father's high expectations of his very young son, and when the child fails to meet these expectations; his father loses control and hits the child. As already explained, starting the program with a focus on victimization allows participants to express their experiences as a victim, which many aggressive children have, and thus affords them an opportunity for cathartic experiences. Moreover, such a start conveys a message that we are here to help them rather than blame them, which helps to reduce the level of resistance to treatment. Finally, it also increases empathy to the suffering of a victim. Although the literary character is a very young boy, I find that adolescents identify with him— probably because they have similar issues with unmet expectations.

The counselor reads the story aloud, with many interruptions by Ron. The first step in our bibliotherapy intervention is to recognize and identify emotions, thus the counselor asks about the literary child's feelings. The difference in the responses of aggressive and nonaggressive students is striking. The nonaggressive participants identify a wide range of emotions, including anger, embarrassment, sadness, and hopelessness, but also love and pride. Dana, for example, says: "He also loves his father and wants to succeed to make him feel proud." In contrast, the aggressive children see only the fear and are angry at the father. For instance, Ron's immediate reaction is, "This father is crazy. He needs to be hospitalized," while the less aggressive children can see the ambiguity in the father's reaction. "He may be tired, frustrated, incapable, and ambitious," they say. Nonaggressive Dana can even identify the father's fear of his own action, and wishes that he were more tolerant. Following her comment, two of the aggressive participants, Natalie and Don, are able to recognize the complexity of the father. Natalie says, "He may be sorry now that he didn't discuss it with his son, before he lost control," and Don says, "He may not be able to control himself." It seems that the nonaggressive participants have a positive impact on the aggressive ones—except for Ron, who insists that the father has no regrets, is hot-tempered and should be punished. Is this the result of his personal experience with his father, or his identification with the aggressor? Both may be true. Yet, despite the ongoing acting out, Ron is participating in the group discussion, as long as the story is involved. The group identifies a wide range of emotions, and the youngsters demonstrate understanding of the complexity of emotions and behavior. They learn from the discussion that a father can be proud of his son and loving, but at the same time angry and punitive. They learn that adults may lose their tempers for many reasons, including personal frustrations, unrealistic expectations, and even reasons that have nothing to do with the child. They also learn that children are sometimes victims of the persons who love them most, and that they can be quite helpless. They can also see the poor consequences of uncontrolled behavior.

The final step in affective bibliotherapy is self-exploration. The counselor asks the participants to close their eyes and recall an incident that this story reminds them of. Before anyone is ready, Ron shouts "I don't have any!"— again, a defensive reaction. However, after group members share their stories, which were quite impersonal, Ron also finds a story. It is to be expected that, at the second session, personal stories will be inhibited, particularly in adolescence, when youngsters are more aware of the risk of self-disclosure in a group. The distance of the stories reduces Ron's anxiety and permits him to participate, but shortly afterward, he returns to his ritual of bugging other group members, especially Don, another aggressive boy. Dana draws his attention to his behavior, saying, "This is an example of verbal aggression." Ron hesitates about reacting to this "here-and-now" statement. He gets up to leave the room, but goes back to his seat and calms down till the end of the session. It seems that Dana's feedback has had an impact on him. The other kids seem to increase their ability to ignore his bad behavior, and thus he has less support for his destructive acting out.

The *third session* starts with the story "The Bully" (Tester, 1974; see Appendix B). This is a story of a bully who takes out his frustrations on a weak classmate. Some classmates and teachers are aware of the bullying that is going on, but do not handle it very effectively. The focus of this text is on both the victim and the perpetrator.

The counselor starts by soliciting the feelings of the victim. The group mentions fear, pain, humiliation, helplessness, and loneliness. Surprisingly, Ron connects these feelings to those recognized in the earlier session. It seems that, despite his disturbances, Ron is attuned to what is going on and internalizes some of the principles of human behavior that he is exposed to. The counselor then discusses the dynamics of the victim's behavior. The victim hides his pain when hit by the bully so as not to give him the satisfaction of knowing he can hurt; he also is afraid to reveal the conflict, because it may infuriate the aggressor even more. He trusts that his teacher and classmates will be of little help.

The youth in the group understands the dynamics of bullying very well. They know that most people are afraid of the bully and therefore do not mess with him. It is the girls, both aggressive and nonaggressive, who talk about the victim's feelings of loneliness and of being left alone. "They are not good friends if they don't help him," says Dana. She is introducing relational issues, which are typical of girls. Following the girls' reactions, Don also mentions the victim's loneliness and pain. All the children express some type of empathic reactions to the victim in this story.

Next, the counselor discusses the dynamics of the bully's behavior. The adolescents understand that the bully is frustrated by his repeated failures in school, and that he is abused in his family, which influences his behavior. They also recognize that he goes after a weak victim, and understand that this is not fair. However, in general, they seem to be comfortable with the transference that the bully does, because it provides a rationalization for their own bullying behavior. Dana, the nonaggressive girl, takes the discussion to another level: "I understand his pain, but he is hurting other people," she says. The discussion then focuses on the unfairness of the situation to the victim, and how the people around the victim could be more helpful. Everyone agrees with this line of thought, except Ron, who now suggests that we may not know the whole story and that the victim might have started the conflict through provocation. Someone tries to convince him that the aggressor was really mean, but Ron insists, "Perhaps it is just like in my case that Shawn is picking on me and I lose my temper." It is not clear whether this is one of Ron's ways to get attention, by playing the "devil's advocate," or whether it is a way to justify his own behavior, as he continues disturbing the group.

Fortunately, the group ignores Ron's statement and moves on to the next activity. They are asked to take sides with one of the characters (one of the strategies of a clarifying process). Johnny chooses the perpetrator, "because I sometimes hit other children." Shawn selects the victim, because he needs help and he would like to help him. Dana selects the victim because he doesn't inflict any harm on others. Most children, at this point, take the side of the victim: they are empathic to his suffering and understand the unfairness of taking advantage of the weak, with the exception of Ron, who insists that the bully "is only responding to provocations."

The consensus regarding the negative aspects of bullying and the empathy to the victim opens the way to Natalie's self-disclosure. She confesses to bullying behavior in the past. She looks at it now and cannot understand how she could have behaved like this. "We thought we are playing out of boredom, but actually we did hurt her a lot. . . .I really don't like myself in this role, and I don't ever want to be dragged into such behavior again." Ron responds cynically; he doubts that Natalie has really changed. She turns to him and says, "See, in the past I would respond to your provocation, but now I just ignore it." What a progress in Natalie's behavior! From the beginning of the group, the two fought like cats and dogs. Ron provoked her in many ways and she responded with verbal aggression. But now she has selected a different response.

Following her self-disclosure, others confessed to some aggressive acts. Ron wants to participate but seems embarrassed; he rambles, doesn't get to the point, and pushes Johnny. Someone laughs, and Ron feels insulted: "But they are laughing at me," he says. Dana assures him: "We are listening." Interestingly, the group seems to have internalized the group rules and do not attempt to take revenge. Ron eventually confesses that he used to bully some young kids in his neighborhood. "I would invite them to play, then hit them, annoy them, just for the fun of it. They were younger and couldn't fight back. …Then I thought that's not nice and I stopped." Whether the change in his behavior is accurate or not, it seems that he is trying to join the group, by openly sharing his negative behavior, and he seems motivated enough to present a better image of himself. But the group is not making it easy on him. "Now he bullies other kids," says Johnny, a frequent victim of Ron's; this is his chance to get back at him.

Shawn, who is not among the aggressors, confesses that he incites others to fight. This is a brave step to take in a group. The participants appreciate his openness and provide feedback to him. "It hurts others and you then get hurt," someone says. "I know," he says, "I'm not strong enough to fight, but I like to see others fight." It is the counselor who takes him off the hook: "Sometimes it is difficult to change our behavior even when we know it is wrong."

This is a turning point in the group. Group participants seem to feel safe enough to share the darker aspects of their behavior, to provide honest feedback, and to accept it. Even Ron, who is still acting out, exhibits a tendency to be part of the group despite his noncompliance with the group's consensus regarding bullying.

Fourth sesssion starts with Johnny's question, addressed to the counselor:

Johnny:	Are you listening to the tapes?
Counselor:	Yes.
Johnny:	Do you hear me well?
Counselor:	I hear you all very well and the sessions are really interesting.
Natalie:	We have lots of stories.
Counselor:	And I want to assure you again that no one else listens to the tapes but me.
Johnny:	Not even our homeroom teacher?
Counselor:	No, not even your teacher.
Natalie:	Do you do this in other classes, too?
Counselor:	No, I selected your class only.
Johnny:	Yeah! We are the lucky ones, we are the chosen (all laugh).

This conversation is not trivial. In the last session, the youth self-disclosed, sharing experiences of their negative behavior—all signs of the group's moving to the working phase—and with this the level of anxiety among participants tends to rise. The counselor understands this and reassures the group. She also makes them feel special. The door seems to have opened for further self-exploration and clinical work.

For the current session, the counselor has brought the poem "What Do You Do When You're Angry" (Benziman, 1992), which deals with controlling anger.

It is about a character whose anger grows and grows, and he doesn't know how to handle it. It starts like this:

> I really don't know what to do
> When I feel angry at you
> I must not hit
> I must not shout
> Say bad words
> Or rage about...

Then it goes on to deal with ways to control one's anger. Ron immediately identifies with the character, saying, "I also have these feelings."

The group members then draw pictures related to what they have heard. Shawn draws an angry face and explains that the boy is angry at his parents and takes it out on another child. None of this is mentioned in the poem; it is his pure projection. The counselor makes a legitimizing statement: "Yes, sometimes that is a way to get rid of the anger." "Exactly!" says Shawn. She further assures him that, when it is difficult to cope with anger, people sometimes take it out on someone else, which makes Shawn feel understood. "What is he angry about?" she asks the group, referring to the literary figure. Perhaps he uses drugs and his parents found out, Ron suggests, saying that the face in Shawn's drawing reminds him of Shawn's brother, which Shawn immediately confirms, adding, "Only my brother is less mean." Ron has actually helped Shawn make the connection to his own experience, as his brother was recently arrested for drug abuse.

After they all shared their drawings, the focus of the group discussion moved to self-control. Each of the participants shared a time when they lost control and explored the pros and cons of the behavior. For example, Don tells the group that often a simple trigger leads him to an aggressive response.

Counselor:	What do you gain?
Don:	I am glad I hit back.
Counselor:	You get a sense of revenge?
Don:	Yes, 'cause he deserves it.
Counselor:	So you get some relief of the anger, you feel strong. But is there perhaps something that you lose?
Don:	I get in trouble, my parents are called in, and I get detention.
Counselor:	Do you consider that a loss?
Don:	Of course!
Counselor:	A loss big enough to consider a change in behavior?
Don:	Yes, I think about it, but I can't always control myself.

The counselor doesn't proceed to the action stage yet, because it is too early for Don and the group. The counselor hopeshat this will come later; meanwhile, some motivation to make a change has been raised. The other group members also continue working on their issues. When one group member goes through a clarifying process, each of the participants asks himself or herself similar questions. This is an important stage in raising motivation to make a change.

The *fifth session* starts with Johnny's request to share something with the group. It is typical of the working stage that group participants initiate participation. Johnny shares an incident in which he threw a raw egg through a bus window onto the head of a passenger, just for the fun of it. When he later told this to a friend, it turned out that his victim was his friend's father, and his friend hit him. When he shares the incident with the group, it is clear that Johnny feels embarrassed. He shares the story to say he wants to grow up. Luckily, he feels comfortable enough in the group to confess his actions.

In the *sixth session*, the counselor has brought a picture depicting a fight between a group of youth (Teaching Pictures, 1974a, b). The group is invited to create a story to explain the fight. Most participants create stories based on violent movies, such as a rich man attacked by a gang, but Don presents a real-life story: "This is a boy who comes from a rich family," he says, "and once the kids discover it, they blackmail him all the time." Whether he is involved in such aggression, we don't know, although we may suspect it, as children usually project on the picture or literature their experiences and feelings.

The counselor directs the group toward the victim's feelings first. They recognize his helplessness, loneliness, confusion, and fear. Then the group discusses the behavior of using force against a weak victim. As the youngsters in this group already understand the dynamics of selecting a weak victim, they move to discussing the behavior of the aggressive group and the bystanders who indirectly support the aggression. They discuss the excitement of the bystanders, for whom the aggressor plays out their fantasies, the indifference that bystanders feel toward the victim, the fear of getting involved to help the victim, and so on.

Finally, to explore their own level of aggression, they perform a clarifying process in response to the question: "To what extent am I aggressive?" Ron is the first to respond, "I am on 11" (10 is the maximum score), another of his provocations, while the rest of the group ranges between 5 and 7. However, when they are asked to place themselves on the continuum on the spot they wish to be, most place themselves between 1 and 2, and Ron is on 5. Usually, following this placement activity, questions are posed to the participants regarding their thoughts, feelings, and behavior in relation to the behavior in question, in this case aggression/violence. The goal is to help them reflect on their own behavior and look at discrepancies between their thoughts, feelings, and behavior. This time, however, there is no time to complete the clarifying process. Nonetheless, it is obvious that the youngsters recognize the importance of changing their behavior—even Ron.

Sixth session starts with Ron's disturbance of the group. He is very restless, eats the plant, triggers Natalie into a hostile reaction, chokes on paper and spits it out, makes fun of a group member who sucks his thumb; in short, he doesn't let the group start. The counselor is extremely patient with him, reminds him of the group rules, offers to let him out to get a drink, but he insists on remaining with the group. The group members are losing their patience, some beg him to stop, others are angry with him, and Natalie curses him back. The counselor has no choice but to ask him to leave the room. He argues and makes promises, but eventually leaves. Reading the transcript of the session, I, too, felt that Ron was just impossible. Sometimes the group leader needs to protect the group from a difficult patient, but if the group is already cohesive, it may be quite painful for group members.

The group gets some relief, but somehow this has damaged the participants' self-image: "It's like a kindergarten here," says one; "Little kids," says another. Members need to respect their group in order to develop cohesiveness. One such group member may affect all members' feelings about the group. Yet, Ron does need help and it was the counselor's intention to help him, despite the constant trouble he gave her and the group.

They now can quietly proceed with the story, "The Smiley Face" (Noy, 1995; see Appendix A), which was planned for the current session. The story tells of a new student to the school whose self-confidence threatens a veteran student. The youngsters discuss the feelings of the newcomer (shy, embarrassed, and lonely) and of the veteran student (threatened, confused, and envious). They understand the dynamics of the behavior of both parties. The newcomer is looking for a chance to be accepted, to make friends, and to be involved. The veteran, worried about losing his powerful position in class, reacts with rejection and aggression. Only after he gets home does the veteran understand how ugly his own behavior was and greatly regrets it.

Following the discussion, group members again perform the clarifying process, this time regarding their level of tolerance. The scores vary on the scale, but they all want to improve. Don, who placed himself on 2 (not tolerant at all) wants to be a 10, explaining: "It is difficult for me to be tolerant in general, not only towards certain people. I do not have the patience to stand in line, to wait for people, or to accept new people." The counselor asks him if he can recall a situation where he was a newcomer. Don shares his experience of moving from elementary school, where he had a high social status ("There I was king," he says), to high school, where he is all alone. "It was embarrassing, very strange at the beginning, it took time, and now my best friends are from this class." Hopefully, Don can develop some empathy to strangers from his own shared experience as well as from the shared stories of others.

In the *seventh session*, Ron is in detention and the group process is much smoother without him. This time the group watches the film *Bazz* (Shtern-Odavi, 1997), which is based on the true story of two teenagers who were extremely violent toward classmates, teachers, and animals, and eventually killed a cab driver who wished to bring them safely home. At this point in the intervention program, group members can easily identify the feelings of the two perpetrators and the people around them. They also understand the dynamics of aggression, the wish to be powerful, and cause others to be afraid of you. But they don't like the characters' behavior, their cruelty, or the senselessness of their hostility.

The clarifying processes that the youngsters complete after viewing this film not only reveal some experiences of being aggressors, but also a clear wish to reduce the level of aggression. Don shares an incident during a soccer game:

Don: He put the ball next to me. I asked, "why are you doing that," and he started pushing me, then jumped on me. I turned around and hit him. I hit him so hard he needed treatment afterwards.
Counselor: And how did you feel?
Don: I was angry! I enjoyed hitting him. I wanted to show him how strong I am.
Counselor: So you found an outlet for your anger. Any other feelings?
Don: I was sorry, I regretted it, as it stopped the game, it got me in trouble.
Counselor: Anything else you felt?
Don: I was worried about him. I was afraid I did real damage ... and it was so stupid, so senseless, just in the middle of a game.

Don doesn't seem to appreciate the use of force as he did before. He can see some of the pain of the victim, and some of the price he pays for his aggression. He is approaching the action stage, and so are some of the other group members.

It is now *eighth session*. As the children like movies, this time the counselor uses *Madi*—a movie that shows how uncontrolled anger may have a tragic ending. After discussing the feelings of both the parties and the dynamics of uncontrolled behavior, the group members cite their own incidents of uncontrolled aggression. This time, however, they assess their use of force as bad behavior. Don confesses that he hit a friend without thinking, could not talk to him because he was so angry at the moment, but felt very bad afterward.

Taking Don's lead, Johnny brings up a fight he had with Ron. He says, "I often fight with Ron, because we both get easily irritated." This was often observed in the group as well. However, Johnny is now taking some responsibility for his behavior, whereas in the past he would always blame the other party. He focuses on a particular incident in which Ron took away his pencil and started destroying it.

Ron: I didn't destroy it.
Don: So I asked him to return the pencil and he didn't want to.
Ron: Because I still wanted it.
Don: So I talked and talked and didn't lay a hand on him, although I wanted to.
Ron: I then pinched him with the pencil, then we started to fight.

The group witnessed the incident and confirm that it was a really frightening fight, where both boys were bloody.

Don: I hit him really hard, I went wild. The teachers couldn't separate us.
Counselor: What did you gain?

Don:	He had to learn a lesson. The group agrees, they don't like Ron, he picks on them.
Counselor:	What did you lose?
Don:	Our parents were called in, we got detention from school. I wish I could have talked a bit longer and convinced Ron to return the pencil or involved an adult.

Ron is resisting; he still can't think of another reaction. This is an example of a conflict outside of the group that was brought into the group and involved its members. The dialog between the two is important; at least one party understands that progress in his behavior is still needed.

The *ninth session* focuses on the youngsters' own "monsters," using the poem "My Monster." Although the poem may seem more suited to younger children, and indeed was used in the elementary group process described above, our experience is that older children, even adults, also benefit from it, not so much because of its content, but rather due to the metaphor of a monster. This time the counselor invites them to create their own monsters out of clay and then introduce them to the group. The youngsters have a lot of fun with the creative art. Ron describes a frightening monster, who kills people in their sleep and takes people to a mental hospital. This is interesting, as Ron is a bright kid, but as he cannot control his hyperactive behavior, he may feel he is losing his mind. Perhaps others in his environment also point to such a possibility. Later on, in the discussion, Ron says that the child feels sorry and regrets what his monster has done, and thinks that "his mother is sorry for giving birth to him." When the counselor asks, "Really, she's that desperate?", Ron answers, "I know such mothers."

The group discussion moves to "something I do not like in myself." Johnny says he has difficulty forgiving others. "I feel like it affects my value if I do. There were so many times I would have gotten out of trouble if I would have apologized, but I just couldn't." Forgiveness is a big issue for aggressive boys. "How can the group help Johnny?", the counselor asks. As the group is at the action stage and change is expected, the counselor directs them to look into alternative behaviors. Some suggest avoiding a fight before it even starts, Natalie suggests thinking about the other person before getting involved, and Dana argues that people who forgive are actually the strong ones. Johnny accepts these suggestions and is ready to try some out.

Shawn doesn't like his own tendency to get other children into fights. This is something he has mentioned before, and now comes back to. Ron criticizes his behavior angrily, and is verbally abusive. The counselor reminds them of the rules and turns the group's attention back to Shawn.

Shawn:	Kids start up with me, but I'm not strong enough to fight, so I get others heated up, so they will fight.

Counselor: You're saying you're not strong enough to fight, so getting some-
                one else heated up is your way of hitting back. [This restatement
                was appropriate to provide Shawn with the sense that he is
                completely understood.]
Shawn: Exactly.
Counselor: What do you lose?
Shawn: The kids hate me.

Although there isn't a chance for the group to offer him alternatives, such insight in itself is of utmost importance for Shawn's progress. Recall that he is not one of the identified aggressors in the class, and yet he has gained so much from this experience.

Don talks about his impulsive behavior that involves him in endless fights. "I regret it immediately after I fight. I think I need to use the suggestion offered earlier to Johnny, think before I fight and talk things over before it is too late." Note that Don has gained from alternatives offered to another group member. It seems that interpersonal learning is taking place.

What strikes me at this session is the openness, the children's ability to connect to their true emotions, the insight they have developed into their own behavior, their self-awareness, and their wish to make a change. These are all goals of our program, goals that are based on the basic deficits of aggressive boys, including difficulties in expressing feelings, endorsement of force, and lack of self-control.

In the *tenth session*, the poem "I am My Own Commander" (Bokek, 1980) closes the intervention. The poem is about a boy who decided to take control of his own aggressive behavior. This poem is suitable for the action stage. After children are able to admit their own behaviors and have expressed a wish to change, it is our goal to help them achieve the desired change. Assisting aggressive children in controlling their behavior is also one of the four goals of our intervention, and is appropriate to be applied as a final step. The poem also provides a nice model for change, and uses a metaphor, which helps children internalize the decision. Adolescents, who strive for a sense of auton-omy, particularly like the idea that a person can be his or her own commander. "He wants to be the one to decide," says Don, and Dana adds, "He wants to decide when to hit and when not to." "He doesn't want to let others drag him into a fight," says Johnny.

The youngsters cite examples of how they manage to control their anger and avoid a fight, and are proud of themselves. "I feel that I am more mature," says Natalie. Johnny says he still has a hard time controlling himself, and Don says that lately he is much better at it. He shares with the group an incident he had with his teacher, and although she was unfair and blamed him for some-thing he didn't do, he convinced himself that it is best not to respond. "I was happy I didn't give in to my anger," he said. Ron was the only one who insisted that he wants to remain the way he is and couldn't find an example of self-control.

At the termination of the treatment of a group, we include a "goodbye" activity. In this group, the counselor suggested providing positive feedback to each other. She used a game in which each child throws the ball to each of the other members and mentions some accomplishments, positive feelings, or impressions. Some of the resulting feedback suggests that group members got to know each other in a more intimate and accurate way. For example, Johnny says to Larry, "In these sessions I got to know that you're smart and we could learn from you." Natalie said to him that he is responsible and she liked the role he took in the group. The members voice appreciation of each others' self-disclosure: "I liked that you told us about yourself"; "You always expressed your feelings and opinions, I learned from you."

The members also expressed appreciation of the progress made in behavior of the group members. For example, Johnny says to Don, "You showed us that people can change." Interestingly, despite the hard time Ron has given the group, he also receives positive feedback. Most of the children say that he is intelligent, good in math, a good student. He also receives feedback about his progress in behavior. Dana says, "I could see the efforts you made to improve your behavior and I see progress." Johnny says, "You are the best student in the class. Do not disturb the class, we want you there." Natalie, who suffered from his behavior throughout the group process, said, "You are smart. Sometimes I envy you. We do not want you to get into trouble, we will help you. We should not respond to your provocations, this will help."

Finally, the counselor asks the children how the group has helped them. "I learned to be less angry and aggressive, to think more about myself and others," says Shawn. Dana adds, "I learned to speak about my emotions, this felt good." Several say that they learned to think before responding impulsively. "Anything you would like to change?" asks the counselor. "Yes, to continue the program," they all said. She gives them a little gift to help them remember the lessons they have learned.

Evaluation

Evaluation was performed by self-reports, teacher reports, and analyses of the sessions. Although we cannot generalize the outcomes to a larger population, the results do provide additional and interesting information on the processes the children went through. For example, all four aggressive children showed a reduction of aggression, as evaluated by teachers who were not involved in the project. The instrument used for both self- and teacher reports was a short version of the Achenbach scale, including 18 items that pertain to aggression and delinquent behavior. Responses are given on a 3-point scale from 0 to 36. Outcomes were measured at three points of time: pre, post, and follow-up (3 months later).

Ron initially scored the highest on aggression, according to the teacher's report (27 out of 36). We witnessed his resistance throughout the group process, and, indeed, at termination, he scored the same. However, at follow-up, the teacher gave him a 20, indicating a perceived reduction in aggression. Moreover, on the self-report measure (the same instrument), there was a much higher reduction in scores on aggression. Ron initially evaluated himself at 17, gave himself a 7 at termination, and a 0 at follow-up. So what happened to Ron? It seems that he noted a change in his behavior following the intervention, which was only partly confirmed by his teacher after a period of time. As Ron is a very smart boy and quite self-aware of his negative behavior, his own sense of improvement seems important. True, his evaluation could be biased, but it is also possible that the social environment doesn't recognize the change immediately. This is unfortunate, because such children need a lot of support at the action stage in order to prevent relapse, and do not always get that support. In fact, teachers tend to hold biased and stereotypical views of their students, which makes it difficult for the children to hold on to the efforts necessary to achieve stable and permanent change. It is the group members, who noticed the change in Ron and were willing to support him in his efforts. I felt that the feedback he received from them was moving. Not only did they want him to succeed in his efforts, but they also recognized their own part in triggering his impulsive response, a very mature stance, especially that of Natalie.

Natalie was identified by the teacher as an aggressive girl, and scored second (16 out of 36) in her class on the aggression questionnaire, as evaluated initially by her teacher. In the group process, we witnessed her strong verbal aggression, directed particularly to Ron's provocations. Since then, she has learned to ignore largely his provocations, has gradually replaced her endorsement of aggression with antiaggressive attitudes, and has developed a self-identity of a nonaggressive person. This is also reflected in the initially low score on aggression that she gave herself (1)—very different from the teacher's evaluation. At times, it seemed that she was pretending and was inaccurate in her clarifying process, always placing herself low on aggression, although in reality she continued to use abusive language. However, even though her scorings were distorted and biased for social desirability, they show that Natalie wanted to change very much. Once a child has the motivation to change, there is a good chance that change will occur. Indeed, the teacher noted great progress in her behavior; she scored 5 at termination and 8 at follow-up. Natalie is a clear case of improved behavior. Is it because she is a female, and girls learn effectively from group processes? That could be; evidence show that girls gain more from interpersonal relationships than boys (Shechtman, 1994). This issue can be answered if we look at the other two aggressive boys in the group.

Johnny initially scored 15 on the aggression scale, as evaluated by his teacher, and although his score decreased at termination, 3 months later it was 15 again. Interestingly, he noticed himself that he didn't maintain the progress he had made for a while: he gave himself a 12 at follow-up, higher than initially, 9. Thus, although he was a constructive group member and had learned from the process, he wasn't able to maintain his achievements. Perhaps other circumstances, in his family or neighborhood, played a role, as we so frequently see.

Finally, Don, who struggled so hard to control himself, was somewhat successful. He scored 14 initially, 10 at termination and remained 10 at follow-up, by teacher report. In other words, just as he said in the group, he doesn't succeed in controlling himself. His awareness of his negative behavior makes him quite frustrated, as reflected in the way he scored himself: 11, 17, 11, giving himself a higher aggression score at termination. This is typical of children who have developed insight, but have not yet achieved change. I suspect that a longer group process would have been helpful.

In general, ten sessions is a very short time for an intervention focused on aggression. When we look at the change process stages, it becomes clear that we are not allowing the children to be in the action stage for long enough periods. For this particular group, we also analyzed the stage of change the children reached in each session. In the *third session*, three of the four aggressive children were at the stage of awareness without motivation to change (Stage 2). Ron was in Stage 1—no awareness of his behavior. Natalie was the first to reach the action stage—in the *fourth session*— and indeed showed the best results. At the *tenth session*, three of the four children arrived at Stage 4, experimenting with actual attempts to change, while Ron reached Stage 2, that is, he developed some awareness but with no motivation to make a change. Was Ron really unmotivated? I suspect he only pretended that he didn't care or want to change. Ron is a smart guy and highly hyperactive; for him, showing that he doesn't care is easier than not being able to control himself. The fact is that he wanted to change and felt he has done so, as reflected in his self-evaluation. He also wanted very much to remain in the group, but had to really struggle for it.

I think the counselor who did the intervention should be applauded for her patience with Ron, for her use of effective helping skills, and for her nonjudgmental approach. The texts that she selected were adjusted to the change process, and she used a lot of paraphrases, reflection of feelings, and encourages—all very helpful in navigating self-exploration and insight.

Did the children indeed develop insight? This was also investigated in this group in the *fifth* and *tenth sessions*. Each statement during the session that indicated self-awareness was counted. Results indicated progress from the *fifth* to the *tenth session* for the whole group: from 25 to 34 statements. Johnny and Don were the two participants who grew most in self-awareness, and Natalie was the only one who was already high in self-awareness at the first measurement. Growth in self-awareness may have helped Don, who really struggled with the issue of self-control, but it didn't have an impact on Johnny.

The group process also may have had an impact on the children. From the termination session, we could see how close group members had become. They really cared and respected each other. This is also reflected in the analysis of interpersonal learning. While in the *fifth session*, there was no evidence of such interpersonal interactions, at termination we counted 52 interactions. This large number is probably influenced by the activity, which required feedback. Nevertheless, feedback was in fact provided and most of it was positive.

The fact that these teenagers terminated the group armed with positive feedback is not trivial. Even those children who did not reduce their level of aggression to a desirable extent still gained support, caring, and intimacy, which are so important for youngsters, particularly adolescents. This is an important reexperience of positive relationships that most difficult children lack in school and elsewhere. Take, for example, Ron: he left the group with a lot of positive feedback, which is very unusual for this boy, as we have seen along the group process. Ron has learned that, despite his difficulties, his classmates respect his knowledge and abilities, and more importantly care about him and don't want to get rid of him. What a therapeutic experience!

As already noted earlier, we compose groups in a heterogeneous way, mixing different levels of aggression and including nonaggressive kids, so as to avoid mutual negative influences. The nonaggressive ones help a lot in the process, as reflected in Dana's communication throughout the group process. Why would a nonaggressive kid want to "waste" his or her time in a group with aggressors? Dana gave us one answer: "It was good to talk about feelings and to get to know other children intimately," she said at termination. Dana is quiet and shy, with an altruistic need to help others. She gained self-esteem, social skills, and self-growth from the intervention, as have many other nonaggressive group members.

The greatest advantage of group interventions is the power of the group. If managed appropriately, the group, through bibliotherapy, becomes a source of change. It provides pressure when needed to change behavior, as we have seen in the case with Ron, and yet remains a source of support and mutual learning. It often is also a place for belonging, which is so important in adolescence, and a source for new friendships.

Finally, the group and the literature together convey to the children that they are not alone in their struggle. A change in one group member provides the hope that change is possible for others. These are strengths unique to the group.

Summary

This chapter has demonstrated two group processes: one with elementary-school aggressive children and one with aggressive adolescents. In both processes, the literary text played a profound role. It provided structure to the discussion and it brought up the complexity of the victim's and perpetrator's behavior. The stories, poems, and films, selected according to the goals of our intervention, helped the participants to engage in the discussion of issues relevant to aggressive behavior, such as anger and its control, empathy to the suffering of the victims, power struggle and misuse of power, and self-control. The participants first identify the feelings of the main characters of each text, then discuss the dynamics of aggression and its consequences, and finally explore their own aggression and make a commitment to change. The process of bibliotherapy starts in an indirect manner, focusing on the literature, then moves to a direct exploration of self, which leads to the development of insight, and ends with the acknowledgment that action must be taken.

Not all children complete all the stages, nor do they start on the same initial level of aggression. Indeed, our large-scale research indicates that about 70% of treatment children arrive at the stages of the will to change and make efforts to change (Shechtman, 2004a ; Shechtman & Ben-David, 1999). However, as illustrated above, there are numerous individual differences that influence the change process: the child's personality, family circumstances, teachers, and schools.

Group dynamics played a unique role in the change process. The group climate, group interactions and feedback, and group support all have positive impact on the process. However, not all children benefit from a group. In both groups, we had one child who was difficult for the group and the group was difficult for him. In the first group, this child couldn't control himself and dropped out after giving the group quite a hard time. In the second group, the difficult child remained in the group and I trust that he benefited from the process to some extent, but the price the group paid was quite high. Moreover, both counselors were novices in counseling, and although they did an effective job in both groups, it was not without difficulties. Perhaps individual treatment would be a better choice for the difficult children and their therapists. Individual treatment, its advantages and disadvantages, and an illustration of the processes, are presented in the next chapter.

Chapter 6
Individual Treatment

Introduction

As mentioned in Chapter 5, some aggressive children are not suited for a group setting, owing to personal or interpersonal difficulties. They may be too aggressive and uncontrollable to participate in a group or too withdrawn to share feelings and personal experiences with others. Sometimes it is the school conditions, parents' refusal, or the counselor's preference that lead us to treat aggressive children individually. Thus, although most of the children we work with are placed in small groups, we also work with individual children using the same intervention. In contrast to the focus on group processes characterizing the earlier chapter, the current chapter will illustrate the processes in individual treatment, at the same time highlighting the different types of aggression, differences between boys and girls and differences between younger and older children in the treatment of aggression.

Treatment of a Young Boy

Background

Nine-year-old Barry is from a middle-class family; he is the middle child with an older brother and a new baby sister. There are no known difficulties in his family; in fact, his teacher reports that Barry's mother is very involved in his schooling, is in close contact with his teachers, and often visits the school to monitor his progress. Barry has been diagnosed with Attention Deficit Hyperactivity Disorder (ADHD). Like many children with ADHD (Barkley, 2002; Frankel & Feinberg, 2002), he gets easily irritated and angry, and responds with verbal and physical aggression. His teacher reports that he is restless in class, is easily frustrated, loses his temper quite often, and tends to get into fights with peers.

This is a clear case of reactive aggression. The decision to treat him individually was based on a combination of professional and practical reasons. His

Z. Shechtman, *Treating Child and Adolescent Aggression Through Bibliotherapy*, The Springer Series on Human Exceptionality, DOI 10.1007/978-0-387-09745-9_6, © Springer Science+Business Media, LLC 2009

impulsive behavior, along with his young age, raised concerns as to whether he could be a constructive group participant. Moreover, his mother's request for treatment after school hours limited the option of adding other children. Hence, treatment was provided after school in ten 45-minute weekly individual sessions. The counselor was a graduate counseling student trained in the intervention promoted in this book. A classmate with a similar personal and family background was selected as control in order to evaluate the progress Barry made following treatment.

Treatment Process

The counselor introduces the goal for their meetings in the *first session*, in the following way: "I shall meet with you on a weekly basis to talk about experiences and perhaps some difficulties in your relationships with peers. We will read stories and poems, watch films, and play card games." Note that the word aggression is not mentioned in order to avoid resistance. Barry wants to know whether there will be homework; "no homework" the counselor assures him, "just discussions of literature; we will have a lot of fun." Barry seems eager to start.

The first activity is the "Legacy of My Name." In an attempt to set a model for emotional self-expression, the counselor shares her legacy first. She tells him that she changed her name after emigrating from another country because children used to tease her about her foreign name, which often made her cry. Following the exposure of her vulnerability, Barry shares with her that kids sometimes call him Bear. He sees this as a great insult; it makes him very mad and causes him to lose control. Aggressive children often mention put downs, insults, and disrespect as triggers of impulsive reactions. Being vulnerable, feeling inconfident and incompetent puts such children on the defense and raises their need to appear strong.

Regarding the therapeutic process, note that this is only the first activity of the *first session*, but the child is willing to open up and disclose his vulnerability. The counselor's modeling probably set the tone for a high level of self-disclosure. On the other hand, the individual setting might also have contributed to the acceleration of self-disclosure by removing some of the inhibitions that children show in a group.

Barry and the counselor then play with "feeling" cards. Again, she goes first, selecting "anger," and she tells him about a grade she got that was lower than she expected. She points to the unfairness of the situation and shares her feeling of helplessness. This was a true experience (counselors are trained to share only meaningful experiences), but adjusted to reflect Barry's situation; after all, the counselor's self-disclosure is not meant to solve her personal issues, but to help her client. Barry is in constant trouble with teachers, feels misunderstood, and complains that they are unfair with him. Yet, he is unable to express his true feelings, as typical of aggressive children (Garbarino, 1999; Gurian, 1997; Pollack, 1998), and thus reacts with hostility. The counselor acknowledges his difficulties, but does not discuss his behavior yet. On the contrary, they end the session with talk of some of his positive achievements. Barry is happy to tell the counselor how helpful he is with his baby sister.

Barry's behavior is typical of children with attention deficit disorders(ADD). Gurian, (1997) stipulates that all boys—let alone children with a deficit disorder— have difficulties in the current school system, which requires them to sit still for longer periods of times than they are comfortable with. Kids with ADHD experience frustration with their academic work because they find it difficult to concentrate, miss homework, get scolded at home, and also have difficulties in relationships with peers. Although they have the cognitive ability to under- stand the social situation, they are often more impulsive and less self-controlled, and therefore get into more trouble (Barkley, 2002; Frankel & Feinberg, 2002). It is clear to the counselor that a focus of Barry's treatment should be self- control. However, as we do not start with behavior change, the initial focus is on anger and its management. Listening to the child's expression of anger is in itself therapeutic; exploring his anger will hopefully lead to insight and change. Seeing how literary figures cope with anger will enhance his efforts to actually change his behavior.

Second session starts with a warm-up game in which Barry is asked to complete certain statements: "When I get mad..." "I get irritated by everyone and everything." "When I lose my temper..." "I hit, curse, and scream." The counselor then introduces the poem, "My Disastrous Monster" (Shilon, 1981), hoping it can help him in dealing with such incidents. The poem describes a monster that has taken over a child's control and causes him to misbehave and embarrass himself. It starts like this:

> Once I said to Mom:
> My monster is a disaster
> In the morning she screams
> Yesterday she also cried
> And at night she wet her bed...

It goes on to describe the bad behavior caused by the monster and the child's fear of losing control.

The counselor first asks about the character's feelings. "He may be feeling good, but others don't feel so great, they are threatened and frightened by the monster," Barry responds. It is clear that Barry feels empathy for the suffering of others, which shows that he understands the complexity of aggression. Asked if the child is happy with his monster taking control over his actions, his response is a clear NO! He goes on explaining that the monster makes him do things that embarrass him and get him into trouble.

They then discuss the situation of losing control. The counselor asks, "How does a child let the monster control his behavior?" Barry replies, "Because it is part of him and sometimes he even likes it." Barry has admitted that he can see the positive side of being aggressive: getting emotional relief, punishing others, and getting even. He also expects others to understand and accept this: "They need to understand that he doesn't always mean to be bad and they don't have to be angry with him all the time; they need to help him," he requests.

Aggressive behavior tends to escalate because aggressive children get negative reactions from their environment, which makes the aggressor even more fearful and helpless, and in turn, also more hostile. This young child tells us what aggressive children need, but who hears them? Most parents, teachers, and society in general judge children by the consequences of their actions, not by their uncovered feelings, or intentions, leading to miscommunication and great frustration for the troubled child.

Later in this session, when they move to direct self-exploration, Barry admits that he is familiar with the portrayed situation. "My monster gets out when I am threatened, then I get really wild," he says, and shows the counselor how he kicks and hits back.

Counselor: How do you feel when the monster strikes?
Barry: I'm not happy, because then I have to deal with people's anger....
                  I hate it when people are angry with me.
Counselor: Would you like to get rid of the monster?
Barry: No, because sometimes I want to be mad and fight.

Barry is in the second stage of the change process. He admits that he is aggressive and can see some of the consequences, but he doesn't want to let go. As Barry doesn't come from a difficult family background and has not learned aggressive behavior in his family or social environment, it is still unclear what secondary gratifications he gets from his aggression.

The *third session* focuses on a poem in which a young child is betrayed by his close friend who refuses to share a new toy with him. He gets extremely frustrated and throws a rock, unintentionally hitting his friend and injuring him badly. Barry understands both parties in the conflict. He seems to understand the child's refusal to share the toy: "Maybe he was worried that something would happen to his new ball," and was empathic to his pain: "He must have felt pain when the rock hit him and was sad that his good friend hurt him." But he can also understand the child who threw the rock. "He must regret the consequences, but he couldn't help it, he was so mad." Barry seems to be an empathic boy who loses control, and so he could identify with the perpetrator despite his empathy for the victim.

In the direct self-exploration that follows, Barry shares an incident in which he hit a younger child who insisted on participating in a game that Barry refused to include him in.

Counselor: How did you feel?
Barry: First, I was still angry, but then when everyone got mad at me, I
                  didn't feel good.
Counselor: And how did the little boy feel?

Barry:	Of course, it was not pleasant for him. He was in pain and embarrassed because there were kids around.
Counselor:	Do you regret your behavior?
Barry:	No!

Barry continues to talk about the punishment, but doesn't let go of his aggression yet. Although he has the ability for perspective taking, his moral development is still quite low. He focuses on the consequences (punishment), but does not yet internalize a nonviolent approach.

In the *fourth session* the counselor uses "The Underdog" (Folsom-Dickerson, 1974; see Appendix B), a story about a fight between two brothers. The older brother hits the younger one because he suspects that he took his ball. Barry understands that the older brother was frustrated, as his friends were waiting for him, and this got him so angry: "He lost control and took it out on a younger victim, because it is easier to fight someone weaker." "If he would just stop for a moment and think. . .," says the counselor, but before she has a chance to finish the sentence, Barry says, "Sometimes it's impossible to stop the anger." The counselor suggests that it feels better when you do control your behavior, to which Barry admits, "This is very true!"

Is this a turning point? In the following exploration stage, Barry completes a clarifying process on the level of aggression in his relationships with his brother. He places himself on 10, because he fights with his older brother often. He is not happy to be on 10, sometimes wants to be on 5, but says it all depends on his brother: "If he won't make me mad, I won't fight with him, but if he annoys me, I will not give in and I'll hit him." Barry still demonstrates an external locus of control, blaming others for his aggression and refusing to own some of the responsibility. Regarding Prochaska's stages of change, Barry is still in the initial stage of awareness without motivation to change.

Fifth session makes use of the poem, "What Do You Do When You're Angry?" (Benziman, 1992). The poem describes the inner struggle in a time of anger, the wish to take it out on someone, yet the need to comply with rules and norms imposed by society. It fits the stage Barry is in well. Barry understands that the character is angry, but does not know what to do with the anger. If he lashes out, then everyone will blame him, and he will have to say that he didn't do it, in defense. "Even if he did?" asks the counselor. "Yes," Barry answers and further describes the cycle of violence, spontaneously talking about himself: "I try to control myself, but at a certain point I cannot hold it in anymore, so I have to curse and hit, and then there is a big problem." He sounds quite helpless and is probably frustrated, but is willing to change. When they continue to discuss alternative behaviors, he mentions "leaving the scene, forgetting [what happened], playing soccer—anything that doesn't hurt others." For the first time, he shares a situation in which someone annoyed him, but he managed to control himself, thus avoiding punishment by the teacher. The counselor reports that this is a turning point for Barry. He is excited about his newly acquired self-control, but is still unsure that he can maintain the change. "It was so hard not to react," he admits.

The *seventh session* deals with "The Bully" (Tester, 1974; see Appendix B), a story about an aggressor who is giving his victim a hard time, and no one seems to be able to help. Barry empathizes with the victim and criticizes the bully; he considers him mean because he takes advantage of someone weak. He then states, "You don't always have to fight, there are other ways." This is the first time Barry initiates a discussion of alternatives to aggression. Yet, when placing himself on a continuum, he is still on 10. "If someone hits me, I will hit back even if the teacher is around, I will never give in, no way!" They discuss the consequences, but he still insists that he does not want to change; he is only looking for ways to express his aggression without being caught. His reaction indicates that he continues to endorse power and force, as typical of aggressive children.

The counselor feels a bit frustrated. She is bothered by his strong identification with the aggressor and his endorsement of force, and she decides to focus more on developing empathy for the suffering of the victims. Empathy is considered a strong buffer to aggression (Feshbach, 1997; Horne et al., 2007). In the next three sessions, therefore, she uses literature that presents the suffering of the victims in a highly emotional manner. In the seventh session, they discuss "The Evil Palm" (Rabikovitz, 1995), a poem about a young girl whose father abuses her in front of her friends. Barry is moved by her embarrassment; "She is very, very sad and hurt," he says.

In the next session, the counselor presents a picture in which a father abuses a child. Barry perceives a father who hits his child and identifies feelings of fear, sadness, and helplessness. He is very angry at the aggressor: "Fathers shouldn't force their children to do things they don't want to do." He then confesses that it happens to him all the time. "I am forced to eat things I don't like, and my father spanks me if I don't." He expects his mother to intervene and calm his father down. In a role-play, conducted a bit later, Barry, playing his father says, "I am very angry at you! You are a bad boy!" When the child starts crying, his father continues, "You are still very bad." There is no compassion from his father.

Can this harsh discipline be a reason for his aggression? We know that it does tend to increase childhood aggression (Dodge, 2002). The role-play revealed a possible home situation that the school doesn't know about, which may explain why Barry holds on to his aggression.

In the next session, they read the story about a boy who is highly rejected by his peers. Barry understands his loneliness and pain, and is further convinced by the teacher's act of showing her scars to the children. He shares his experience with new immigrants who are rejected by his classmates, doesn't think it's right, and even suggests helping them. But when the counselor asks him to remember when he was a victim, his response is, "Nobody ever hurts me!"

Following the focus on empathy in the last three sessions, *nineth session* goes back to dealing with anger and aggression. The poem, "Yaron is Angry" (Omer, 1978; see Appendix A), is introduced, in which frustration leads to aggression that is directed to an object rather than a person. Barry understands that Yaron chose not to hurt anyone, but rather to express his anger in a nonviolent way and thus to avoid getting into trouble. He shares several instances in which he took out his anger on objects:

Barry:	I broke a lamp in my room, my computer, a book shelf.
Counselor:	How did you feel?
Barry:	Good, although I had to pay for some of the things.
Counselor:	Was this the right way?
Barry:	No, but I couldn't control myself.
Counselor:	Are you willing to be more self-composed?
Barry:	Yes, I could use the money for better things.
Counselor:	How could you change your behavior?
Barry:	I could go out and relax, kick a ball, watch TV, or destroy a piece of paper like Yaron did.

There is an obvious change in motivation and a step further toward behavior change. Barry is referring to alternative models of behavior that were introduced in the poem, but he also suggests some from his own experience. There seems to be a major change in attitude.

In the last session gains are summarized and goals for future behavior are clarified. Barry doesn't like the idea of termination and begs the counselor to come at least once more, explaining that he feels he has changed, but needs her continuing support.

Barry:	I use to say stupid things, to curse, to go crazy, and to fight a lot. I don't do it that much any more. I am still angry sometimes, but not that often, I have learned to let go of it and to restrain myself. I don't always succeed, but I know now that being nice to others and talking nicely leads to better results.
Counselor:	What made the difference?
Barry:	The stories, in particular "The Scars." I have learned that cruelty is so mean, that people shouldn't suffer from the bad behavior of others.

So what did really work here? We met an angry child who couldn't control his behavior. His anger may have been directly associated with ADHD symptoms and related failure in his academic and social life. It could also be a result of the misunderstandings expressed by meaningful people in his social environment, including his father. Difficulties of controlling himself, might have lead to helplessness and despair. It seems he was holding on to attitudes endorsing aggression in an attempt to cover up his sense of helplessness. For him, therapy was a slow process of realizing that there are better ways to deal with his anger. The question, however, is what made the change? Indeed, Barry himself mentioned the stories, but the content he was exposed to cannot be the whole answer. Discussions of the literature not only provided alternatives to improved behavior, but they actually served as the basis for self-expressiveness, increased empathy, and enhanced self-exploration. I believe that the counselor's deliberate move to increase his empathy for victims of aggression was a good one. Barry needed to change on an emotional level before he could change his perception of violence. The change process is reflected throughout the treatment. But is it evident in Barry's actual behavior?

Evaluation

Levels of aggression were measured through one dimension of Achenbach's adjustment scale—namely, the 18-item aggression scale. Responses are on a 3-point scale from 0 to 2, making the range of possible scores 0–36. The instrument is both a self-report and a teacher-report measure, and was completed at three points of time: pretreatment, posttreatment, and follow-up 3 months later. On the self-report measure, Barry moved from a score of 17 at pretreatment to 13 at posttreatment, where he stayed (13) at follow-up, compared to the control boy, who remained virtually unchanged (19, 18, and 20, respectively). Results of the teacher's report were quite similar: 17, 13, and 14, compared to a slight increase in the scores of the control child (20, 22, and 22).

Barry was also evaluated on empathy, using Bryant's empathy scale. Responses on the 19 items of the scale were yes/no (0/1), with a possible range of scores being 0–19. Barry started with an extremely low score of 6, moved to 15 at posttreatment, where he remained (15) at follow-up, compared to the control child who started higher, with a score of 9, but did not change (9 at posttreatment and 10 at follow-up).

Finally, the children completed a 10-item questionnaire on self-control, with a score range of 0–10. Barry rated himself as 5 at pretreatment, 7 at posttreatment and 6 at follow-up. The control child rated himself 4, 5, and 5, respectively.

In short, slight progress is revealed by the different measures, with the greatest progress being on the empathy scale, as argued by Barry himself in his final feedback. Self-control remains a major problem, suggesting that Barry still has a long way to go. Overall, compared to the control child, there is evidence of change in the experimental child's behavior. His progress is modest, but one needs to take into account several factors at play: Barry's ADHD, his very young age, and the brevity of the treatment. A result based on a single-case treatment is obviously not convincing, and was brought here only to complete the case illustration. Other large-scale studies have indicated that children with learning disabilities, including ADHD, do benefit from such treatment, are as constructive in the therapeutic process as children without LD, and show favorable outcomes on a variety of measures (Shechtman & Katz, 2007; Shechtman & Leichtentritt, 2008). It is obvious that Barry could benefit from more sessions, as he needs continuous support in changing his endorsement of power, maintaining control over his behavior, and preventing relapse.

The next case study is of a young girl. Although of a similar age, the process may be quite different, because girls think differently and express their anger and aggression in a different manner.

Treatment of a Young Girl

Background

Michelle was introduced in Chapter 4. She is a second grader, evaluated by her teacher as highly aggressive, both verbally and physically. She and her mother are on the run from her violent father, and she recently arrived in this particular school from a shelter for abused women and children. She is rather neglected by her mother, her appearance is messy, she is pale, often seems hungry, and sometimes steals from other children. Obviously, she is highly rejected by her classmates, and this is her main problem. Although she is extremely vulnerable, she plays it tough.

Treatment Process

The *first session* of Michelle's therapy process begins by her getting acquainted with the school counselor. Asked how school is for her, she starts a long monologue, saying basically that she hates everyone and they all hate her. She is self-expressive and connects easily, but is angry and disappointed in people around her. She likes to draw and is happy to use the crayons the counselor provides for her. She draws the schoolyard during recess, placing a single girl in a corner watching the kids playing. She then explains that the girl doesn't care, because she doesn't like the others and is actually waiting to go home. The counselor makes no interpretation at this point, but the identification and projection processes are quite clear, providing important information about the young client. Michelle is also interested in the counselor and interviews her about her personal life. She wants to know whether she has children, and particularly why she picked her out of all the kids in her class. The counselor tells her that she is a graduate student and needs the experience as part of her school assignment. She also says that the teacher recommended Michelle as someone who can benefit from the contact with her and because she can help the counselor with her assignment. Michelle seems to like the response and promises to be of help.

Knowing the harsh background of this young girl and the social rejection she endures, the counselor decides to focus on victimization as a starting point. First, she introduces the film, *Dumbo the Flying Elephant* (1941). Dumbo's peers are giving him a hard time because his ears are unusually large. Michelle has an opportunity to identify with the feelings of the rejected literary character. She expresses her empathy for Dumbo spontaneously: "He is embarrassed because everyone made fun of him, they didn't like him at all." When the children write a letter to Dumbo, Michelle writes, "I feel lonely just like you."

In the *second session*, the counselor introduces the story, *The Ugly Duckling* (Anderson, 1843), which is appropriate for her age and social situation. Michelle strongly identifies with the ugly duckling, who is humiliated and rejected by his fellows:

> He is so lonely, and he can do nothing because they are all against him, and he is ugly and different, poor thing. . . .Only his mother is protecting him. . . .Why do they care so much about his appearance? After all, what is important is what he is like on the inside, like with me, I am a good person, but kids don't see it.

Through this process of identification, Michelle is able to express emotions, feel some empathy, and start dealing with her own issues.

In the *third session*, the story, "The Present" (Sade, 1990; see Appendix A), is introduced, which presents a harsh father who spanks his young child because he failed to meet his expectations. Michelle expresses a lot of anger at the father, who cannot understand the needs of a young child, who takes out his frustration on the poor victim, and who cannot control himself. She also expresses a lot of sympathy for the young victim "who suffers only because his father is so stupid." Her identification with the victim is quite understandable, as she, too, suffers from an abusive father.

At *fourth session* the counselor reads to her the poem, "The Evil Palm" (Rabikovitz, 1995), which tells about a girl who was badly abused by her father in the past and, although many years have gone by, still cannot forget and forgive. Michelle starts crying and shares her sadness raised by the poem. She perfectly understands the humiliation of being spanked in front of her peers; she accepts the character's need to convince people that her father indeed abused her; and she expresses a lot of anger toward the abusive father.

Following this session, Michelle exhibits a greater sense of closeness with the counselor. She moves her chair to sit very close to her and becomes more emotional, sharing her sadness following the death of a loved animal. She seems more vulnerable, making less of an effort to appear strong. The counselor notes that she noticed her anger at violent people and asks her if she ever gets angry or aggressive herself. At this point, rapport has been established with the child and the counselor feels she can introduce communication that is more direct. They draw a sun and surround it with situations that lead Michelle to an aggressive response. She mentions insults, put downs, and social rejection. In such cases, she fights back, but sometimes she just runs away.

In the *fifth session* , the counselor introduces the story of a fight between two brothers. Following the discussion, Michelle is asked to place herself on a continuum from 1 to 10 on aggression. Michelle gives herself a 10, explaining: "My brother always hits me; if I don't hit him back, I get very edgy.... I need to get it out so I won't be taken advantage of . . . and I do want to remain on 10, because I want everyone to be afraid of me, and to know that I can win."

However, during recess that day, Michelle seeks out the counselor and says that she has been thinking about the continuum they did earlier, and she wants to redo it. She now places herself on 7, because she wants to stop fighting and hitting: "I don't want to be in conflict all the time." She seems to be developing awareness of her own aggression and shows a clear motivation to change. This encourages the counselor to move a bit further into the action stage.

Counselor:	How are you going to achieve this?
Michelle:	I can ask for the teacher's help.
Counselor:	That's one possibility. Anything else you can do?
Michelle:	I don't have to argue over every little thing, and when someone wants something from me I don't have to refuse, because I always say NO.

Here is the beginning of self-exploration and insight, following some cathartic experiences. Michelle is able to come up with alternative behaviors herself, even without being directly taught specific social skills.

In the *next session*, she continues sharing her sense of loneliness:

Michelle:	I feel sad when the girls play at recess but refuse to include me. I feel very lonely then. ... I would like to be friends with Renee—the queen of the class—because then nobody would reject me.
Counselor:	Do you have an idea how to do this?
Michelle:	I can beg them to include me.
Counselor:	Any other way?
Michelle:	I can talk to Renee, tell her that I'm a nice person who it's worth getting to know, that I can be a good friend.

This clarifying process was powerful and opened the way for Michelle to change.

Evaluation and Comparison with Barry

In her feedback on the intervention, at termination, Michelle says that she now has more friends, including the "queen" of the class, and that she gets into fights much less. Indeed, her scores on aggression reflect the change. She started with one of the highest scores in aggression—on a scale of 1–36, she had a self-report of 17 and a teacher's report of 26—and she ended up at posttreatment with scores of 6 and 12, respectively. She also increased her self-reported score on self-control; on a scale of 1–10, she moved from 2 at pretreatment to 8 at posttreatment and 9 at follow-up, 3 months later.

From the beginning, Michelle is verbal. She easily expresses negative feelings and does not need modeling to express herself. In this, she differs from Barry. Moreover, she invests in creating rapport with the counselor, shows interest in her as a partner in a relationship, and is happy to be of help to her. She is also much more empathic to the suffering of others than Barry was. The major problems that she brings up are relationships with classmates, the suffering of social rejection, indicating the relational aggression typical of girls. She easily expresses empathic feelings to characters in the literature and to others.

Like Barry, she, too, is angry, and for a while she also holds on to endorsement of aggression. But in contrast to him, she lets go of the need for power in favor of relationships. It is easier for her to change her aggressive behavior than for Barry, because she doesn't suffer from ADHD. Her progress is impressive; she has actually solved her social problem and her level of aggression has been sharply reduced. It is clear that Michelle's ability to express her real feelings has helped her to experience catharsis and to develop insight into her aggressive behavior, and that her ability to establish a close relationship with the counselor helped her change her disruptive behavior. Hence, relationships are the key to the problem and its resolution, in this case, and very different from the case of Barry.

The following describes individual treatment of two adolescents, a boy and a girl. Both teenagers live in a group foster home, having experienced violence and neglect throughout their lives. They were also treated by the same counselor, which makes the comparison more reliable.

Treatment of an Adolescent Boy

Background

Vincent is a 13-year-old boy whose parents are divorced. His mother is addicted to heroin and his father is an alcoholic; both are violent. Vincent and his younger sister were initially placed with a foster family, where his experience of abuse only continued. He particularly remembers being hungry in that family. He was later placed in the current group home, in which he has now resided for 1 year. He still resists the place and acts violently, but admits that at least he is not hungry anymore.

Vincent represents the case of both proactive and reactive aggression. He has seen violence throughout his life and uses it to gain emotional and social gratification, as well as to fill practical needs; in this sense, he is a proactive aggressor. However, he has accumulated so much frustration in his life that he may also be considered a reactive aggressor. The two types of aggression often go together, despite the attempt to separate them (Dodge & Schwartz, 1997). A boy with a similar background served as control.

Treatment Process

The meetings are held in the group home after school hours by an experienced counselor. Vincent has agreed to attend 12 sessions, even though they take away from his free time, and to have the sessions taped. The purpose of the meetings, as introduced to Vincent, is to learn about adolescents' difficulties, for which the counselor trusts he can be of great help. He responds positively and is willing to help. It is not easy for an adolescent with a background such as Vincent's to trust someone new, but on the other hand, he is in dire need of individual attention. Hence, his personal needs, coupled with his altruistic tendency, lead him to give up his free time.

Already at the *first session*, in an activity of getting acquainted, Vincent admits that he likes to fight, particularly to hit his younger sister, and hates to clean his room. Is he trying to impress the counselor with his violent behavior, or test her ability to tolerate him? Or is this a true response expressing his self-concept? All may be true.

Next, when they talk about a meaningful object in their possession, Vincent refers to the ball that he keeps playing with as they are talking. He seems quite restless, and so the therapist changes activities rather often. When they play with "feeling" cards, he selects "hatred," explaining that he hates all children and particularly his sister. Finally, in the Telegram activity, in which he sends a message to himself, he notes that he likes to make others laugh, but he himself does not enjoy laughing. In short, the counselor meets a restless, sad, and lonely adolescent who is full of hostility, particularly to the most significant people in his world.

When they discuss the poem, "My Monster," Vincent immediately states that it reminds him of himself. "I too push, shove, and hit kids at home and outside." He feels OK with it, "its fun," he says. "It feels good to be strong. . . .Sometimes I feel sorry for the kid . . . .At first, I am happy, then sometimes I feel sorry, but not always . . .actually, I don't feel anything." This sense of emptiness is described in many books on violent children. The interpretation that clinicians provide is that denial of one's own feelings leads to indifference toward other's suffering as well (Garbarino, 1999; Moeller, 2001; Pollack, 1998). In an attempt to increase the connection to his own feelings, the counselor asks him how he feels when he gets hit.

Vincent: I'm angry. Wouldn't you be?
Counselor: Yes, I would, but sometimes I also feel sad, hurt, insulted.
Vincent: No, I don't feel anything.
Counselor: What do you do when you are angry?
Vincent: I throw chairs, hit, shout ... I know I get in trouble, but I can't help it.

The counselor challenges him on this discrepancy: "You talk about your aggression as if you don't care, but you also seem to doubt your response and are not too happy with it." Vincent answers, "Well, I get into trouble too often." He continues telling about a serious incident in which he used a knife and was almost kicked out of the home. Vincent is honest about his behavior, even concerned about the possible consequences, but feels quite helpless regarding change. "A person can't change in one day," he says.

In the next session, in which they discuss a picture of a fight among children, he sees a bully who hits his victim and invites all the guys to come and see how strong he is. "He is showing off his power," he explains. "That's the way it is here, too, you want to establish your status in the group ... I do the same," he confesses.

The next session they watch the film, *Madi*, which shows the horrible consequences of impulsive aggression. One of the two children in the movie causes the other to fall down a two-story building, leaving him paralyzed. Vincent gets restless, claims he is hungry, and wants to leave. This is a very unusual reaction to the movie; most kids realize the danger in being so violent. The counselor reminds him that he is here to help her, and he sits down again. In contrast to many children, Vincent identifies with the aggressor and cannot see anything wrong with his violent response. He understands the aggressor's violent reaction as the result of anger that had to find an outlet, and as the victim was weaker, he was the perfect target. Vincent continues defending the aggressor by interpreting the whole situation as an accident. In the direct self-exploration part of the session, he cannot remember any serious incident in which he himself was involved. I guess this was too threatening to recall, and also the reason for his defense of the perpetrator. But he did mention that he gets very angry when he is hungry, insulted, or threatened.

For the next session the counselor selects another movie (*Victor*) showing a milder type of aggression. The film depicts an immigrant boy who faces many learning difficulties and eventually gets into a fight. The situation is less violent and therefore permits Vincent to connect emotionally. He talks about his own failure in school, admits that there is a girl in the group that he repeatedly bullies, and mentions his disrespectful behavior to a teacher. But to the counselor's question "How do you feel about that?" he responds angrily, complains that he is hungry, and leaves the room.

This is an important lesson to all who work with aggressive children. Pushing them toward expressing their feelings too much or too early is not effective. Once they feel judged, they react with avoidance or violence. The session was difficult for Vincent because there was too much pressure on him to talk about his behavior, which he is ashamed of but cannot stop because he gets gratification out of it. It seems that aggression helps him get rid of tension, and so he picks fights. But he doesn't understand the function of his fights yet.

The next session starts with a talk about Vincent's difficulties in the previous session. There is no need for literature, as the counselor reflects on his difficulty with his own behavior. She reframes it to focus on the positive aspects of his personality. "You find yourself in a loop in which you pick a fight to get out your anger, it escalates to the point that someone is hurt, and you dislike yourself." "Exactly!" he says, and gives an example of a girl who rides the bus with him to school. He picks on her, she reacts by rejecting him, which he perceives as a put down and uses to justify his aggression, but then he feels bad about himself. He is willing to change, he admits, but when the counselor asks him to pick one behavior that is worth changing, and offers to draw up a contract, he says he wants to go to sleep. He again reacts in avoidance because he cannot trust himself.

They move to a clarifying process. The counselor asks if he wants change, if it's worth it for him to make an effort. Vincent is not sure, cannot think of any benefits, but eventually says that it would be best for everyone if he could be less aggressive. She further probes because it does not seem to her that he is serious about change.

He eventually chooses to stop picking on that one girl, but cannot promise that he will succeed.

When they discuss, at a later session, the story "The Smiley Face" (Noy, 1995; see Appendix A) he is already quite critical of the aggressor. The story is of a new student to school whose success and self-confidence threaten a veteran student. Worried about losing his status in class, the veteran reacts aggressively. Vincent expresses empathy for the newcomer, saying that the perpetrator treats him unfairly. The counselor is impressed with the change in his newly acquired perceptions, and plays the tape of former sessions to show him how much he has changed. Vincent admits that he avoided getting involved in a fight and instead went to sleep, a big accomplishment for him. Still, he has a hard time accepting the counselor's compliments. I tend to interpret his behavior as fear of not being able to maintain the change.

In his feedback at termination, Vincent emphasizes improvement in his level of verbal aggression. "I do not curse that much anymore," he says. To the counselor's question of what in the process made him change, he says, "that you listened to me." This feedback is very moving, yet not surprising. Sometimes it seems to me that all that these very aggressive children need is individual attention, the caring and support that is missing from their personal lives and the lack of which makes them aggressive in the first place.

Evaluation

Interestingly, Vincent's self-evaluation of the progress he has made is quite modest. On the self-report adjustment scale, he reported a score reduction from 25 at pretreatment to 17 at posttreatment (on a scale of 0–36), compared to the control boy, who gave himself a 10 and 8, respectively. The teacher's report, in contrast, shows more favorable outcomes: a pretreatment score of 23 and a posttreatment score of 13, compared to 17 and 14, respectively, for the control boy.

Throughout the process, Vincent didn't seem to trust his own ability to change. Thus, it is not surprising that he doesn't recognize the progress he has made. The teacher's report is more objective and more reliable in this respect. Moreover, weekly observations by his homeroom teacher indicated that Vincent started with 3–4 aggressive episodes a week during the initial stage of treatment and ended with 1–2 at the end of treatment. Based on this accumulated data, it is clear that the level of aggression has decreased following the treatment of this young man.

Treatment of a Teenage Girl

Background

Nancy, aged 13, also comes from a family of divorce and drug abuse, with a father who is highly disabled and a dysfunctional mother. She lives in the same group foster home as Vincent. However, she is a veteran there, having lived there for more than 3 years. Nevertheless, she still feels uncomfortable, mostly because of many interpersonal conflicts with girls of her cohort. Her communication with her younger sister, who is placed in the same group foster home, is also extremely violent. Nancy is a highly aggressive girl.

Treatment Process

As is common in our treatment, the initial sessions are devoted to establishing a therapist-client alliance. The therapist therefore plays getting acquainted games with Nancy. Nancy immediately shares her major dislikes with the counselor: she doesn't like it when children brag about their achievements, she doesn't like the girls in her cohort, she likes private communication with one person, and she likes to be home whenever she can (a fantasy that she has despite the terrible conditions in her home).

Next, Nancy is invited to share a meaningful object with the counselor. She selects a microphone and tells an embarrassing incident in which she didn't show up for a play the cohort put on. Everyone was mad at her afterward. They then have an imaginary birthday party. Nancy invites her parents, although they were explicitly excluded from the game. "I don't like anyone else," she explains. In this *first session,* Nancy discloses her difficulties with relationships, her antisocial behavior and her indirect resistance to authority. Being a girl, relational aggression is expected in her case.

In the next session, they discuss the poem, "My Monster." The monster reminds her of a girl in her cohort who always triggers her (Nancy's) aggression. She describes a fight with her, which became so violent that Nancy ended up with a handful of the victim's hair. "I took all my frustration and anger out on her." It seems that she had a lot of anger locked inside herself, considering the level of violence that took place, which was not necessarily provoked by the victim. No, she says, she doesn't feel good afterward, but she needs to take out her anger, and the victim just happened to be there. She recalls another guy that she hit; she didn't like it that time either, but couldn't help it. At this point, she doesn't see any other way to handle her anger. She does not trust the adults around her, and therefore doesn't involve them in her conflicts; she feels she needs to resolve her issues all by herself.

In a later session, the counselor shows her a picture of a fight between youngsters and asks her to make up a story behind the picture. Nancy tells about a group of teenagers who live together but don't get along. There is one girl that they particularly dislike for no obvious reason. One day they decide to teach her a lesson, and this picture is the result. Asked if she's had a similar experience, Nancy cannot recall any time that she was a victim, but she has participated in such abusive groups, she admits.

For several sessions Nancy pretends to be powerful and strong, the perpetrator rather than the victim. Eventually, however, she shares a conflict she is having with her roommates and the house mother of her cohort. She feels disrespected and hurt after a fight with her roommates. She is blamed for the fight and feels that is unfair. As a result she hasn't eaten in two days and is hungry. She relates at length that it all started in a simple conflict with another girl who was celebrating her birthday. This girl gave Nancy a look that she interpreted as disrespectful, and made Nancy respond with verbal aggression. As a result, she is rejected by the whole group including the house mother. The house mother invited her for a talk to clarify things, but Nancy felt highly insulted. She needs the house mother on her side, but instead of trying to communicate with her openly, she ran away. The whole home was out looking for her until midnight, when she was found. Even then she kept silent and wouldn't respond to any attempt to communicate with her. "I feel that everyone hates me here, the kids and the adults," she discloses to the counselor. She wants to get out of this mess, she says, but doesn't know how.

The counselor tries to explore the situation with her. "How did it all start?" she asks. "I don't know" is the response Nancy gives to this question and several others. The counselor tries to help by providing clues—a word, a curse, a touch, a glance? Nancy picks the last option. The exploration process reveals that Nancy was jealous of the attention her friend received on her birthday, and this made her so hateful. Nancy realizes that people respond to her anger and hatred with rejection, and is unhappy because she is so sensitive to rejection. "I hate it when people are angry at me, but I don't think there is a solution to the situation," she sadly confesses.

The counselor then introduces a story about conflict between two brothers that escalates into violence. It all started when the younger brother destroyed a car that his older brother built. Their mother instinctively blames her older son for hurting his younger brother, but when she listens carefully to the older boy, she understands his anger. The story shows how listening to him was important to restore understanding. Following the discussion of that conflict, Nancy understands that she should have involved the house mother before the conflict escalated and explain the situation. "Yes, I can see why the house mother is so angry with me; she puts so much effort into building a relationship with me. She's probably disappointed that I still don't trust her, and rather than talking to her, I just took off." As Nancy still doesn't trust her own ability to communicate with the house mother, they role play a possible conversation with the counselor playing the role of the house mother.

Counselor:	I am angry and also insulted that you didn't involve me, and just ran away. I was so worried about you, I couldn't sleep.
Nancy:	Because you can't help me; you are effective with others, but not with me.
Counselor:	If I can help others, I may be able to help you. Please help me to help you. Please trust me, tell me: how did you behave that made everyone so angry at you?
Nancy (grumbling):	When I am angry, everyone suffers.
Counselor:	What would you like to change, one small step?
Nancy:	It's difficult to choose, very difficult; I would like to resolve the issue, to improve the climate in our group, to get rid of the tension, but I just don't know how to do it.

She eventually decides to talk to the house mother as a starting point.

This session is a turning point in many ways. For the first time, Nancy has stopped pretending to be tough and indifferent. She has shared a conflict as it is happening. She has started to examine her own feelings and her own part in the conflict, rather than just blaming others. She is now honest about her own anger, vulnerability, and helplessness. The counselor seems to have earned her trust, and lack of trust seems to be a major drawback in Nancy's personality.

In a later session, when they discuss the poem, "The Evil Palm" (Rabikovitz, 1995). Nancy is more open with the counselor. Although it is very difficult for her, she discloses physical abuse she suffered when she was much younger. "I still remember it, and whenever I see a group of guys, I think it is them." After discussing the abuse, they go back to the current conflict with her roommates. She notes that she managed to restrain herself and avoid further escalation, but she doesn't feel happy at all. "She thinks she is better than me because I don't respond," Nancy says, and it bothers her.

Counselor:	You feel weak because you don't insult her back?
Nancy:	Exactly!
Counselor:	Could it be that self-control is a strength rather than a weakness?
Nancy:	I understand that it may be a strength, but what about them? Would they see it as a strength, too?

The counselor assures her that being in control is a strength, and Nancy promises to continue being in control until the next session.

At a later session, when they discuss ways to handle anger, the counselor asks Nancy to make up a list of unacceptable ways to express anger. She puts cursing at the top of her list. She often uses abusive language and feels embarrassed afterward. She would prefer to avoid the situation, get out, leave the room, or write in her diary. In terms of alternative behaviors to aggression, Nancy seems to be progressing and offers sublimation as part of her solutions.

Toward termination, Nancy shows signs of progress in her behavior as well. She updates the counselor about her attempts to control herself. She had an argument with a girl who really insulted her, telling her "I don't eat from your hands." "Normally, I would curse and even fight with her, but instead I hit the wall in her room and wrote in my diary." Yet, Nancy admits that she doesn't feel good about her progress. The counselor reinforces her for making an effort, and, as a result, Nancy promises to continue.

The internal struggle that Nancy is going through is quite clear. This is a young woman who never had a chance to learn how to resolve conflict. Aggression and violence is what she has seen throughout her life and is part of her current life as well. Coming from a background such as hers, one can understand her difficulty trusting others. The counselor developed a rapport with her that permitted Nancy to share feelings and even some repressed as well as current experiences. Although she seems to accept the need for change in her behavior, she cannot be sure that others in her environment will see it as positive. Realistically, she may be right. In a climate of aggression and norms that endorse power, restrained behavior may indeed be interpreted as weakness and lead to further victimization. In such circumstances, little progress may be expected in this short time of treatment.

Evaluation

Although, in her final interview, Nancy reports that she is using abusive language less often and refrains from getting into fights, the scores on the questionnaires do not support her progress. She remained quite high on the aggression measure, by both self-report (18 to 15 for pre- and posttreatment, respectively) and teacher report (16 to 15). The lack of favorable outcomes, in her case, may also be attributed to the acute conflict that she was still involved in at termination. Termination was definitely done at the wrong time.

When asked about what she liked about the intervention, she mentioned the stories ("I could see that other kids also have problems") and the fact that the counselor listened to her ("My gut is not full of so much anger anymore."). In more professional language, it was the catharsis that helped her release some of the tension. This catharsis was made possible by the positive alliance with her therapist. In addition, the universality of her conflict and feelings, as reflected in the literature, helped her better understand her own situation and perhaps even learn from literary characters how to resolve her problems.

Comparison of the Therapeutic Processes of Boys and Girls

Boys and girls are expected to present different types of aggression, according to the literature (Connor, 2002; Crick & Bigbee, 1998; Yogan & Henry, 2000). Boys are expected to show more direct physical aggression, either of a proactive or reactive type, while girls are expected to show more indirect relational aggression. These differences were indeed reflected in the cases illustrated above. At an early age, Barry and Michelle expressed different patterns of aggression. Barry had more difficulty expressing feelings than Michelle, he was more focused on the need to show power, and he was less empathic. Michelle, for her part, demonstrated patterns of relational aggression in terms of her relationships with classmates and the counselor.

The difference between boys and girls is even more obvious in the case of the two teenagers, because they shared a similar background and were treated by the same counselor. The two adolescents reacted very differently during treatment. From the beginning of treatment and throughout the process, Vincent proudly presented his externalized behavior, expressed endorsement of power, and referred mostly to his actions. Nancy, on the other hand, talked about relationships and intimacy; she wants to be home, likes private communication, hates the girls in her cohort, and expresses passive, indirect aggression (e.g., doesn't show up for the play). Vincent's ability to relate to and express feelings is quite limited, with one exception: anger. Both youngsters see themselves as victims who only respond to provocation, but the type of behavior is different: he hits and she pulls hair. At termination, they both state that being listened to is an important therapeutic factor. However, Nancy adds the cathartic experience, the expression of strong feelings. In short, she demonstrates relational aggression while he demonstrates reactive and proactive aggression, despite their similar backgrounds and present circumstances. Indeed, these differences are evident among the younger children as well.

While boys endorse physical power and appearing strong is their main concern, girls don't feel comfortable with such an image, as can be seen in the following example:

> Martha is being treated in a group of high risk dropouts from the regular school system. Although these girls talk about their own aggression freely, they do not feel comfortable with it. At one session, Martha shares an incident in which she hit a boy who insulted her: "I'm quite a strong person and I can take care of myself, so I hit him, because there is no other way with him, he just doesn't understand. But, on the other hand, I feel disgusted with my behavior, as if I was a man." Martha used aggression but didn't like it, because it doesn't fit the image of a "lady."

Such a process is more typical of girls than of boys, particularly in adolescence, when the development of self-identity is intensified.

Summary

This chapter provided illustrations of individual treatment of aggressive boys and girls using bibliotherapy as an adjunct to the treatment. As already noted, for various reasons, we sometimes end up treating aggressive children and adolescents in individual settings. This is sometimes due to practical considerations, but usually it is because some children are not ready for group treatment. In order not to endanger the group process and to secure their own well-being, these clients are invited for individual treatment. I recently read a report of a group treatment in which a teenager was removed from the group in the ninth session. The counselor wrote, "Don constantly hindered our group process; I wish I had asked him to leave earlier, for the group's sake. The group members indeed made efforts to accept him, but they paid a high price. Thinking back on the process, Don shouldn't be in a group."

The illustration of the individual process of treatment also permitted a comparison of the type of aggression displayed by boys and girls, as well as their process of treatment. Regardless of age, girls display more indirect relational aggression while boys show more physical aggression. This difference seems to be associated with the attitudes characteristic of each gender. While boys need to express their physical power, girls are more concerned with their relationships.

Both genders reacted positively to the same stories, poems, and films. However, the discussions of the literature was obviously limited to the single treatment child's experiences. In a group situation, the discussion and interpersonal exchange of ideas and feelings is much richer, permitting more intensive interpersonal learning experiences and the acquisition of interpersonal skills. Perhaps children with extreme difficulties may start in individual treatment and move, when ready, to group treatment to enrich their experiences. Such a stage-like approach is supported in the literature on treatment (Yalom & Leszcz, 2005). Another intermediary option is to provide treatment in pairs. This approach, which provides a degree of interpersonal learning, is discussed in the next chapter.

Chapter 7
Treatment in Pairs (Duo-Therapy)

Introduction

As explained in Chapter 5, we prefer to work in groups whenever possible, not only because it is cost effective, but because children help each other to learn about themselves and others. The discussion of the literature text is richer in a group and, if conducted in a positive climate, allows children to learn new and more constructive behaviors from each other. However, as pointed out in Chapter 6, it is not always possible to form a group. Sometimes the solution is to work with a pair of children, and they, too, can be helpful to each other. This is a relatively unknown model, referred to in the literature as "duo-therapy" or "peer pair therapy" (Scheidlinger, 2001). This method has been successfully employed with children who were unsuitable for group treatment, either because they were too fearful and withdrawn, or because they were too impulsive. The duo setting, devoid of the multifaceted stimuli inherent in traditional groups, provides each child with the opportunity for an intense relationship with a peer and an adult.

Two children can be paired incidentally, because there are no other suitable children able to attend. Another possibility is for children to be selected based on friendship relationships, with the intention of supporting each other. This interesting variant is represented by a designated patient's selecting a friend to join him/her in the treatment sessions. The theoretical basis for this method is Sullivan's concept of "chumship" (Sullivan, 1953) or best friendship. Best friends are a major source of support for children (Hartup, 1993), and their presence may be very meaningful in a child's change process. Finally, children can be paired based on rival relationships, to help them resolve the issues, which not only influence their relationships, but also affect the whole class.

Z. Shechtman, *Treating Child and Adolescent Aggression Through Bibliotherapy*,
The Springer Series on Human Exceptionality, DOI 10.1007/978-0-387-09745-9_7,
© Springer Science+Business Media, LLC 2009

Treatment of Two Close Friends

Background

Joseph and David, both 10, are best friends. Joseph was selected for treatment based on a questionnaire completed by classmates, who identified him as the most aggressive child in class—data confirmed by his homeroom teacher. He first refused treatment, but when he was allowed to bring a friend, he selected his best friend, David, who also scored quite high on aggression. Both boys are the youngest of four children in families of an average socioeconomic class. Their friendship started in first grade when they were classmates. However, in third grade, the school authorities decided to separate the two into parallel classrooms because they supported each other's negative behavior in class. This made them sad but did not break up the friendship. They both love sports, particularly soccer, and often meet after school to watch violent movies together. Their behavior is characterized by lack of boundaries, classroom disturbances, and aggression toward peers. Joseph instigates most of the negative behaviors and David seems to be a trusty follower. This pattern became quite obvious from the start.

Treatment Process

In the *first session*, Joseph and David play getting-acquainted games. Although they know each other, the therapist does not. Moreover, getting acquainted is an ice breaker which helps to set norms of self-expressiveness and mutual acceptance. Joseph is the first to respond to each question and David just copies his behavior. Throughout the session, they make an effort to complete each other's sentences and actually get in each other's way very often. At the end of the session, their greatest fear is that they may be separated for the rest of treatment, and they ask the counselor about it. She assures them that she has no intention of punishing them. She also acknowledges their self-awareness that they misbehave together, and invites them to use this insight in their change process. As you can see, the therapist presents these children with a new role unknown to them in their school reality: she is building on their positive aspects of behavior rather than using punishment. This is very important to establish rapport and increase their motivation to participate in the treatment process. It is clear to her that Joseph has a devastating influence on David and she wonders whether it is to their benefit to work as a pair. But it seems there is no other option, as Joseph refuses individual treatment.

The counselor starts the *second session* by showing the boys a picture of a group of boys fighting (Teaching Pictures, 1974a, b) and asks them to make up a story about what led to the fight. Joseph starts, as usual, telling a story of a group abusing a single boy: "The boy must defend himself," he suggests, "and he will be successful," he believes. In his projection, there is a rejected boy whom the group and the teacher insult. The boy must use violence to take care of himself, because there is no one else to protect him. Joseph quickly shifts to talking about his own experiences, stating that he doesn't feel comfortable in his own class and would like to be transferred to David's class. David reacts to this with clear empathy and support: "It is not fair how they treat you, you were actually all right with them, and they took advantage of you." Now, armed with his friend's support, Joseph continues sharing some of his violent acts with quite a bit of pride. David watches him with admiration, laughing at his horror stories. "This is how you teach others to respect you," he says to Joseph. Joseph goes on telling about a visit to another friend's home. That friend invited him, but when he got there, the friend's mother refused to let Joseph in. He had to stay outside in the cold until his mother came to pick him up. To this, David again responds with emotional support, "He's a jerk, he does it to others, too, he is really mean." It is clear that Joseph feels rejected, as he probably is. Yet, at this point in his treatment, he is unaware that the rejection may be a consequence of his aggressive behavior. Instead, he is enthusiastic about his own power, which gives him much satisfaction.

The *third session* they read the poem, "The Bad Boy" (Goldberg, 1959), in which a boy loses his temper and becomes verbally and physically abusive. Joseph tells about a girl who made him angry and, when he responded to her provocation, he was blamed for choking her. Joseph sees himself as a victim whose only choice is to defend himself; he expresses no empathy for the real victim. David supports him again: "She is lying." This reminds David of a time he was unjustly blamed for pushing someone, and he shares this with Joseph and the therapist. While Joseph provides immediate support, saying "What a liar!" he also states, "but in your case, they believe you." Joseph is expressing his vulnerability and sense of rejection; he is in a worse situation than his friend. He seems to feel some respect for his best friend, and maybe even some envy. This is a good sign for the therapist, as David may be of help in Joseph's treatment process, even though Joseph seems to be the stronger one. Interestingly, Joseph continues to probe David: "But is it possible that you did push him accidentally?" David accepts the version provided by his friend and admits that he did push the boy, but was blamed for doing so intentionally. David learns from Joseph's response and develops some insight into his behavior.

When the counselor asks them about their feelings in the course of such incidents, the two boys differ in their responses. Joseph totally denies any feelings, stating "I just move on, I don't care." David, on the other hand, admits that he feels insulted: "I also move on, but I don't feel good." For the first time, David reacts authentically despite Joseph's influence. He is taking a risk, as we can see from the next reaction. "I didn't know you're so sensitive," Joseph says to him. This is a put down, but David ignores the tone and says, "I'm not sensitive, I'm angry." He is developing some ego strength, a good sign for independent thinking and a buffer against Joseph's negative impact.

In the *fourth session*, the poem, "What Do You Do When You're Angry?" (Benziman, 1992) generates a discussion of anger and its management. Joseph appears very angry and refuses to respond to the poem. For a while he is very quiet, although he seems ready to explode. After a while, he shares the incident that made him so angry. He tells about a fight he had with another classmate, whom he was blamed for hurting badly. "Everyone blames me," he says, "the children and the teacher." He feels rejected, misunderstood, and tired. "They all hate me," he says. The main point is yet to come; among the children who complained about his behavior was his best friend, David, and this he cannot tolerate: "How could he blame me when I always protect him, and I often get in trouble because of him?" Losing the support of our best friend is difficult to handle, it makes us feels quite lonely.

The therapist effectively uses this here-and-now situation to teach the boys some communication skills, suggesting that they talk to each other about what happened. David immediately apologizes for offending him, but adds that he couldn't lie to the teacher. The therapist emphasizes the apology, but Joseph does not accept it easily: "He pities me, that's why he apologizes," he says, "and I don't need his pity." For aggressive boys, it is difficult not only to apologize, but also to forgive. Apologizing and forgiving are both signs of weakness, in the eyes of the aggressor. To this, David responds directly to Joseph: "I don't feel pity for you! I apologize because I hurt you as my friend, because I betrayed you . . . but I also felt pity for the boy you hit. You were very wild; I didn't like your behavior." David is honest and strong enough to provide constructive feedback, which Joseph seems to accept, as he says, "When people put me down, I respond with force, I am not perfect." This is the beginning of insight, as Joseph is willing to admit, for the first time, that aggression is not all positive. Could this be a reaction to the feedback he received from his best friend?

When they discuss the story, "The Bully" (Tester, 1974; see Appendix B), in the *fifth session* the two boys are both back to stories in which they endorse aggression as a means of solving all their problems. It seems that David is trying to regain his friend's trust. Is there a cause for concern about the negative impact Joseph may have on David? Not really, because in the next session, Joseph's influence seems to diminish. Discussing "My Monster," Joseph says that it is impossible to control the monster, while David feels that it is certainly possible. Joseph says that controlling the monster means fighting yourself, which he cannot do, while David suggests taking the anger out on something else (sublimation) as a solution. He further suggests that asking for forgiveness is another option, and shares how he solved a recent conflict with his girlfriend by writing her a letter of apology, and that he feels good about himself. Joseph listens to this, but doubts the effectiveness of such an approach: "They will think I'm weak."

In an attempt to increase Joseph's ability to apologize, the counselor introduces a poem on "Forgiveness" (Nir, 2000) in the next session. David admits that his parents have taught him he needs to apologize or else he gets punished—he can't watch TV, play on the computer, or see his friends. Moreover, when he apologizes, people are less angry at him, and he feels better. Joseph, on the other hand, is never punished; even when his mother threatens to do so, she never actually carries it out. When his father wants to punish him, "my mother saves me." Joseph has never been asked to apologize and doesn't intend to do so. Although David's modeling is not effective, there is some information in this interaction that is worth noting. The two boys do not come from similar homes. David is socialized to be prosocial, while Joseph is brought up with no limits or boundaries. Moreover, he gets distorted messages at home, with a manipulative mother who is inconsistent in her upbringing of her son. These differences in socialization may largely explain the differences in the boys' behavior.

Indeed, in the last session, following a discussion of "I am My Own Commander" (Bokek, 1980), Joseph empathizes with the character's lack of control, while David thinks that the character is angry with himself and regrets his behavior. He also thinks that the boy is aware of the consequences and therefore is trying to control himself. Joseph continues making jokes about the consequences of aggression. When they place themselves on the continuum of aggression, David gives himself a 5 (mid score) because he is violent only when he loses control, while Joseph gives himself a 10 (the highest score) and argues that he wants to be there because he chooses to be aggressive. It is interesting that David is not able to influence Joseph, as hoped, but he was also not affected negatively by Joseph, an important outcome in the light of literature that cautions against such negative influences (Dishion et al., 1999).

Evaluation

In this case, we did not measure outcomes, but we did measure processes. Specifically, we measured client behavior over the eight sessions, based on Hill's Client Behavior Responses (Hill & O'Brien, 1999). Joseph made about 20 statements of resistance in the first five sessions and overall mostly unconstructive responses, such as restatements, but these declined from the sixth session on, dropping to 7 and 3 statements in the last two sessions, respectively. David had much fewer statements of resistance overall 2–3 per session at the most, throughout the treatment. That is, the two boys had different responses to the program. Their initial differences, their parents' behavior and their therapeutic progress were different. Both children need further sessions to progress.

The intent of presenting this case was to highlight the contribution a close friend can make in the treatment of a violent child. This begs the question: how important was it to include David in Joseph's treatment? Despite research that cautions against the negative impact of aggressive children on similar children (Dishion et al., 1999), my answer is that David's inclusion was very important. First, Joseph refused to be alone in treatment; were it not for his best friend, he wouldn't have gotten any help at all. Despite the disappointing results for Joseph, we may expect that something has been absorbed. Second, David certainly was favorably affected by the process and his presence in the treatment was valuable to him and to his friend. He, too, might have skipped treatment if he hadn't been invited to join his friend. This case illustration suggests that highly aggressive children do not necessarily have a negative impact on less aggressive peers in a treatment process. Moreover, it points to the effect that the initial level of aggression has on the change process; it seems more difficult to change the extremely aggressive boys than the more mild cases.

Treatment of Two Rival Classmates

Background

Steven and Jack, 10-year-old classmates, are in constant conflict, often fighting each other. They were selected by their teacher as the most aggressive kids in her class. Two other classmates with similar scores on aggression served as controls. The two treatment boys come from middle-class families, their mothers are housewives, they are both the youngest children in the family, and they both mentioned in the intake interview that watching violent movies is their favorite activity.

Treatment Process

Steven and Jack were quite surprised to find themselves in the same treatment room, but the opportunity to skip class and play games convinced them to give it a try. They quickly understood that they were selected because they misbehaved in class, but it didn't bother them very much.

In the *first session*, they play getting acquainted games, such as sharing a meaningful object, a meaningful event, and a fantasy. They both share a valued object they possess and both also mention a fantasy of having a dog. To some extent, the two are imitating each other; nevertheless, this makes them recognize that they have a lot in common.

Next, they play a game in which they throw a ball to each other and ask a question. Jack asks Steven, "How do you feel when kids call you fatso?" Note that Jack himself is one of the children who abuse Steven by calling him that name. This seems to be a risky question, but surprisingly Steven responds honestly, at least regarding his emotions. "I feel humiliated," he says, "but I don't retaliate, because I'm strong and I could kill someone." We know that Steven is aggressive and is often in fights, but it is probably too early to admit to his aggression. This is only the first session, and he probably wants to impress the counselor with his appropriate behavior. Nevertheless, he does not deny his feelings, which most aggressive boys do. This seems to be an extremely important step in establishing a relationship between the two boys. Authentic communication usually helps to connect and to become more intimate.

The next activity is "feeling" cards. For Steven, *Anger* is evoked when he feels helpless (e.g., when older kids take away his ball); he feels *Happiness* when he dances; and he has a lot of *Self-confidence* because he is physically strong, which makes it possible for him to help victims. When the *Violence* card is chosen, he admits, "Yes, "I'm very violent. I bite and hit, I want to kill the guy. I can't control my behavior." Jack chooses *Love*, which he feels for his girlfriend; *Control*, as he likes to control Steven ("I make him do things he doesn't like and I feel good that I win")"; and *Violence*, recognizing that sometimes he can't control his own hands: "I hit with hatred," he confesses.

While both boys are aware of their violent behavior and their difficulty in controlling it, it is not yet clear if they are disturbed by it. This should be further explored in future sessions. For now, it is important to close the session in a positive way, to make them feel accepted and confident. Indeed, the counselor suggests that they give each other awards. Steven gives Jack an award for helping children in need, and Jack gives Steven an award for being generous and being a good soccer player. The session ends with both feeling good. Steven says, "Most of the time, children curse and insult. It is nice to hear good things about myself."

In the next session, the counselor continues to build a climate of trust, but also starts developing some understanding of aggressive behavior. The boys are first asked to write postcards to themselves from classmate. The aim of this activity is to see how they perceive their social status. The postcards are sealed, to be opened at termination. Without making any direct attributions to their own actions, the counselor then asks them to identify disturbing behaviors in class. They mention fighting, pushing, cursing, and insulting.

In the next session, the focus shifts to aggression, based on the poem, "My Monster." Steven says, "The boy doesn't like his monster, because it's selfish and gets him into trouble. In fact, it frightens the boy" because it gets into his dreams. This is Steven's projection of his fears. The counselor asks him why that happens. "Because when someone annoys the monster, it doesn't want to show its vulnerability, it acts out of fear," he replies. He then starts to talk about his own monster, which he tries to fight, but with little success.

Steven: It happens often, not because I want to get into a fight, but because I get mad easily and can't control myself. ... But the monster also does good things for me; it shows that I'm brave.

Counselor: And what are the bad things?

Steven: It can be dangerous in a fight, as it may hurt someone.

Steven is starting to see the negative aspects of aggression, but continues to endorse the use of force. The monster is brave, children admire its power, why give it up? This, of course, is only the *third session*, and most aggressive children are still unaware of their aggression or unwilling to change their behavior at this stage of treatment.

Jack sees the monster as a power that takes over, even when the child doesn't want to fight. The child feels helpless, so controlling is the monster. He admits that when he gets insulted, the monster takes over. He sees only bad aspects in letting the monster control his behavior because the consequence of aggression can be horrifying. In contrast to Steven, Jack does not seem to be conflictual about aggression; he only feels helpless. He is at a more advanced stage than his friend. He seems to fear his own aggression and mostly needs help controlling himself, whereas Steven still needs to change his attitudes toward aggression.

The *fourth session* focuses on a poem in which a child hits his fried because he has betrayed him and refuses to share with him a new toy. The two boys understand that the boy loses control when his friend refuses to share his toy, and that he is jealous; "he (the boy who betrays his friend) has everything and he (the aggressor) has nothing," says Steven, and Jack agrees. They quickly shift to talking about their own envy: "I envy children who look nice, who have a good body, and I am sad that I don't look like them," says Steven. "When kids call me fatso, it hurts me a lot, I cry and get violent," he continues. Jack, referring to the relationship in the "here-and-now," admits that he envies Steven, who gets many new things, like a TV in his room. Steven in turn admits that he envies Jack for being a successful soccer player.

Again, the two differ in their perceptions of violence. Steven has an excuse (others hurt him) and therefore it seems right to him to react aggressively, while Jack continues to talk about lack of control ("Ron threw a rock because he couldn't control himself.").

Next, the counselor deals with the consequences of lack of control, using the story "The Smiley Face" (Noy, 1995; see Appendix A), in which a veteran student responds violently to a newcomer because he is worried about losing his social status. Steven strongly identifies with the aggressor rather than the victim: "It is not fair to take away his status; after all, he was there first." Later, he admits that he was jealous when a newcomer befriended his close friend, and hated him for it. In an attempt to raise empathy, the counselor explains the discomfort of the newcomer. This reminds Steven of his own experience of being new to the school and to the soccer team, when he felt extremely embarrassed and shy because of his appearance. This feeling of loneliness, however, does not change his mind. "I still agree with the veteran," he concludes.

Jack hesitates about whom to take sides with. He tries to convince Steven that the aggressor was just terribly jealous of the newcomer's self-confidence, and further provides feedback to Steven: "You are too preoccupied with your own status, that's why you think the veteran student is right." This is pretty accurate feedback for Steven, which the latter seems to accept, as he doesn't respond. Steven is indeed sensitive to how the other kids relate to him. Being able to accept criticism from a peer is an important step.

The counselor further explores the consequences of aggression by airing the film, *Madi*. Again, the boys react differently to the movie. Steven clearly identifies with the perpetrator. He understands his anger and frustration, which he takes out on the victim.

Steven:	It happens to all children when they're angry.
Counselor:	How does anger deteriorate into violence?
Steven:	Because when you're angry, you don't think, you just hit. . . . This is probably a pattern in his [Madi's] behavior, and even though he may later regret it, he can't control himself . . . believe me, that's how it happens.

It is clear that Steven is speaking from his own experience. Indeed, he then shares an episode in which he was extremely violent.

This is already the *fifth session*, but it is the first time that Steven openly admits to his aggression and mentions possible regret. Is this a turning point in his treatment process? Possibly, as he now places himself on 5 on the continuum of aggression during the clarifying process, because he takes out his anger on teachers when they threaten to call in his parents. He wants to be on 4 and stop cursing, "because it is not nice." This is a small step, but it is in the direction of change. As the child shows some self-awareness and motivation to change, the counselor may now begin guiding the change process. Referring to Steven's aggression reaction to his teacher, she asks, "How could you avoid such a response?" He replies, "I don't have to argue about everything. I can give her my journal [to write a note to his parents], then explain to my parents what happened. I make it worse by refusing to cooperate."

Jack has been silent most of this session, but joins the discussion at this point, saying that the film clearly shows how easy it is to escalate from anger to aggression and how dangerous it is. He says that while Steven was doing the continuum, he was thinking about himself—how he sometimes finds a weak victim and takes out all his anger on him. He doesn't like his behavior, sometimes feels ashamed of it and wants to move from 7 to 2 on the continuum. Jack is clearly at a more advanced stage of change. He is less occupied with the issue of power, but suffers from serious lack of self-control.

The counselor now begins to deal with the issue of self-control, using the poem, "Yaron is Angry" (Omer, 1978; see Appendix A), to focus the discussion on this motif. But beforehand, they try to resolve a violent incident in which Steven was involved during recess. It all started when he accidentally threw a ball out of the schoolyard and refused to retrieve it because they are not supposed to leave the yard. The child whose ball it was nagged him to the point where he couldn't bear it anymore and hit the child.

Steven:	I couldn't stand his nagging.
Counselor:	How do you feel?
Steven:	I don't feel good, but I can't control myself when I'm angry.
Jack (joining in):	It happens to me too. I like to torture animals, especially cats. I don't like it, I feel ashamed for using helpless creatures to take out my anger.

Counselor:	I understand the difficulties you both have. You both seem unhappy with your behavior. Can you think of other ways to resolve interpersonal conflict?
Steven (going back to the incident):	I don't know, I am angry at him, but also at myself. I'm like the veteran in the story ... Actually, I'm not angry anymore. I'll look for the ball after school. (Turning to Jack:) Will you help me?
Jack:	promises to help.

They then move on to the poem, in which a boy is frustrated by his failure to draw a picture and takes out his anger by destroying the piece of paper. This presents a good opportunity to discuss alternatives to aggression. This is the first time that both boys criticize aggression openly. "He is hot-blooded, he doesn't think," says Steven, but also admits that he behaves in a similar way when his brother makes fun of him for his poor grades. Jack, too, shares his aggressive behavior toward younger kids. The two seem to gain courage from each other to connect to their real behavior, but also to the disturbing feelings that follow their aggressive acts.

Counselor:	Are you happy with your response?
Steven:	No, but I forget that I need to stop.
Jack:	At first I'm happy, because I release my anger, but then I feel ashamed that I give in to my anger.

The two boys agree that taking anger out on a piece of paper is the right way to release anger (as the poem suggests), "because it doesn't hurt anyone."

They then make up a list of their destructive behaviors and are asked to select one behavior they most want to change. Steven's list includes hitting, kicking, spitting, and cursing. He wants to get rid of his physical aggression because "I don't want to hurt other kids. I want to be like Bill [a nonaggressive classmate] because he is always so self-composed." The clarifying process involves identifying the pros and cons of Steven's behavior, pointing to the disadvantages of his aggression and the advantages he can gain by letting go of his aggression. He identifies the negative consequences of getting punished, not getting rewards (being excluded from a classroom enrichment program), and being unsuccessful in school, as well as the gains of doing well in school, being invited to serve on committees, and being the team captain in sports. Asked how he can improve his behavior, his response is "to avoid problem kids." He promises to monitor his behavior for one week and see how he is doing. Steven is aware and ready to take action.

Jack's list of his disturbing behaviors includes torturing animals and hitting little kids, "because they cry and I feel sorry for them." When discussing the pros and cons, he borrows many of the gains that Steven alluded to, but with regard to the disadvantages, he says, "I can't lose anything [by letting go of aggression], because I don't care if children see me weak." As you may recall, Jack never held on to power, as did Steven. His issue is losing control, and he is still not sure he can overcome it: "Sometimes I feel like I'm addicted to fights. I need others to constantly remind me that there are other ways." This time Steven offers his help, saying: "I can remind you whenever I'm around."

The two boys have learned to relate to each other, rather than being in constant rivalry. They have learned to reach out, perhaps because they found a common ground and supported each other in their similar difficulties. Interpersonal learning has also taken place; they learn from each other's experiences and ways of coping.

In the next session, Steven is absent. Jack, who is usually less prominent in the dialog, has an opportunity to use the whole session. He starts by reporting that he wasn't in any fight that week and feels proud of myself. They read the story, "The Bully" (Tester, 1974; see Appendix B). Although Jack understands the aggressor's motives for bullying the victim, he also shows empathy for the victim and is critical of the aggressive behavior.

In the *eighth session*, the counselor brings a picture of a fight between two kids and asks the boys to make up a story about the cause of the fight. Steven tells about a fight with a friend, and shifts to relating a personal experience.

Steven:	I was at a friend's house, we were watching TV. I told him he reminded me of the person on the show and he kicked me out of his house. I wanted to continue watching, so I didn't want to leave, and I hit him.
Counselor:	How did you feel?
Steven:	Bad, because all I wanted to do was enjoy the show with him a bit more.
Counselor:	And how did he feel?
Steven:	He probably was also sad, because maybe I insulted him. That's why he hit me.
Counselor:	Could you have avoided it?
Steven:	Of course. I just have to keep my mouth shut.
Counselor:	That's not easy; sometimes, words just slip out of your mouth. Could you do anything else?
Jack:	He could talk to him, tell him that it was a lousy comment, apologize.
Steven:	Jack is right. I should tell him that I said it as a joke, that I didn't mean anything bad, instead of getting into a fight.

This is an important turning point in Steven's behavior. He is introduced to the method of direct communication, which is probably the most advanced behavior in a conflict situation. Interestingly, he accepts Jack's advice without resistance. In general, Jack seems to be very helpful in the progress Steven makes.

The next session focuses on behavior change, without the use of literature. The boys select some of their own experiences and discuss possible alternatives to aggression. It is clear that they are now critical about their own behavior. "I shouldn't scream at my father in front of my friends," Steven says, and Jack states, "I don't have to hit back before finding out what actually happened."

Counselor: How would you handle this today?
Steven: I would try to convince him [his father], explain that my friends are all waiting outside.
Jack: It wasn't that important, I could ignore the whole situation.

Both boys find constructive alternative behaviors to aggression. We cannot be sure that they will use them in a time of conflict, but they are now more insightful about their aggression and more familiar with other ways to resolve a conflict.

Termination takes place in the *tenth session*. They first draw their feelings following the treatment sessions. Steven draws two boys and a counselor sitting in a circle and laughing, and Jack draws a sun lightening up the room. The climate seems to have been positive for them. Next, they express positive perceptions of each other. Steven mentions how Jack excels in soccer and how he is willing to include him in games even though he is not so quick. Jack applauds Steven's generosity in giving away some of his marbles. They then summarize their gains following treatment. Both mention that they feel much more calm and relaxed. "I listen more in class. I want to go to university and have an honorable profession," says Steven. Jack says that he is in much fewer fights.

Next, they open the "feedback postcards" that they completed in the first session (which they imagined other children writing to them) and say how they expect others to see them now. Steven initially wrote that friends would say he is angry and aggressive. Now they will say he is a good friend, and doesn't cheat or fight. Jack originally wrote that some friends think he is crazy because he loses control. "Now they will probably say I'm a normal kid," he says.

Summarizing the sessions, they both say that they love each other and have become really close friends. "We are now like brothers," Steven says, and Jack adds, "I feel much better in class now because I am not alone anymore, I have Steven." They both feel that they have changed for the better, as does the counselor. In her farewell note, she writes to Jack, "You are a sweet child. You have learned to listen to your friends. You have a strong desire to change your behavior. Go for it, and thanks for participating." To Steven, she writes, "You have many strengths that you are not aware of. Once you decide to change, you will find them. I enjoyed your participation."

Evaluation

Was the boys' own evaluation realistic? Teacher reports point to progress: Jack reduced his score on aggression from 31 to 22 (out of 36) and Steven moved from a score of 31 to 20. The control children remained with the same scores (both boys moving from 29 to 30). The teacher's evaluations confirm to a certain degree the progress that the children have made. Their scores in aggression are still high, and whether a follow-up would point to sustained progress or a relapse is unclear. We weren't able to obtain follow-up scores, but clinical experience has shown me that it takes time for teachers to evaluate the progress that aggressive children make. In this case, it is important to note the progress the boys themselves felt they had made; they, too, understand that they have still a ways to go. I would certainly advise continued treatment of these two boys to prevent relapse.

The importance of the close relationships established between these two rival kids cannot be overstated. Close friendship is vital to the psychological well-being of children; it is the best buffer for loneliness and the most important source of support. Steven and Jack have learned to be attuned and empathic to each other, which in turn has enhanced their empathy for the suffering of victims and changed their attitudes towards aggression. They have even learned alternative behaviors from each other. Hence, the experience in pair treatment was positive and may be helpful when a group is not available, as suggested by Scheidlinger (2001).

Treatment of a Young Youth Leader, Paired with Brother and Friend

The following case study is of individual treatment that also included a few sessions with a significant other. It is interesting to see how interaction with brother and friend contributed to attitudinal change and progress.

Background

Dean, 17, is a leader in a youth group, responsible for a group of 10 adolescent boys. Part of the group activities, particularly during long school vacations, is to take the youngsters out on field trips. On his first trip as youth leader, on a very hot day, one of his charges died of dehydration because Dean didn't allow him to drink and refused to call a doctor. Moreover, when the other boys told him that someone was sick, he made fun of the boy, calling him a "spoiled jerk" and a "sissy." Dean convinced the group that, if they want to be real men and good soldiers in the future, they have to overcome such minor problems. He argued that dignity is more important than life—until his actions led to the fatal consequence. Dean was found directly responsible for the boy's death and sentenced to 12 months of community service in a home for physically challenged children. The kids in the home complained that he was very strict with them, controlling, and bossy, and tended to put them down and be verbally aggressive. At this point, Dean dropped out of school. He refused psychological treatment. A graduate student, who met him in the home for challenged children and witnessed his internal struggle, offered her help through the use of stories and poems. He initially refused but later agreed, saying he likes literature and will give it a try.

In the intake interview, Dean tells the counselor about his family. His father, who died 2 years beforehand, was a career officer in the army, and he wielded considerable influence over how Dean and his older brother, Ron, were raised. Their mother was a submissive wife and a housekeeper, who was somehow pushed into the background when it came to socializing the children, because "women have an adverse effect on boys," his father used to say. His father's main goal was to prepare his sons to be good soldiers and to follow in his footsteps. To achieve this, he would practice survival and combat skills with them from a very early age. He made many statements endorsing self-sufficiency, power, and aggression and cautioned them against putting faith in others. He also inflicted cruel punishments and psychological abuse, such as criticizing Dean's gentle appearance and his lack of assertiveness. As a result, Dean doesn't like himself, and doubts if he could ever meet his father's expectations.

His older brother, Ron, refused to follow his father's career path. Extremely disappointed, his father severed all ties with Ron, who left town and cut himself off from his family for many years. Dean remained his father's only hope, and he indeed took on the role of his father's follower. Dean admires his father and will do anything to satisfy him, even in death. He plans to have a military career, where he can put to use his father's legacy. The way he led the youth group was pretty much based on his father's modeling and his own experiences with him.

The counselor tells Dean that she can help him through literature and that he can help her to complete her university assignment. He seems proud to be of assistance and promises to do anything necessary "to help you get a good grade." They decide to meet once a week, after work hours.

Treatment Process

The first session is based on a poem written by a suicidal soldier. Although unfamiliar with the story behind the poem, Dean understands that the commander's aggressive behavior results from his being an overachiever, and that the soldier's aggressive reaction is meant as revenge. He can also see his own ambitious goals for the group of boys he led, but he doesn't see the connection between what happened and revenge. "I wanted them to be the best group," he says, "and I used the tools my father gave me. But I shouldn't blame him; I just didn't use the tools I got from him in the right way."

Dean seems extremely intelligent. He understands that he should seek parallels between his own behavior and that of the literary figure. But he is unable to see anything wrong with his behavior: he only wanted what's best for the boys, just as his father wanted what's best for the soldiers under him and for his children. Interestingly, Dean takes the blame for his poor results; his father remains on a pedestal.

The next session starts with a reflection on the previous one. Dean admits that he thought about his harsh response to his boys and came to the conclusion that he acted out of anger and frustration. The situation with the sick child frightened him; he felt, by giving in to a moment of weakness, that all the boys would feel helpless and he would not be able to make them into the best group. He also mentions that boys who cry make him nervous, because he never cries. "I haven't cried since the age of six, when my father spanked me for it, telling me that only girls cry," he confesses.

For the current session the counselor brings a poem named "Pity," in which pity is portrayed as a weakness. According to it, you must be strong and perfect, so that no one feels sorry for you.

Counselor: Do you know such perfect people in your life?
Dean: My father.
Counselor: What about you?
Dean: I can't tolerate failure of any kind. I have to be the best! ... My
             father never failed, but his theory of life, which I inherited from
             him, seems to fail for me.
Counselor: Do you mean your interpersonal aggression?
Dean: Exactly! It seemed to work for him, we saw it as assertiveness, but
             in my case it appears as aggression.

Dean seems to recognize the negative outcomes of his aggression, yet still cannot see any negative aspects of his father's behavior. He seems quite puzzled: on the one hand, he believes in conforming to the family norms, but on the other hand, he realizes that following his father's path has led him into trouble.

At this point, Dean brings up his brother, Ron, who refused to follow his father's lead and in fact rejected his father's theory of life.

Dean: My brother, Ron, is visiting my mother this week. He chose not to
        conform to our family, abandoned my father's path and left home. We
        haven't spoken to him since he left. I feel angry at him and proud of
        him. He was an achiever, although in an unexpected area, but I am
        angry that he made me lose him.

Dean is debating whether to "betray my father's will and see my brother." He ultimately decides to meet his brother in the presence of the counselor.

The session with Dean and Ron is based on the film, "The Problem with Evan," which deals with abusive family relationships. They watch the film together, agreeing to pause it whenever someone feels that he wants to say something. Ron immediately stops the tape, saying that he is going to say harsh things about his parents, although he knows that they meant well. He recalls an incident in which their father punished the two of them when they were 5 and 9 years old. Their father wouldn't listen to their reasons for their actions and punished them brutally. Ron remembers feeling humiliated and hating his father. Dean also recalls the horrifying punishment, but feels respect for his father and remembers that he accepted the punishment without argument or resistance.

Ron also talks about how his father bossed them around. He recalls how he insisted that Ron choose the same career as himself and wouldn't accept Ron's choice, which Ron made nevertheless. He expresses sadness that Dean hasn't realized his many interests and talents. "He used to write poems and draw beautiful pictures," Ron says to the counselor, "but he never pursued his talents because our father didn't consider them appropriate for the macho image he held for boys." In response, Dean tells them that he is now writing poems, and both show interest in his creative work. Later, Dean admits that his father was wrong in imposing his will and choices on his children, and says he can see how he feared, and still fears, his father. Ron suggests that Dean tried to please their father his whole life, to live up to his expectations, but in doing so, lost his own self. Dean can now see this, too: "I guess I can be sensitive and creative and a man at the same time, but it is still only in my head, I don't know how to do it in real life. In fact, I wanted to hug my brother rather than just shaking his hand." Ron admires this openness, saying, "I liked that."

Later, Ron stops the movie when it discusses how childhood pain turns into violence. "I think that Dean's aggression is a direct result of our father's behavior," he says. This helps Dean see the cause of his behavior and he thanks his brother for providing such a clear link. Dean says, "I didn't dare making this connection myself. Can you give examples?" Ron provides many examples, and together they recall many incidents involving put downs, insults, and harsh punishments to prove that those who hold power are superior. Now Dean feels disappointed not in himself, but in his father. "I can't believe that a father would do such things to his own children," he concludes. He also mentions sadness, pain, and freedom: "I shouldn't blame myself only. This is a freeing thought, actually. I feel that I don't care." Ron is happy with the progress, but Dean seems restless and admits: "It's not easy to grasp the change in perceiving your father as a crazy man rather than an angel." Having said this, he feels more relaxed. "It's so important to talk about feelings," he admits, "I used to hold in everything until I blew up at the first available victim." He feels exhausted and leaves the room for a few moments, but immediately comes back to thank his brother for his great help in his therapy. His brother confesses that he likes the change he just witnessed in his brother, has been happy to assist, and hopes to maintain a relation with him.

Pairing Dean with his brother has been an extremely meaningful step in his progress. Ron is able to open Dean's eyes so he could see a different father, one who shouldn't be worshipped and admired, but rather is an object of anger and disappointment. Moreover, so long as Dean accepted his father's behavior, he had full justification for being aggressive himself. It is not until he can see his father's true colors that he can let go of his aggression and take responsibility for his own behavior. The film has helped the two brothers to recall, express, and reflect on their past experiences. Stopping the film whenever they could identify with certain motifs has further eased self-expressiveness.

To the *fourth session*, Dean brings a poem he wrote, expressing his difficulties with interpersonal relationships. The poem is about the loneliness in his life. Dean explains that, until now, his father was the closest person to him; now that he has lost his father, he feels very lonely. Taking responsibility for his own behavior has made him lose confidence in his ability to establish any close relationship, because he has so little to give to others. Exploring his opportunity for a friendship, he comes up with Jim, another leader in the same youth organization who has wonderful relationships with his boys; they all love and admire him. Although he used to be in constant competition with Jim, Dean can now recognize his strength. He would like to be a leader of such caliber and would like to befriend and learn from Jim. The counselor asks Dean to invite Jim to the next session.

In the *fifth session*, Dean, Jim, and the counselor discuss a poem about a bear who befriended a man; trying to save him from the nuisance of a fly, the bear throws a stone at the man and kills him. Dean immediately relates to the piece in terms of his new perception of his situation. Now that he cannot hide behind his father's philosophy anymore, he must take responsibility for his actions. Thus, all the excuses of being the best or doing the right thing are gone, and he is left with a sense of self-blame. He refers to himself as a murderer, as he "killed the boy," and feels that everyone sees it this way and will never forgive him. Jim argues with him about perceiving the incident as murder and suggests that it was a horrible mistake, which any human being is entitled to make. To support his viewpoint, he shares with Dean and the counselor a tragic mistake that he himself made in the past. Jim gets extremely upset to the point where he bursts into tears. He tells them that this is the first time he has ever talked about this and therefore is so sensitive. Dean, very moved by Jim's self-disclosure and the expressiveness of his emotions, hugs him and cries with him. The significance of this event cannot be overstated; Dean has not cried since the age of six. Following this cathartic experience, the two seemed more relaxed and much closer to each other. Dean continues asking about the family of the young boy who died and how they perceive him. Jim reassures him that everyone considers it an accident and offers to join him in visiting the mourning family. He adds that everyone is talking about how different Dean is now, more relaxed, less angry, more attuned to others, and that they are all look forward to his return to the youth organization.

Jim has provided support to Dean on several levels. He has expressed his own favorable feelings toward Dean, he has provided information about others who see the change, and he has offered instrumental help. But most meaningful is his altruistic self-disclosure; admitting to his own failures, which has provided a clear message that accidents happen to many good people. By revealing his vulnerability, Jim has helped Dean get in touch with his own feelings. This has been a good opportunity for Jim to go through a cathartic experience, as well as a lifesaver for Dean, who admires Jim so much.

Dean and Jim become best friends. Together they go to visit the mourning family and learn that Dean has indeed been forgiven. His ability to feel, to express feelings, to be close to another person, and to stop blaming himself have freed the way to intimate friendship and love. At termination, Dean reflects on his accomplishments in therapy. He understands now that his overly high expectations and his competitive attitude led to disappointment, anger, lone-liness, and aggression. It is good to get close to meaningful people—his brother, a good friend, a lover. But most important is the connection to his real feelings and getting to know his real self, his interests, and his creativity. Overall, "it was good to talk to myself and not to my father," Dean concludes the gains from therapy. In a letter to his therapist at the end of his 12 months of service, Dean writes, "I was reborn in ten meetings in which I have learned what it means to feel, for myself and others. I am leaving the place more vulnerable and yet stronger than ever."

Summarizing the experience, the counselor points to several strengths of the therapy. First and foremost is the use of literature. Being an indirect technique, and because Dean happened to like reading and writing poetry, it allowed him to agree to the sessions in the first place. Without the literature, Dean wouldn't have accepted therapy at all. Second, involving other people in his therapy was highly important. The sessions with Ron and Jim were the most effective ones. Finally, it was very important to empower Dean, because of his low self-esteem and his self-blame. The positive feedback provided by the therapist, his brother, and his best friend was immanent in the change process.

Summary

This chapter has discussed the provision of therapy in pairs. Duo-therapy is offered when group therapy is not possible and yet we want to enrich the individual therapy process. Three illustrations were provided—two with young children and one with a young adult. In all the three cases, the partner was helpful in providing support, offering a different point of view, helping to reframe the case, and modeling alternative behavior. In the two illustrations with young children, the pairs worked together throughout the therapy process, whereas in the third case, the partners were guests who were invited to specific sessions. This is another variation of pair therapy that seems to work. In all the three cases, the intimacy established over the therapy process was transferred to relationships outside of treatment. Even a rival relationship ended up in a close friendship. This is an important side effect of pair therapy, as close friendship is the most important buffer against loneliness and one of the most important sources of social support.

So far, I have focused on the direct treatment of aggressive children. However, significant people and caregivers play an important role as well. How they approach these children's aggressive behavior can reinforce or alleviate it. Treating the important people in the children's lives is therefore the topic of the next chapter.

Chapter 8
Working with Caregivers

Introduction

Children's behavior in general depends a lot on the significant people in their surroundings, particularly family members (parents and siblings) and school personnel. Aggressive behavior in particular is associated with the socialization process at home and in school (Connor, 2002; Dodge, 2002; Pettit et al., 2001). Even the most efficient intervention with aggressive children may be only partly effective if the grownups in their lives are not involved as well. After all, children go back to their families and continue to be in contact with their teachers, which influences their behavior.

Despite the benefits that can be gained by working with parents and teachers, along with child and adolescent treatment, very few such interventions exist. In this chapter I illustrate some of the work done with parents and with teachers of aggressive children using a similar program, and provide outcomes of research on the contribution of mothers' treatment to children's outcomes on aggression.

Working with Mothers

Considerable research has revealed relationships between the ways parents manage and cope with children's antisocial behavior and the level of that behavior (Dodge, 2002; Lochman et al., 1999; Pettit et al., 2001). In a series of particularly relevant studies, Eisenberg and colleagues (Eisenberg & Fabes, 1994; Eisenberg, Fabes, & Murphy, 1996) investigated mothers' emotional reactions to their children's negative emotions. They found that maternal responses of distress, minimization, and punishment were associated with children's avoiding behavior and lower levels of social competence, whereas encouragement of the expression of emotions, problem-solving, and maternal comforting were correlated with children's constructive verbalization of anger and positive social functioning (Eisenberg & Fabes, 1994; Eisenberg et al.,

Z. Shechtman, *Treating Child and Adolescent Aggression Through Bibliotherapy*,
The Springer Series on Human Exceptionality, DOI 10.1007/978-0-387-09745-9_8,
© Springer Science+Business Media, LLC 2009

1996). That is, high levels of parental distress, a tendency not to take their children's situation seriously (minimization), harsh discipline, and frequent punishment all increase aggression. Moreover, children need to be encouraged to express negative affect, to be comforted when in pain, and to acquire conflict resolution skills in order to be able to refrain from aggressive responses. Similarly, Pettit and colleagues found high psychological control (use and often misuse of power, frequent punishment) to be associated with higher levels of anxiety, depression, and delinquency, while high levels of monitoring (paying attention to the child, being involved in his/her life, providing guidance) were associated with lower levels of delinquent behavior (Pettit et al., 2001). In other words, parents who are irritable and nonsupportive of prosocial behavior during conflict situations induce aggressive behavior in their children (Dishion & Patterson, 1997) through social learning and identification processes (Dodge, 2002). In addition, parents of children with high levels of aggression tend to engage in child-rearing practices that sustain and escalate child dysfunction (Patterson, Debaryshe, & Ramsey, 1989). Much of the research to date suggests that family-based interventions are the key to maximizing change in children's aggressive behavior (Horne et al., 2008; Lochman et al., 1999; Southam-Gerow & Kendall, 1997). In their description of the Bully Buster Program (Horne et al., 2007), now a widely accepted program in the United States, the researchers suggest a comprehensive program including the education of mothers and teachers. The authors of a recent book on the subject (Horne et al., 2008) dedicate it to the education of mothers of aggressive youth. But despite the favorable outcomes of this program, it is not frequently used, owing to its high cost.

Besides the cost, I have personally found in my practice that it is not easy to engage parents of aggressive children in psychological treatment. I was once invited to a parent event in one school to lecture on the topic of childhood aggression. This was a private school of 600 children in a highly affluent neighborhood. Only about 100 parents attended the event and none appeared to be the parents of aggressive children. In fact, they were parents of the victims, who came to complain about bullies and other aggressive students that were giving their own children a hard time.

Why didn't the parents of aggressive children attend? It is my belief that most of them are not aware of their own aggression and devastating modeling, and those who are aware often do not have the motivation to change their behavior. Many people who exhibit deviant behaviors are not aware of it. Prochaska (1999), who developed his theory of change based on extensive research, suggests that most people with a problem, no matter what kind (e.g., alcoholism, heavy smoking), are not aware of its magnitude at the initial stage of treatment. Most aggressive people and children that we work with are also unaware of their destructive behavior.

Parents' general lack of understanding of the problem was clear from their reaction to a short poem that I read to them at the lecture. The poem was about a very young boy who misbehaved, and, in his anger and frustration, used abusive language to his parents. As the audience was too large to lead a dialog, I asked them a general question: "How would you react to your child in such a case? How many of you would punish him or her?" About half of the audience raised their hands. Following this experience, I am not surprised that there are high rates of childhood aggression even in "good families," as there are high rates of harsh discipline.

My goals in working with parents of aggressive children and youth go beyond educating the parents about aggression. Just as we work with children, I want to help them reduce anger, frustration, and stress before I teach them the skills of parenting. Once they are more relaxed, parents are able to respond to their child better. Moreover, after experiencing catharsis themselves, they can better appreciate the emotional expression of their children and encourage them to express their anger and frustration in a constructive manner. Finally, in the group experience, they learn to appreciate the healing power of being listened to and receiving emotional support, which will assist them in becoming better listeners and supporters of their children.

In a study of mothers of children with (LD) and (ADD) (Shechtman & Gilat, 2005), many of whom had issues with aggression and violence, we applied a comprehensive intervention in which self-expressiveness and support were highly emphasized. We compared the 56 mothers who were given treatment to a similar group of mothers (with children attending the same school), who received an educational program based on lectures. The intervention focused mainly on the mothers and their unique emotional needs, though in relation to their interaction with their children.

Cathartic experiences were frequent in the treatment groups; the mothers talked about their despair and helplessness. School authorities were constantly complaining about their children's behavior and they felt inefficacious in handling the difficult situations at home, let alone in school. Many spoke of their loneliness in dealing with their difficult kids. They also expressed a great deal of anxiety about the future of their children. We analyzed the verbal behavior of these mothers using a scale that measures clients in therapy (Hill & O'Brien, 1999). Most of their verbal responses were of affective self-exploration, and usually included cathartic experiences, adding validity to our intervention.

The results of the study indicated reduced parental stress, improved coping skills, and improved child behavior in school, even though little direct guidance and education was provided. These improved attitudes were also expressed with regard to another sibling in the family who didn't have a LD. Finally, the fathers (who didn't participate in the intervention) showed improved scores on all the same measures as the mothers, both with regard to the child with the disability and the nondisabled sibling. All these results were compared to the educational program, which did not produce any change in parental behavior. In fact, on some measures of distress, the scores in the control group increased.

We concluded the study with our belief that parents need a more comprehensive and personal treatment to make a change in their parental style of coping with difficult children. Indeed, Miller and Prinz (1990) suggested a broader based treatment model to address parental concerns that could impinge on a child's behavior. Adding a group treatment component to parental training has proved effective in several studies (Pfiffer, Jouriles, Brown, Etscheidt, & Kelly, 1990; Webster-Stratton, 1994). My colleagues and I have had several opportunities to treat mothers of aggressive children with bibliotherapy, similar to our intervention with the children, although adjusted to the parents' age and needs. Following are a few examples.

Bibliotherapy with Mothers

A group of mothers participated in a bibliotherapy group in 14 sessions. In one session, we discussed the story, "The Present" (Sade, 1990; see Appendix A), mentioned often in this book. You will recall that the story describes a frustrated father who spanks his 4-year-old son for not being able to tell time. When we work with children, the focus of the discussion is on the child's emotions in the story, but with adults, we focus on the character of the father.

One of the youngest mothers, Shelby, admits to the group that she has a bad temper. She explains that she is very harsh with her 5-year-old daughter, and often spanks her for failing to do small chores correctly. For example, she expects her to clear her plate off the table, and if her child spills something along the way, Shelby gets very angry and spanks her. Following the discussion of the story and reflecting on the participants' own thoughts and feelings, Shelby expresses her wish to behave differently. She already realizes that it is wrong to hit her child but is unsure that she can change her behavior. She describes her aggressive reaction as automatic: "This is how my father used to treat me and this is how I treat my daughter."

Several weeks later she shares her progress with the group:

> Every time I come back from the group I share with my daughter and husband what I have learned that night. After the session in which the story of an abusive father was discussed, I also told them that I had shared with the group my behavior at home and realized that I am ashamed of my reaction, and that I never want to spank my little girl again. A few days later, my daughter accidentally spilled a glass of milk. I was raising my hand to hit her when she said to me, "Haven't you learned that it is not right to hit me?" My hand remained in the air and I have never spanked her since.

Shelby is an extremely kind and sensitive person; she is a successful kindergarten teacher. But at home she was using the automatic responses she had learned in her family of origin. It wasn't very difficult for her to change her attitudes in regard to child rearing, but it was a challenge to change her automatic response. Sharing perceptions and feelings honestly in direct communication with her daughter turned out to be an effective way to change.

Not only did Shelby change, but she also decided to pass on her positive gains to others. She was aware that two of the children in her kindergarten were being abused at home and decided to educate their parents in the same way. She set up a parent event and read "The Present" to the attendees. Before she could get to the discussion, one of the abusive fathers angrily left the room. She was rather worried when she saw him waiting for her after the meeting. It turned out, though, that this was a turning point in their relationship. The father shared with her his miserable life with a mentally ill wife. He had to take care of the children before he went to work, and so he often loses control and is impatient with them. He told her that the story about the abusive father was very moving, he feels guilty and ashamed, and that's why he left the room. After that meeting, their communication became much more intensive, Shelby became an important source of support for this father, and the abuse at home stopped.

This case illustration presents the personal and professional progress made by a mother who was counseled in a group using bibliotherapy as an adjunct to the therapy process. She not only changed as a mother, but she was also able to change another parent and in turn help another child.

Another interesting incident happened in the same group, following the discussion of the above story. A general debate evolved regarding physical punishment. Several of the mothers support mild physical punishment, feeling it is impossible to raise children, particularly young ones, without it, as talking to them is ineffective. After listening to the debate for quite a while, I expressed my clear resistance to any form of physical punishment as a method of child rearing, although I can understand that mothers are sometimes unable to control themselves. Some group participants agree that it is a matter of self-control, while others express cultural attitudes endorsing harsh discipline. Mary is particularly insistent that physical punishment is sometimes a necessity. To make her case, she challenges me by sharing the following story.

Mary has adopted a 6-year-old child with severe learning problems, who is far behind in his academic achievements. To help him progress, she reads with him quite often. "Strangely," she says, "sometimes he reads with no mistakes at all, and at other times, he reads the same paragraph with lots of mistakes." She interprets this as resistance, as something he does to hurt her; therefore, she thinks that mild physical punishment is appropriate. She expects everyone in the group to support her, but, following the discussion of "The Present," they express their firm belief that it is unfair to use power against a helpless child, and convince her that physical punishment is inappropriate.

A Mother Providing Treatment to Her Child

The next case illustration shows how a trained mother can help her own aggressive child. Olga is the mother of 12-year-old Gary who recently began junior high school. Gary suffers from a severe LD and ADD. He is frustrated because of school failure and social rejection. In an attempt to find a social niche, he recently joined a group of youngsters on the verge of delinquency, and together they act out and behave violently. Olga, a teacher, raises Gary and his younger (nonaggressive) sister, Joan, alone, as their father has left them. Gary is angry at his mother for the separation from his father, but he also blames himself for the desertion, thinking that his poor functioning caused his father to leave them.

Following a training course in bibliotherapy, Olga decides to use our program to treat her son, together with his younger sister. As part of her training responsibilities, she is expected to record all sessions. The following illustration of the therapeutic process, held at home, is based on these records.

From the very *first session*, it is clear that Gary suffers from an extremely low self-image. They are playing the "Personal Award" game, in which each child gives himself/herself an award for some personal achievements. While Joan can find plenty of reasons to get an award, Gary has none. His sister offers to help and provides positive feedback, which Gary accepts with great appreciation.

When they discuss a poem about an exceptional child, Gary identifies himself with the character's loneliness and sense of rejection. He never talks about such feelings, he prefers to keep them to himself, he says. But when his mother (acting as therapist) suggests that keeping all feeling inside is not very healthy, Gary admits that this is often the case for him. "Yesterday I had a stomach ache because I don't have friends, I feel lonely," he says. He doesn't know how to share things and with whom, he says, and he asks Joan to invite him to share with her. She accepts the challenge with pleasure. Again, his sister appears as an important potential source of support.

At a later session, they discussed anger and how to cope with it. Gary recalls many situations where he felt angry mainly as a result of his loneliness. "I feel like this all the time. I hate my class, and I can't control my anger.... I feel like I've swallowed a ball of fire and can't chill out, my head explodes with anger." He agrees that sharing feelings with others is a good option. During the clarifying process, in response to the question "To what extent do you share feelings and experiences?" Gary places himself on a 2 on the continuum, but wants to move to 5—that is, to be able to share his difficulties, "because otherwise I become too angry." Gary is now aware of his stress and wishes to make a change, at least in this regard.

When they discussed the poem "My Monster," in another session, Gary draws a monster and attaches to it the following words: sadness, anger, frustration, hell, and dead, while Joan lists screaming, shouting, and cursing. One would expect the opposite to appear, but actually Joan's list confirms her ability to express her pain, while Gary's suggests how he internalizes it. He wishes he could control his monster better, but doesn't seem to be able to do so.

After reading and discussing the story, "The Bully" (Tester, 1974; see Appendix B), Gary identifies with the victim's frequent suffering. Although he is considered aggressive by his teachers and mother, he perceives himself as a victim. The victim-aggressive combination is well known, typical of children who feel helpless in the face of their difficulties and react in frustration and fear.

When they later discussed self-control through the poem, "I Am My Own Commander" (Bokek, 1980), Gary identifies with the character's impulsive behavior and lack of control, while Joan recognizes his strength and self-confidence, as expressed in his ability to control himself. Gary cannot accept this, he turns to his sister and gently disagrees with her. "I have something to say to you," he says. "Don't you see how aggressive he is, cursing and hitting without control?" "But once he decided to change, he's able to do it," Joan responds. Gary is impressed and says, "I can see that now," and expresses his hope for himself that he will not respond impulsively: "I will try to check things out with the person who insulted me, before I respond." He also accepts his sister's point of view that the literary character is indeed self-confident when he decides to take control.

There seems to be a shift in Gary's social information processing (Dodge & Schwartz, 1997). Gary now seems to perceive self-control as a favorable behavior and to be willing to control his own impulsive behavior. He seems to be moving from the stage of awareness with no wish to change his behavior to the stage of motivation to make an actual change (Prochaska, 1999).

When Joan provides Gary with a feedback, "You often react to me impulsively," he admits, "That's true." Surprisingly, his nonaggressive sister also admits that she sometimes reacts angrily, screams, and even cries. Her reaction is extremely important, as it adds to the normalization of Gary's behavior. He is now not the only "bad guy"; other people who are not considered problem kids, such as his sister, are also sometimes impulsive. During the clarifying process, referring to the level of impulsivity, Joan places herself on a 5 but wants to be on 10: "I never want to be ashamed and regret my behavior," she explains. Although she is not aggressive at all, she wants to improve in this respect. This again normalizes the situation for Gary. He is not the "designated client"; everyone can improve. Gary places himself on a 5, too, and also wants to be on 10.

Whether it is his own wish or he is imitating his sister, it is clear that he really wants to change. He even suggests a few alternative behaviors that may help him, including "saying that I am angry rather than acting out, and leaving the scene until I relax, I don't know what else I can do." Joan suggests taking the anger out on an object or doing something he likes. To this, he responds: "I would like to be my own commander, but it is very difficult. I'm not sure I know how." They continue discussing alternatives and he selects two: getting out the anger by sharing his feelings and doing things he likes to do, like watching TV and playing on the computer. He seems not only to be learning from his sister, but also to be capable of presenting extremely relevant goals, such as expressing feelings, an ability that so many aggressive children are lacking (Pollack, 1998).

Olga summarizes her experience:

> I took upon myself the treatment of my son because the school personnel couldn't provide help and I was quite desperate. My goal was to enhance Gary's insight into his impulsive and aggressive behavior. I was hoping that getting in touch with his feelings will help him become more relaxed and able to control his behavior. I saw much progress in his ability to express himself. He started with an attitude that "anger

must be hidden," but reached a point where he could express his sadness, anger, and frustrations. He also understood the consequences of his negative behavior and was even able to find alternatives. I see him struggling, he does not always succeed in controlling himself, but he is trying and he knows what he wants to achieve. I am glad I used bibliotherapy; it helped Gary to discuss his problem, it helped me to navigate the therapeutic process, it helped me understand myself better, and it helped us become a closer family in which feelings are welcomed.

According to his mother-therapist, Gary now feels more relaxed in school, he is doing better at academic work, and his self-image has improved. This is an exciting example of how training mothers not only helped the parents themselves to reduce anxiousness, but also provided them with a tool to help their children further. Involving a sibling is an additional way to support an aggressive child in his or her change process. Gary's sister had a profound impact on his change of behavior throughout the process, by supporting, modeling, and guiding Gary. Needless to say, Gary's successful sister stopped being a competition and a threat and became his close friend. In general, the family climate improved a great deal.

Research Supporting the Treatment of Mothers of Aggressive Children

An empirical investigation examined how treatment of mothers contributed to the reduction of their children's aggression. Three conditions in the group therapy of aggressive children were compared: child-only treatment, mother and child treatment, and a nontreatment control. The study population was Druze living in two nearby villages in Israel. The Druze are Israeli citizens who belong to a unique ethnic group. They are Arabs who closely guard their own religion, traditions, and cultural customs. They live mainly in segregated cities or villages and have their own school system, through which they transfer their traditions to the next generation. They are characterized as a collectivist and patriarchal society. They consider the family the most important institution; the men work to support the family and make the major decisions, while the women stay home and care for the household and children. The parental practices of Druze are seen as somewhat inconsistent: authoritarian and harsh, but also warm and caring (Ali, 1997).

The 75 participating children, from fifth and sixth grades, were assigned equally and randomly to the three conditions, 25 children in each. The mothers of these children also participated in the study, with 25 of them treated in groups and the rest only filling out questionnaires.

Both mothers and children were treated in small groups, using the program described in this book. The mothers in the treatment groups attended ten 90-minute sessions, with the aim of increasing their understanding of their children's aggressive behavior. Like the process in the children's groups, each session with the mothers started with a literary text. Although the selected literature was more appropriate for adults, the structure and dynamics of the discussion were similar. The mothers, too, discussed emotions that lead to aggressive reactions, the struggle for power, consequences of aggression, and methods of self-control. There was a great deal of cathartic experiencing and supportive exchange of feedback. Unique to the mothers was the application of the content discussed in their groups of their children's behavior, as well as exploration of their relationships with their children.

Results revealed that children in the two treatment conditions showed a significantly greater decrease in aggression scores than those in the control condition, for all the three report sources (self, mothers, and teachers). Children whose mothers also received treatment reported a greater reduction in aggression than those in the child-only treatment condition, although such a difference was not observed based on teacher scores. Compared to nontreated mothers, those mothers that participated in the therapy groups reported less distress, less of a punitive response style, more encouragement of their child's emotional expression, and less minimization of their child's stress. These results were sustained after 3 months. Finally, an association was found between the mother's reduced distress, increased encouragement of emotional expression, and decreased minimization, on the one hand, and the child's reduced level of aggression, on the other.

The following illustrates the change process for one of the mothers. Dara is a mother of six, two of whom have been diagnosed with ADD. The two boys give her a hard time at home; they fought a lot with their siblings, had discipline problems both at home and in school, and recently started shoplifting. "They are wild," according to their mother. When she feels helpless she spanks them, a common action in her culture. When the children misbehave, Dara's husband blames her for doing a poor parenting job. He is out working all day and expects her to do the child rearing on her own. When she feels stressed and helpless, she reacts in anger at her children and husband. Recently, in great despair, she left home for 2 days, an unusual act among the Druze. Anxious following her move, her husband took over the disciplinary role for a few days, but then became extremely violent, and the whole house was in an uproar.

Dara, in tears, tells all this to the group after they read the story, "The Present," mentioned earlier. Following the discussion of the father's behavior in the story, she understands her own loss of control and that of her husband. She decides to involve him in the process gently, by sharing her experiences rather than requiring his intervention. But most importantly, she admits that by listening to the story, she has realized how universal parental aggression is. The acceptance that the group expressed to the literary character made her trust that they would accept her as well. In tears, she sums up, "It is so good to have a place to share all this. I'm less angry lately, and I manage to respond to their acting out with simple conversations rather than with physical punishment."

In sum, the child-and-mother treatment combination improved the mothers' coping strategies and reduced their children's scores on aggression. The three maternal coping responses that were associated with the child's improvement are actually highlighted in our intervention. The program is aimed at reducing maternal distress through the encouragement of self-expressiveness and cathartic experiences. It also stresses the development of empathy, which could be reflected in reduced minimization of the child's pain or stress.

As the study is based on correlations, which cannot indicate the cause-effect direction of relationships, results can be interpreted in at least two ways—namely, that the mothers' improved coping positively affected their children's behavior, or that the children's reduced aggression affected the mothers' coping style. Future research is needed to sort out the complexities. It is possible to conclude, however, that the intervention offered in this book works for mothers as well as children, and that treating mothers of aggressive children adds uniquely to the reduction of the child's aggression.

Working with Teachers of Aggressive Children

Many teachers do not understand the dynamics of aggression. In fact, one of the greatest challenges for teachers is coping with behavioral problems (Almog & Shechtman, 2007). The literature distinguishes between restrictive and supportive teacher strategies (Cunningham & Sugawara, 1988), and concludes that, while most teachers prefer supportive strategies, they tend to have restrictive reactions to child behavioral problems (Almog & Shechtman, 2007; Jack et al., 1996). These responses become even more extreme when faced with childhood aggression and violence. Aggressive behavior frightens teachers and puts them in a position of helplessness, unless they have the skills to cope with it. Although aggressive children and particularly youth appear strong in their acting-out behavior, they are actually extremely vulnerable, as we have seen in many illustrations throughout this book. Thus, first and foremost, teachers need to understand what leads children and adolescents to act aggressively. Following are some examples illustrating the importance of the teacher's understanding of aggressive behavior.

Wanda is an extremely strict teacher who perceives her role as being responsible for discipline and nothing else. She truly believes that if she can keep her homeroom class quiet, there will be no problem kids. But she is dealing with one of the most difficult classes in the school, and the more she tries to be authoritarian, the more trouble there is. One afternoon, one of her students commits suicide, hanging himself near the classroom. Following this devastating incident, the school counselor gets involved to help the children in the class to cope. She uses a classroom climate intervention program to help children identify the dynamics in the classroom, and she insists that the homeroom teacher be part of the intervention.

Led by the counselor, the children begin to talk openly about their emotional difficulties. They share difficult mornings in which they leave home without a meal, cope with family problems, and try to deal with their schoolwork.

Listening to their stories, Wanda feels much closer to her students and realizes that she needs and wants to play a different role in their lives. She becomes more supportive, the climate in the class improves, and the frequency of aggressive behavior decreases.

Another illustration concerns Donna, a special education teacher whose students give her such a hard time that the principal decides to suspend all the five girls. Terry, the girls' homeroom teacher, makes an attempt to understand the situation. Listening carefully to the five, she realizes that their aggression is in response to Donna's treatment of them with disrespect. Terry suggests an open dialog between Donna and the girls. In an attempt to avoid mutual blame and further escalation of the situation, Terry prepares the girls to communicate constructively, using "I" messages. When they are ready, the meeting takes place. Susan is the first to speak: "When you call me stupid, I get very angry and respond with violence. But what worries me more is that, when I leave school and think about it, I can see that I am stupid." Donna is in shock. She apologizes, saying, "I had no idea that this is what I'm doing," and the conflict is resolved.

Another incident took place in a junior high school in which I worked with the personnel: One class has long been giving Judy, the foreign language teacher, a hard time. For several days in a row before she enters class, all the plants are overturned and the class is full of mud. First, Judy tries to deal with the situation on her own by threatening them with poor grades. Next the vice principal is involved. Finally the principal announces to the class that their yearly trip is canceled.

I was informed of this incident when I came for one of my sessions with the faculty. I first asked about the reactions of each person involved. Judy said that she was so angry that all she could do was scream and threaten, and so did the others. I was surprised that no one asked the class *why they did it*. I argued that there must be an underlying message and suggested that they communicate with the class openly. Natalie, the homeroom teacher, agreed to do this. She is surprised to hear from the students that Judy verbally abused them, so they were very angry at her. "Why didn't you use legitimate channels of communication?", probed Natalie. It turned out that they did complain to the principal, but her response was that teachers cannot be fired in the middle of the year. Feeling helpless, as no one would listen to them, the students found a "creative solution" to their problem. The direct communication continued with Judy, leading to a resolution of the conflict.

Another misunderstanding happened in another school where I was working with the faculty on changing their attitudes toward children's misbehavior. Specifically, they wanted my help in creating a school constitution, and they were particularly interested in the types of punishments. There was a huge gap between my perceptions of education and theirs. They felt that I was naïve, thinking that school discipline can be maintained without punishment, while I felt that they were expressing and modeling aggression.

One day there was an incident in which a group of kids, frustrated at being excluded from a special class, threw stones at a closed door. The next day, Robin, the principal, investigated who was involved and threatened to call in their parents and exclude them from the yearly school trip. One of the girls involved in the incident called her father, who immediately came to school, shouting at and threatening the principal. Robin had to hide from him and even threatened to call the police before he finally left. Rather than calling the police, she decided to wait for a consultation with me at our next meeting.

When I came, I met a group of agitated people who were willing to use any punishment that was possible, but they were unable to convince me that such a course is appropriate. My calm reaction really egged them on. I suggested calling in the father for a therapeutic conversation. As Robin was not sure how to do it, I suggested the following opening sentence: "You must have been very angry last time. I am here to listen to you," and insisted that she let him talk as much as he needs to without interrupting. "What about all the children who saw the show he put on?," someone asked, "and what about the punishment we already promised?" asked another. I suggested that, following a constructive conversation with Robin, he be asked to talk to the class and explain his behavior. At this point they were absolutely sure that I was being strange, but they agreed to give it a try.

The next day, I found the following message on my answering machine:

> You wouldn't believe what happened! The father came in with his wife, I opened the conversation with the sentence you offered and he talked for about an hour. He expressed a lot of frustration related to his three children in school, and concluded the conversation with the following sentence: "I am so glad you invited me back. I was so embarrassed following my outburst, I feel I'm speaking to you like we are close friends."

Robin responded in a similar fashion. Then she goes on to express her concern about the kids who witnessed the incident. Before she can complete the sentence, he offered to enter the class and talk to the children. She was still worried and asked him if he would like to prepare himself, but he had no doubts that he could do it immediately. His message to the children is as follows:

> I had an embarrassing incident here the other day. I feel ashamed that as a grownup I acted so violently. Anger shouldn't be expressed in such an aggressive way. I hope for me and for you that this doesn't happen to you because it is very unpleasant.

This is the end of the message on my machine and of the incident. The teachers now understand that there are many other ways to resolve a conflict than through punishment.

Teachers who endorse punishment provide a poor example of behavior, but many schools know no other way to handle aggression. The two schools mentioned above at least exhibited an interest in learning alternatives that were more therapeutically oriented responses to children.

All aggressive people, children and adults alike, need support rather than a harsh reaction that only escalates the problem. One of the greatest challenges for aggressive children who try to change is the danger of relapse. They are so used to their pattern of behavior that changing it requires a lot of encouragement. They need the teacher to acknowledge their efforts and be patient with their ups and downs.

This is clear from the case of Daniel, an elementary school boy who had been treated for several sessions. While the class is on a field trip and they were waiting for the bus, one of his classmates pushed him and he bumped into his teacher. He was quite embarrassed, as it wasn't his fault, but he certainly did not expect the following reaction: "What a waste of time it is to treat you; you will never change." Having lost confidence in his ability to change, Daniel droped out of the program.

Educating Teachers

One way to deal with misunderstandings is to educate teachers about childhood aggression. I don't mean just to teach them theories of aggression; teachers, too, have to change their attitudes and behavior, and such change usually doesn't happen through cognitive learning alone. Thus, we offer programs using bibliotherapy as an adjunct to our intervention with teachers, as we do with children and adolescents and their parents. Teachers must learn about their own aggression before they can understand another's aggression empathically. Only afterward do we also provide them with some tools to help their students.

The following is a reflection provided by one of the teachers at termination of one such program:

> The program gave me an opportunity to look at myself; I saw my own aggression that was always a reaction of frustration. Even small frustrations made me lose my temper, mostly at home with my family. I guess I felt confident enough to express my anger to them, but I also see the damage I did. I was like a caged lion because I couldn't express my needs and wishes openly. I now feel much freer, I can see my needs in a clearer way, and I like myself more. . . . My son is considered an aggressive child. Teachers complained about him constantly and I sided with them. As a teacher I felt frustrated that I cannot control him, and the more frustrated and helpless I was, the angrier I got and the more I punished him. I now understand my son much better; I listen to him and hear that he is helpless, too. He recently told me that he is aggressive only because he doesn't want other kids to perceive him as weak, but he doesn't like his behavior, and in tears asked me to provide him with some tools that will reduce his aggression. I have never felt so close to my son as in those moments.
>
> With my students, too, I listen to their pain and lack of control and, rather than being judgmental, I am now attuned to their needs and ready to help them. I now feel that I also acquired the tools needed to be effective in helping them change.

What permits such a profound change? A dynamic group process helps participants reconnect to their own emotions—the confusion, disappointment, despair, and helplessness in difficult situations—and to face their own aggression. For example, in one of the first sessions, we used an activity to identify the causes of our anger and explored our response to each. Very quickly we came to the conclusion that it is frustration, disappointment, anxiety, and helplessness that lead to an aggressive reaction. As adults, we don't always explode, but we certainly use direct and indirect verbal aggression, active or passive. From this point, it is easy to progress to seeing the reactions of our students as a response to similar feelings. However, without going through this self-exploration stage, it is difficult for a profound change to occur.

Stories and poems help teachers to increase their participation in the group. I once entered a *fourth session* assuming that a group of mature teachers would be able to progress without a helping device, but the request came from them: "Can we use a poem?" One group member explained that it is easier to connect with a literary character than to initiate self-disclosure; somehow it helps overcome some barriers, she said. Another used her own experience with children to argue that the story or poem helps the kids to connect to emotions and helps her to guide them through the process.

Teachers Applying the Intervention to Students

The following examples were drawn from the teachers who applied our program with their aggressive students. They point to the profound changes that took place in the teachers' professional as well as personal lives.

One of the teachers, who works with high-risk adolescents, wrote the following reflection about a treatment group she was leading:

> I was astonished at the level of aggression I initially experienced in this group. I felt unconfident, disappointed, confused. I wanted to leave the room and never come back. But I didn't, and rather forced myself to listen to their stories and experiences. The children's narratives were so painful that my response to them has gradually changed to love and caring. A sense of trust and hope replaced my initial sense of despair. The group members noticed the change and connected with it. Even the toughest "men" in the group started to disclose their vulnerability. A few months later they initiated a petition to the principal and asked her to give them another opportunity to attend a group "in which we can have tea and share our difficulties."

In one of our studies (Shechtman & Effrati, 2008), the same teachers conducted an intervention with aggressive children with and without bibliotherapy as an adjunct to therapy, using each method every other session. At the end of treatment, they were asked which method they liked more. Most of them said they preferred bibliotherapy, because the children liked it more, and because it was easier to navigate the process as the literary text provided some structure. Teachers are less prepared to do process therapy than counselors or psychologists; for them, the story or poem decreases the anxiety caused by a lack of structure.

A group of 20 teachers who were trained in the program was interviewed following their experiences with a group of treatment children. Many of their responses support the use of literature. One male teacher said:

> The stories gave some structure to the intervention, which was helpful because I had no idea how to talk to these kids. The truth is that, until now, aggression really frightened me; a violent child aroused a lot of anger in me, so I tried to avoid violent children. The intervention made me more involved in their lives. I understand their unique needs now; it seems that empathy is what they need most.

Another male teacher wrote:

> I am more cognitive oriented. I never thought that stories would be part of my teaching repertoire, but I have learned from the children's reactions to them that they can be very helpful.

However, the use of literature is only a part of the program's effectiveness. It is the therapeutic process that follows the reading of the literature that has a profound impact. Self-expressiveness, exploration of feelings, catharsis, and growth in insight all contribute to the change process. Here is what a teacher in a special education program said

> My boys were so restless that even the stories couldn't calm them down. I needed more films to help them be attentive. But all these were only stimuli to the therapeutic conversation and cause of change. It was their ability to express anger and my ability to contain that anger that made the difference. My modeling of behavior, including my self-disclosure and expressed acceptance, made the difference.

When teaching highly aggressive children, listening to the expression of violence and their stories of aggression and cruelty, especially in a bragging tone of voice, is disturbing to many. As one teacher stated:

> The restlessness and bullying, even in the group, frightened me. I first tried to direct the conversation, but learned to give in and be directed by them. I often asked myself if I can do this, if I am up to such a task. The relationships we established with each other increased my confidence that I am doing the right thing. I never had such close relationships with my students. This was the most enjoyable part of my intervention.

Many feel that it is the sharing that helps move the process ahead, but the issue is how to get the children to talk openly and honestly about their aggression. One teacher came to the understanding that the program should be presented as one that deals with self-expressiveness rather than aggression. "They act out their anger. Giving them the opportunity to express their anger and communicate their needs will automatically prevent their anger," he stated. This is a great truth about aggressive children and youth that is rarely recognized by teachers, who generally see their main role as providing knowledge rather than treatment. Teachers are usually not trained to deal with highly aggressive children or to help students talk about their emotions. In this respect, Rogers (1980) was right when he argued that schools invite students to bring their head to school and allow the body to come along as a must, but require that feelings stay at home. This is still true for teacher education programs nowadays.

Often teachers do want to invite feelings to school, but don't know how. As already mentioned, expressing feelings is not an easy task for "macho" boys. Teachers need tools to provoke a discussion of feelings. One such tool is the use of literature, as is evident in the following group process.

The teacher asks the children in the treatment group to share an event that made them feel regret later on. As there is no response to her direct question, she uses the poem "Forgiveness" (Nir, 2000). Sandy, new to the school, shares that she felt a lot of regret when she was held overnight in jail. She tells them how she was caught shoplifting, as a result of which she was kicked out of school and put on probation. The group reacts angrily to the school's act of involving the police. But Sandy actually appreciated it: "Involving the police helped me; otherwise, I would be in jail now." Her honest self-exposure opens the way for other children to share their stories of violence and even legitimize their expression of regret. In the next session Tommy admits that he was forced to apologize in front of the class and didn't like it, but when he apologized in private, he felt good about it, and so did other group members. This teacher is able to develop a highly important topic for aggressive children—forgiveness— in a very effective way, because she uses the right poem and has been trained to develop a therapeutic discussion—training which most teachers lack.

The program gives teachers tools for effective intervention, which enhance their sense of professional self-efficacy. Most participating teachers mentioned that they increased their knowledge, understanding, and skillfulness. Moreover, it is the progress made by difficult kids that encourages teachers to go on despite the hardships. "When Alex said that he used to bully John for fun, but realized that he might be insulting him, that was such huge progress that I felt I wanted everyone in the school to be touched by this program," one teacher testified.

Summary

Children are certainly not the only target of treatment. Parents and teachers must receive help with their own aggression and with their understanding of aggressive children. They are irritated by children's aggression because it threatens them, causing them to feel inadequate. Understanding the helplessness of aggressive kids helps grownups in their lives to befriend rather than fight them and to assist rather than reject them. It is the intimate relationship between the adult and the aggressive child that makes the difference, and the slow but discernible change that encourages parents and teachers to continue supporting children in the change process. Once parents and teachers feel efficacious, they continue their efforts.

Beyond an understanding of aggression and of therapeutic relationships and processes, the therapeutic tools acquired by parents and teachers enable them to offer help to the children. The right story, film, poem, or therapeutic game is handy when direct questions are not efficient enough.

In short, the best treatment combination is not only to help the aggressive children, but also to help the significant people in their lives to help them. Indeed, parents and teachers are caregivers who must be trained in helping aggressive children. However, as we have seen in the earlier examples, siblings and peers are also important in the change process of aggressive children and youth. While access to siblings is quite rare, reaching out to classmates is easier, for example, through classroom preventive programs. Such an intervention is discussed in the next chapter.

Chapter 9
Using Bibliotherapy as a Preventive Intervention in the Classroom

Introduction

This chapter differs from earlier ones in that it focuses on a preventive intervention. As my goal in this book is to help highly aggressive children, the focus of intervention, so far, has been on changing the behavior of those children and adolescents identified as highly aggressive. However, neither can we ignore the social context in which these kids interact, nor should we ignore the positive impact of preventive interventions on the reduction of aggression and violence of children in general.

The growing awareness about child and adolescent social and emotional well-being has shifted the focus of counseling from treatment to prevention (Bauer, 2000; Seligman & Csikszentmihalyi, 2000; Tolan & Dodge, 2005). At a broad conceptual level, two major dimensions characterize primary prevention: individual and ecological (Durlak & Wells, 1997). The individual dimension pertains to the child's unique characteristics, such as temperament, aggression, empathy; the ecological dimension pertains to the child's social environment, such as the family, school, neighborhood, and community. Hence, while the intervention for highly aggressive children focuses more on the individual dimension, the preventive intervention focuses on the ecological dimension (Espelage & Swearer, 2004).

Research suggests that the classroom climate is highly associated with the level of classroom aggression; this relationship is higher than that between aggression and individual social skills (Shechtman, 2006b). These findings are supported by studies attesting to the high impact of classroom and school social dynamics on the level of children's aggression. Salmivalli and colleagues (1994), for example, pointed to the roles that children adopt in the classroom as indicators of the level of aggression. They identified a large portion of the students as indifferent—the "silent audience"—and another of the large portion who supported the aggressors directly and indirectly. Other researchers referred to the classroom climate in terms of social intimacy. Social withdrawal and excessive feelings of isolation are common early signs of potentially violent behavior (Dwyer, Osher, & Wagner, 1998), and social affiliation is related to

Z. Shechtman, *Treating Child and Adolescent Aggression Through Bibliotherapy*,
The Springer Series on Human Exceptionality, DOI 10.1007/978-0-387-09745-9_9,
© Springer Science+Business Media, LLC 2009

decreased violence (Baker, 1998). Preventive interventions in the school, especially those that increase intimacy among children, tend to decrease violence (Dykeman, Daehlin, Doyle, & Flamer, 1996; Horne et al., 2007; Howard, Flora, & Griffin, 1999; Olweus, 2001). School programs, and particularly classroom programs where teachers are involved, have been found to be highly effective (Kolbert & Barker, 2006).

A wealth of classroom and school programs have been mentioned in the literature on coping with aggression (see the review by Horne et al., 2007). In this chapter I present a classroom intervention program that is different in principle, uses literature as an adjunct to the intervention, and is supported by research.

The Preventive Program: Classroom Climate Intervention

Meeting Basic Needs

The program I am referring to is based on group counseling principles that address basic needs of people in a group. Luft (1984) identified five such needs:

1. A sense of belonging: the need to know you are part of the group and share both power and responsibility.
2. Acknowledgement by others: the sense of being liked and recognized for your strengths and uniqueness.
3. Freedom of self-expression: the need to express an opinion, provide feedback, and be free of destructive criticism.
4. Opportunities for self-disclosure: the need to express emotions, to be honest, and to be authentic.
5. Open communication: the need to resolve inevitable group conflicts in empathic and rational processes, free of labeling and stereotyping.

The extent to which these basic needs are met establishes the climate of the group and its level of aggression. To achieve these goals, we involve the group in open discussions about the intrapersonal and interpersonal aspects of their relationships in the classroom. Our aim is to increase the awareness of those relationships, including the level of aggression and victimization. I have learned that much of the bullying and aggression in the classroom is the result of a lack of awareness or a lack of sensitivity to the needs of others. Name calling and minor physical aggression are sometimes an expression of boredom, the need for attention, and a way to gain social status rather than a reaction to frustration or anger. In classrooms where such awareness is not developed, victims are routinely abused without much thought, and they are too weak to cope, particularly in an indifferent environment.

In a poor classroom climate, two major norms are missing, the ability to express feelings and the ability to provide support. These two abilities usually interact; when members trust the group enough to be able to disclose feelings or share personal experiences with each other, they increase their sense of caring and empathy toward others, because you don't want to hurt someone with whom you feel intimate. The opposite, of course, is also true; you cannot make self-disclosures unless you feel accepted and supported. In most classrooms, and in most groups of children and adolescents in general, self-disclosure is not the common language of communication; rather, what is common is put downs, insults, and bullying (Benbenishty & Astor, 2005)—unless intervention is offered in the classroom.

In the preventive program offered here, we try to respond to Luft's five basic needs using a variety of methods and structured activities, including bibliotherapy and clarifying processes as an adjunct to the educational process. We introduce the intervention to the children as an attempt to learn about and improve relationships in the classroom. After one or two sessions of activities that "break the ice" and begin to build a climate of openness and trust, we initiate a cognitive exploration of the classroom situation, then develop a language of self-expressiveness and acceptance, with an attempt to empower individuals in the group, and finally make a commitment to change negative interactions or dynamics in the group.

Positive Climate

Activities aimed at getting to know each other on a more personal level establish a more intimate climate. Classmates interview each other, ask questions of interest to each other while throwing a ball, or write positive feedback on each other's backs (see Shechtman, 2007, for more details).

Cognitive Exploration

Cognitive exploration is intended to identify interpersonal relationships in the class. For instance, the "I Wonder Statements" activity helps to map the social situation in class. More specifically, participants identify the extent to which each student feels comfortable to state his/her opinion or to express feelings without being blamed, judged, or rejected. The children receive a list with several questions to which they respond on a continuum from 1 to 5. For example they are as follows:

- In our class, each student can express freely his or her opinion.
- In our class, each student has an equal opportunity to show his/her ability.
- In our class, students resolve their problems through an open, fair discussion.
- In our class, there are students who do not cooperate with the rest of us.
- In our class, there are students who are insulted or bullied.

Such "wonder statements" can be adjusted to the particular situation of each class. In highly competitive classrooms, for example, the issue of freedom may be raised; in highly heterogeneous classrooms, the issue of equality should be stressed; and in highly aggressive classrooms, the topic of victimization should be emphasized. The students mark each continuum regarding both the real situation and the ideal one.

By mapping the social situation, students identify disturbing behaviors in the classroom. The gap between the real and ideal situation raises their awareness of the difficulties and the need to make a change in the classroom. Sometimes it is advisable, as a next step, to rank those issues that need to be resolved by their level of importance. We do so through an activity called "The Most Urgent Issue." Students identify classroom behaviors that are most disturbing to them, which in turn raises a commitment for change.

In most classes, the disturbing behaviors include social rejection, disrespect, put downs, and bullying. For example, in an intervention in one third-grade class, 26 out of 27 students rate insults and bullying as the most disturbing behavior in reality and all 27 state that this is the most urgent goal to achieve in their class. The huge gap between the real and ideal situation generates an interesting discussion in which the children hear that victims feel sad, angry, or even depressed. Mark says, "I feel suffocated," to illustrate his situation. They also hear that aggressive children sometimes feel guilt and regret. They identify the ways in which they make each other feel bad: when they are insulted, when they are blamed for no reason, when others talk behind their back, and when there is gossip. The discussion ends with the children's commitment to improve the classroom situation. Some of the commitments are to include every child in games; to apologize when you hurt someone; to speak nicely to each other, thinking about your tone of voice and not only the words; to help and support a child who is insulted or bullied. Even if the children don't always follow through on their commitments, the mere fact of putting them on the agenda influences classroom behavior.

This is a powerful activity that quickly raises the children's awareness of what needs to be changed in the classroom, with a particular focus on disturbing interpersonal relationships, including bullying and aggression. The fact that the children autonomously identify the difficulties helps to shift the responsibility for resolving the problems to them.

Another activity that achieves similar results is to help children establish their own classroom rules. We offer two activities to achieve this goal: "The Ideal Classroom" and "Classroom Rules." In the first, children are asked to write down what they envision as their ideal classroom. From these accounts, we can glean and discuss disturbing behaviors in the classroom, and encourage commitments to make a change. Similarly, in the second activity, children write anonymous notes about behaviors they dislike in class (on small pieces of paper of one color) and those they wish to see in class (on paper of another color). Their responses are then collected and discussed, and a group commitment is made.

In one sixth-grade class, the teacher starts the program with "The Ideal Class-room" and "Classroom Rules" based on the children's needs. In their ideal classrooms, respect from teachers and other students is mentioned the most. They particularly dislike situations when children fight or bully others. In their anonymous notes, they did not want to have any lonely or rejected children in class, they wanted for all to be friends, and to cooperate with each other.

In one of the more difficult classrooms, involving an extremely disadvantaged adolescent population, the 17-year-old youngsters are asked to envision their ideal classroom. They are so surprised to address such a question that all they could agree upon is a pleasant climate, without being able to express their wishes in greater detail. In a follow-up activity, in which their needs were discussed in a group , they come up with more detailed desires, such as being more appreciated by classmates, more respected by teachers, and more acknowledged for their efforts. These needs reflected the great vulnerability of these youngsters, many of whom have LD and a long history of school failure. These difficulties, along with their poor socialization, triggered them to act aggressively. Indeed, when they were asked to rank the needs they mentioned that the most important one is to resolve a conflict with the help of an adult in order to avoid escalation. This is a considerable progress for such youth, who are characterized by an antiauthority attitude, and who usually resolve their conflicts amongst themselves, violently.

Developing a Language of Self-expressiveness and Acceptance

Cognitive exploration and identification of problems is a first and necessary step to increase awareness regarding interpersonal difficulties, but not sufficient for children to make a profound change. A real change doesn't occur until children can actually state their opinions without fear of being rejected, and can express their true feelings, such as pain, shame, or fear, knowing that they will be accepted. As verbal support is not the common language in most classrooms, we first need to develop such language among classmates. We do so with the help of structured activities to promote positive feelings about the self and others, such as the "Personal Award" or the "Personal Tree."

In these two activities, personal strengths are identified and shared, and positive feedback is exchanged. The rationale for these two activities is that children identify their own strengths and feel comfortable sharing them with the group without fear of not being accepted or even being rejected. The first activity is more suitable for younger kids, while the second is better suited to adolescents and adults. Here are a few illustrations of the activities and their results.

One teacher uses the "Personal Award" activity in a fifth-grade class character-ized by disturbed relationships. The children receive a drawing of an award in which each child first writes some possible reasons for receiving it and reads them out to the class. The role of classmates is to add reasons for receiving the award in order to empower the speaker. Indeed, they tell one girl "you are good-hearted" and another that "you are very creative." Everyone likes to get positive feedback once in a while, but the impact on nonproblem kids is usually moderate. For Jack, however, the implications are dramatic. Jack has been identified as highly aggressive, and is normally rejected by his classmates and often blamed by the teacher for disturbing the class. It is difficult to talk about such a child in positive terms. Indeed, he is able to name only one achievement for which he is deserving of an award—taking care of his dog. However, the rest of the class makes an effort (because this was the expectation) and provides quite a lot of positive feedback: "you are smart," "self-confident," "you dress nicely," "you're good in sports," to mention but a few. Jack seems very pleased. After adding all the feedback from his peers to his award, he is able to come up with some more of his own.

In another fifth-grade class, Shari, a new student, has had an extremely hard time breaking into the social circle. She was quite lonely and withdrawn before the "Personal Award" activity. Surprisingly, she has no trouble giving herself an award and receives quite a lot of supportive responses, such as "you are an interesting girl," "you are serious and responsible," and "you are a good student." This opens the door to two new friendships in class, which Shari has wanted very much but never dared to initiate.

The "Personal Tree" activity requires more sophistication and maturity. The roots of the tree represent abilities, talents, and the like, while its branches represent achievements. In one ninth-grade class, in a vocational school for drop-outs from regular schools, the "Personal Tree" activity is extended to two sessions because it has raised so much interest. These adolescents are more interested in hearing what others think about them than in talking about themselves, so they ask to reverse the process; first, the group will provide feedback, then they will add to their tree. The request makes it clear that the boys and girls in this class are still fearful of each other and do not trust that they will be accepted. Following the exchange of some positive feedback, they realize that the climate is safe and are ready to talk about themselves. Several students share their strengths with the group. One is responsible for managing all the family expenses, another takes care of her two younger siblings. The group expresses much appreciation.

Then Yusuf, a minority (Arab) student who is extremely rejected, shares with the group—after a long period of hesitation—his difficult life circumstances. He works before and after school in two jobs to support his family. The group members first react with pity:

Sam:	Don't you want to be a normal kid, for instance, play the computer?
Mary (angrily):	And who said you are normal? I would also like an after-school job.
Sam:	But your story is very different, you don't need it. It must be difficult.

Counselor:	Can you ask him directly how he feels about it?
Sam:	Isn't this very difficult for you?
Yusuf:	I am used to working; I've done this from age 9. I know how to do lots of things.

The counselor suggests that Yusuf read his tree to the class. In his roots, he wrote hard worker, knows many tasks, not lazy, and a loyal son. In his branches he mentioned: making money, being a good friend, being physically strong. The group moves from pity to appreciation. The change in Sam's attitude is particularly notable, as he is the one who has constantly bullied Yusuf.

This session is a turning point in Yusuf's relationships with his classmates; they even invite him to a party. In the next session, he shares with them that he feels tired. They are interested in knowing why. Because of their attention, he is willing to share that he had a big fight with his father the other night. Such sharing is quite unusual for an Arab adolescent, as talking against one's family is taboo in his culture. Other children join him in this hot topic so that he does not feel uncomfortable. Yusuf is now a respected group member, no longer subject to put downs or bullying in class. This also illustrates how self-disclosure promotes empathy and reduces aggression. The class has had an opportunity to get to know the real Yusuf and has learned to respect him and other classmates. This activity in itself has contributed greatly to the reduction of tension in the class.

In a climate of social support and trust, it is possible to move a step further and deal with interpersonal conflicts in a direct way. This can be achieved through activities, such as "The Empty Chair" (see below), but at this stage of the process, it sometimes also happens spontaneously. For example, in one third-grade class, in the eighth session, John initiates a discussion about an incident that happened the day before "I feel hurt, because everyone was against me. I was very lonely, as if you all snubbed and excluded me," he says. The class is very quiet and attentive as he speaks. They respond in various ways, but always with respect. Some say that they were not involved and he didn't notice them. Others provide feedback on his behavior, showing why it caused the harsh reaction. Some apologize for getting so heated up about it. John closes the session by thanking them all for listening. He admits that he, too, had a part in the conflict and states his hope that such things won't happen again. "I couldn't sleep last night," he shares with the group, a statement that must raise empathy for the victim.

In a later session, the counselor uses the "Empty Chair" technique to increase interpersonal intimate communication. In this activity, an empty chair is offered and any child can choose to sit in it and express his/her feelings or problems. The child is directed to use "I messages" to make his/her case and to avoid blaming others. John feels so comfortable in class that he decides to share his learning difficulties with his classmates. There is more mutual sharing and provision of both emotional and instrumental support: "We all have days like that," "The bad feelings will disappear in time," and "Maybe I can help you with your homework," to cite a few of the reactions. Sara then takes a turn in the "Empty Chair" and talks about her loneliness in class: "I don't have many friends here and it makes me feel very sad." The girls' reactions are highly empathic: "We didn't know you feel this way; it's too bad that you didn't share your feelings earlier," "There are girls who would like to be your friend," "You are a nice girl, gentle and generous." Sara thanks the group for listening and seems to feel a lot better. The number of students who want to continue using the "Empty Chair" is so high that the counselor has to extend the session.

The same technique is used with a group of difficult boys who dropped out of the regular school system and are currently enrolled in a vocational school. Muhamad, a minority student in an all-Jewish class, talks about his sense of loneliness and despair because of his classmates' constant bullying. The group, which practiced "I messages" for two sessions prior to that meeting, responds with empathy to his shared feelings, and David, his main adversary, says, "I now understand that when I joke around with Muhamad I actually hurt him a lot while I am laughing like an idiot." This is a huge shift from the typical behavior of these youngsters, whose verbal behavior is quite abusive.

The direct communication approach through "I messages" not only promotes self-expressiveness, but also helps resolve conflicts in a rational way. Children learn to take responsibility for their own behavior and for the behavior of their classmates.

Bibliotherapy

Stories, poems, and films help us to deliver the classroom program, just as we do in small groups. A story such as "The Smiley Face" and a movie such as *Victor* are a means of addressing issues of inclusion and rejection, a topic that bothers so many kids in school.

For example, *Victor* is aired to a class of new immigrant boys. There is a lot of identification with the hero, Victor, a new immigrant to the United States from Mexico who not only has to deal with learning difficulties, but also has to adjust to a new culture and different norms. In the film, Victor hits someone to protect his younger sister because that is his role as older brother. Many of the new immigrants in this class feel the same, because "machoism" is a strong norm in their culture. The film permits catharsis through a process of identification, and generates a discussion of how to adjust to the new norms. Rather than being blamed as usual, the boys feel understood.

Another major issue that comes up in all classrooms is bullying and victimization. A story such as "The Bully" (Tester, 1974; see Appendix B) and a poem such as "The Lonely Drum" (Goldberg, 1989) help us discuss the issue of victimization.

The teacher of a third-grade class reads "The Bully" to them. The children perceive the bully as indifferent and strong and the victim as fearful and helpless. They soon reach the conclusion that the victim's main problem is that no one comes to his rescue. They understand that the group has the power to prevent bullying if they all get together and make a decision that, if something similar should happen, they will all cooperate against the bully to protect the victim. It is hard to know if this promise will be kept, but at the very least their attitudes have changed.

"The Lonely Drum" (Goldberg, 1989) is used in a class of adolescent boys. The poem describes a man's execution with people standing around him in silence, and no one coming to his aid. The youngsters share incidents in which they felt lonely and nobody came to their rescue. Interestingly, the reactions in the class indicate that they are not ready to help a victim unless it is a close friend. They accept violence as part of life; sometimes they must get hurt and other times they hurt others. It is difficult to convince them to help someone in need, because their social life is arranged in cliques, and their loyalty is devoted to the people they are close to, similar to the culture of gangs. Nonetheless, awareness of the suffering of victims has been raised.

Positive Feedback

The last stage of the intervention is based on positive feedbacks shared among classmates. At this point of the intervention, the children already know each other on a more personal level and are already more skillful in providing support. Several activities can be used to reach the goal. One activity that we commonly use is "Feedback on your Back," in which each child wears a blank sheet of paper on his/her back and the others write positive statements on it. Kids like this activity not only because of the positive feedback provided by many classmates, but also because it involves movement. I recall one fifth-grade boy who looked at his sheet at the end of the activity and jumped up in air, shouting: "I didn't think you like me so much!"

Another way of achieving this goal is to have students turn to a classmate and tell that person how he/she has been helpful to them. In a very difficult group of adolescents who dropped out of the regular school system and were in a vocational program, some of the interactions are:

David: Yusuf once helped me bake pita bread. I have not forgotten it, and I'm looking for a chance to return the favor.
Nancy (to Mary):   You helped me overcome my fear. I am afraid of heights and you helped me by joining me, then I could do it on my own.

This particular group started with a very poor classroom climate. One of them described the high level of indifference to being in New York. At termination, following the positive feedback exchange, the counselor asks if they still feel like they are in New York. No, they say. "We are now a cohesive and intimate group," Nancy sums up.

Termination

Termination is a very important stage in such a program and must end in a positive tone because the kids continue to be with their classmates after the intervention ends. In fact, such efforts should continue throughout the year to decrease the chances of relapse.

Description of a Complete Program

The following case study is of the classroom climate intervention applied to a sixth-grade class in a high socioeconomic neighborhood. This particular class was identified by school personnel as highly problematic in terms of interpersonal relationships among students. The class was comprised of high achieving, extremely competitive students, which teachers felt was affecting students' performance. The program included eleven 45-minute sessions conducted by the school counselor and the homeroom teacher.

Session 1: The Ideal Classroom

The assignment for the children is to present their real and ideal classroom through drawings (using symbols). For the real classroom, most children draw many small cliques and themselves in the circle or in a corner of one of the groups. For the ideal group they draw one circle with themselves in the center. Asked to write about what the ideal classroom would be, they respond: one group with no rejected children, we respect and help each other, we refrain from abusive language and violence, we cooperate with each other. This activity highlights the gap between the real and the wished-for situation, developing awareness of the social and emotional needs of children in the class.

Session 2: Classroom Rules

This session is a continuation of the previous one, but focusing on classroom rules, through the activity of writing little notes. The students are asked to put the notes about those behaviors they like in class into one pile and the ones they want to get rid of in another pile. The first pile includes friendships, the teachers, the level of achievements, the style of learning, and the seating arrangement.

Things they want to get rid of (the second pile) include fights, aggression, destructive behavior, cliques, unfairness, and "snobbish" relationships.

Sessions 3–4: "I Wonder Statements"

In the *third* and *fourth sessions*, the counselor uses "I wonder statements." The activity reveals that expressions of individual thought are often rejected by those in another clique. This is continued into the next session, where the focus is on the following specific statement: "I wonder to what extent children in our class feel intimidated." Some admit that they are the victims and tend to withdraw when intimidated, while others feel that they have to respond with aggression to defend themselves. This is an extremely "hot" session in which one can feel that the children do care about each other.

Session 5: Urgent Disturbing Issue

"What's Urgent" is the major activity in the *fifth session*. The children are asked to rank the importance of the issues that bother them in class and select the most urgent ones to be treated. They mention such issues as group cohesion and stopping intimidation. The children also discuss those things they are willing to do to achieve this urgent goal. "I am willing to be a friend of kids I have not yet befriended," says Sally. "I'm ready to stop being violent, provided they stop nagging me," says Dan.

Session 6: Communication

The *sixth session* focuses on communication skills. A topic for discussion is introduced to the class and they have to argue for or against it. It is obvious that the children lack communication skills, but they do learn the skills of "I messages," which we find to be very important in our program. Sam says, "When you call me names, I only pretend that I don't mind, but honestly I feel quite insulted."

Session 7: Positive Feedback

Positive feedback is given through the "Palm Activity," a variation of the "Personal Award" game. Each child makes two identical drawings of his or her palm. On one of them, the children write positive things about themselves, one on each finger. The other they give to five classmates, each of whom writes a positive thing about them on one of the fingers. In this way, the children can see what positive things others think about them and how similar or different others feel about them.

Sessions 8–9: Bibliotherapy

In the *eighth session*, bibliotherapy is introduced. The story "The Bully" (Tester, 1974; see Appendix B) has been selected to increase awareness and understanding of victimization. The class understands that if they become united, they can resist such behavior and help victims in class.

In the following session, to continue the topic of the silent majority, the counselor uses the poem, "The Lonely Drum" (Goldberg, 1989). The children understand how cruel it is to let someone be executed. The children share with each other times of loneliness, death, car accidents, and the like, and they talk about their need for support in such situations.

Session 10: Self-Expression

"The Empty Chair" is used to deepen the children's understanding of victimization and increase the expression of honest feelings in a supportive climate. The first child to sit in the chair is Jeremy, a rejected child who can't find a friend to share his room on a two-day field trip. Margaret and Janet also share their sense of isolation. The climate is one of acceptance and understanding, and some of the children even apologize.

Session 11: Termination

The last session is a party and a summary of gains. In a summing-up activity, the children are asked to answer three questions in writing: What has changed in class? What has not changed? and What do I take with me to middle school? Here is one such response written by Ron:

> (1). Relationships among kids have improved and in general we are more cohesive.
> (2). There are still classmates who tend to intimidate others but less frequently. (3). I know better how to relate to others in the new school.

Outcomes

The project was accompanied by evaluation of the outcomes in the experimental class compared to a control (nontreatment) class. On the Anger Scale (Buss & Perry, 1992), a well established instrument to measure anger and aggression, results indicated a significant reduction of anger, hatred, and general score, compared to the control class. On all these variables, the scores for the experimental group decreased, while those in the control group increased. This, however, is only a demonstration of one intervention and its outcomes, offered to complete the case illustration, and meant to demonstrate a sample of classroom activities to improve classroom climate and reduce aggression.

Evaluations of the Intervention

Several evaluation studies of our classroom climate invention have obtained positive results. An elementary-level study (Shechtman, Weiser, and Kurtz, 1993) involved two experimental and two control classrooms. Following the intervention led by a school counselor, the experimental students expressed improved perceptions of social relations in the class, gained an increased sense of closeness to classmates, and improved on the social and behavioral dimensions of self-concept.

A secondary-level study (Shechtman, 1993) involving 600 students examined the impact of the program on similar social variables. Following the intervention led by school counselors, adolescents in the experimental group reduced their support of authoritarian attitudes, and their perceptions of relationships in their classrooms improved.

A third study (Shechtman, 1997) was of a larger population, involving both elementary and secondary students, with a distinction between regular and special-need students in the classroom. Regular elementary school students improved significantly in perceived classroom climate, but not special needs students. In contrast, the special needs students improved on four of the five dimensions of adjusting behavior, as evaluated by their teacher. Results for the secondary students were different; gains on both classroom climate and social acceptance were revealed for special needs students compared to control. No progress was revealed on teacher evaluations of adjusting behavior among the adolescents. These results are based on the individual student as the criterion for measurement. When the classroom was the unit of analysis, results were less favorable (a direct result of the small n), yet even so, social acceptance was improved in the adolescent sample. These findings point to the favorable impact of the intervention on adolescents' perceptions of classroom climate and on the adjustment of special needs children.

The most recent study (Shechtman & Afargan, 2008) involved 905 students in 13 schools, three classrooms in each school. In one of the three classes a classroom intervention was conducted, then compared to small counseling-group treatment and to no treatment (control). It measured, in addition to social climate, the level of aggression in the classroom. Compared to control.(no treatment children), the treatment children reduced their level of verbal and physical aggression, anger, and hate, and decreased in both internalizing and externalizing behavior. Moreover, the level of classroom aggression and victimization decreased in the experimental classes compared to the control ones.

Teachers' and Counselors' Feedback

In order to implement the intervention program introduced in this chapter, teachers and counselors must be trained in its content and delivery. Training involves three components: (a) knowledge of the subject matter, that is, the dynamics of the aggressive child; (b) experiencing the program, that is, using the activities for their own self-growth; and (c) implementing the program under supervision.

Feedback that we have received from teachers and counselors reflects the importance of all the three components. However, most meaningful seems to be the third one (implementation), as it promotes the teacher's or counselor's professional status in the school. This is reflected in the following self-reflection written by one school counselor:

> The course, the articles, and the class discussions helped me understand what makes children act aggressively, and I appreciate this. However, what convinced me that the method works was to witness the change in climate in my class. They became closer friends and the bullying disappeared. Moreover, one student initiated a meeting with the principal to convince her to start programs like this at an earlier stage in schooling in order to prevent harm to so many kids. When I was asked by other teachers to apply the program in their classes, I knew I was capable of bringing change to the school.

For some teachers, it was more than just professional growth, as is evident from the next written self-reflection:

> Beyond learning about aggressive behavior, I learned a lot about myself. I stopped criticizing, judging, and moralizing to aggressive children and instead started listening to their life events and connecting to their pain and lack of control. In my private life, things have changed, too. My son is quite aggressive in school and teachers complain a lot about his behavior. I have learned to listen to him, too, and to discuss his behavior with him in a constructive way. The other day he told me, in tears, that he cannot control himself and asked me to help him with his problem; never in my life did I feel so close to him.

One of the male teachers in our group of trainees had a hard time connecting to the emotional focus of the program. When we were exploring our own aggression, he was rather silent. Working with highly disturbed adolescents, he felt that harsh discipline is needed to keep these youngsters in line. "They must learn to obey authority first," he kept arguing in class. However, at termination his reflection indicated quite a change in position:

> I am more of a cognitive sort of person and most of the interventions I've chosen to do up to now were of a cognitive type. I discovered that [this approach] is not so bad after all. Moreover, I have learned the importance of self-expression, and have come to realize that verbal self-expressiveness is actually an alternative behavior to aggression.

Several school counselors applied both the classroom intervention program and small counseling groups with highly aggressive kids. Some of them liked the classroom intervention better than the small group treatments. Here is what one counselor wrote:

> For me, the classroom program was more meaningful. In my particular classroom, about half of the boys were identified as highly aggressive, and yet progress in class was evident. A large group of students took part in the discussions and made commitments to change. Indeed, an improved classroom climate and a reduction in aggression has been noted by the students themselves, their teachers, and even their parents. Most impressive was the change in the classroom discourse; the fact that children could talk to each other on an emotional level and use "I messages" was astonishing. Even the classroom teacher who joined me in all the sessions has changed and continues working on the climate in class. In contrast, in the small group of highly aggressive children [I worked with], I felt that I needed more time to make a profound change.

Summary

This chapter has focused on primary prevention or classroom intervention. Most of the literature on treatment of childhood aggression focuses on the ecological aspects of aggression, suggesting that such interventions considerably decrease the level of classroom and school aggression (Horne et al., 2007; Olweus, 2001). The reason I have left this topic for the end of the book is not because I disagree with the importance of primary prevention, but rather because so little is written about secondary prevention. My intention in this book has been to focus on the treatment of aggressive children. Still, primary prevention should not be ignored.

This chapter illustrates a classroom program that involves the social community of children and promotes children's awareness of the challenges of aggressive kids and their victims. It also empowers them as a group to take action and resist aggression in their immediate communities (classrooms). Drawing from group counseling principles and addressing the basic needs of individuals in group, the program increases the children's sense of belonging, and it teaches them to earn respect and offer it to others, to express thoughts and feelings, and to resolve conflicts through direct communication. Bibliotherapy as an adjunct to treatment is helpful in classroom programs, just as it is in small groups. In classroom interventions, too, we need to be aware of the resistant nature of aggressive children to change. Using an indirect method for treatment promotes cooperation and helps the counselor or teacher to navigate the process.

Classroom interventions have been proven to promote a positive classroom climate and to decrease the level of classroom aggression to a certain extent. However, they cannot serve as a substitute for the (separate) treatment of highly aggressive children. Such children need special professional attention, which can be provided through small counseling groups or individual therapy. In fact, the best intervention is probably a combination of the two: classroom intervention and treatment of the aggressive children at the same time.

Chapter 10
Summary and Conclusions

Introduction

Having presented the use of bibliotherapy as an adjunct to therapy, and its appropriateness for helping to reduce aggression among children and youth, it is now time to sum up. After briefly describing the concepts of childhood aggression, this chapter reiterates the rationale for using bibliotherapy with aggressive children, how it should be implemented, and its use with significant people in the aggressive child's life. Finally, I address the question of effectiveness and present the evidence base for the program in question.

Description of Childhood Aggression

Aggressive behavior is defined as any intentional act to hurt others, physically or psychologically, directly or indirectly. Extreme cases of childhood aggression, such as school shootings, receive a lot of public attention. The milder types, however, often remain hidden from the public eye, despite their high frequency and the devastating short- and long-term effects they have on children and adolescents, perpetrators and victims alike.

School is the arena where children face violence and aggression the most. Children often do not feel safe in school because classmates hurt them, hitting, pushing, shoving, intimidating, disrespecting, and rejecting them. Aggression violates one of the basic needs of children—for safety (Maslow, 1998). It creates a toxic climate that bears negative consequences for the student's academic and social life (Elias & Arnold, 2006), as well as for future adjustment (Farrington, 1994; Olweus, 2001). It is difficult for victimized children to concentrate on learning tasks knowing that someone may make fun of them or will get them after class. Children who grow up as victims develop a poor self-concept and mistrust toward others that follows them throughout adulthood. Similarly, the aggressors and bullies grow up with a self-image of "the bad guy," which impacts their self-esteem.

Z. Shechtman, *Treating Child and Adolescent Aggression Through Bibliotherapy*, 197
The Springer Series on Human Exceptionality, DOI 10.1007/978-0-387-09745-9_10,
© Springer Science+Business Media, LLC 2009

Because we are currently aware more than ever of the consequences of aggression, schools have invested great efforts to reduce it. There are two contradictory paths to achieve the goal. One is the Zero Tolerance movement, which aims to reduce aggression and violence through harsh discipline, strict rules, and punishment. The other is the Well-being movement, which aspires to decrease the level of aggression by improving the child's social environment and empowerment.

Zero Tolerance has gained strength recently, particularly following cata-strophic events, such as school shootings. The public has reacted in panic, in the hopes of stopping such incidents immediately, and zero tolerance seems the natural reaction. Detectors have been installed in every high school to prevent students from bringing weapons to school; more involvement of police in the school has been sought; and any small rule violation has received the immedi-ate attention of authorities. Suspension, detention, and time out have become the most frequent responses to children's aggressive behavior. The problem is that they have not proved particularly effective in reducing aggression (Skiba & Peterson, 2000).

There are several reasons that may explain the inefficiency of these methods. First, some are punitive methods that by definition represent adult aggression; whether in school or in the family, punitive education tends to increase rather than decrease aggression (Dodge, 2002). Second, aggressive children need treatment rather than solely disciplinary action. They have cognitive misper-ceptions and emotional difficulties that require attention. If we champion the "No child left behind" cause, this also includes kids with socioemotional diffi-culties who cannot be left untreated.

The most frequent reaction of school personnel to a violent act is suspension. The following example underlines some of the problematic of this "solution":

Mitchell is a fourth grader who is often suspended; for a minor infraction he gets sent home for one day and for a more severe one he receives three days of suspension. He always returns to school covered in bruises. When I meet him, he has come back to school with his older brother after such a suspension. Not only is he physically hurt, but he seems depressed. His older brother brings him to the school office, saying, "We took care of him, don't worry, he'll never do it again." I ask the principal if she realizes what's going on in his home when the child is under suspension and she admits that he always gets physically punished. "Does it indeed prevent another aggressive act?", I ask. "You must be kidding," she replies. "Then why do you continue sending him home?", I persist. "What else can I do? I have a whole school to take care of," she responds. This is one of the most frustrating incidents I have experienced in a school. There is no empathy for the child, no understanding of the consequences for him, and no alternative reactions to his behavior.

In contrast, the Well-being movement uses positive psychology to reduce aggression. It takes a primary preventive approach, emphasizing both a positive social environment and enhanced social skills. Classrooms in which there are no bullies and in which children do not feel rejected or scapegoated have less aggressive kids. In fact, in almost all the extreme cases of school violence, like shootings, the perpetrators have been lonely and rejected students (Garbarino,

1999). A wealth of preventive programs has been reviewed in the literature, and most studies report positive outcomes (e.g., Horne et al., 2007).

However, even with the best programs implemented in class or the school, there will always remain a core of youngsters (5–10% per class) who continue to demonstrate aggressive behavior. This group presents varying types of aggression. Dodge (Dodge & Schwartz, 1997) made the distinction between reactive and proactive aggressors. Olweus (1993), among others, established the concept of bullying, suggesting that bullies have unique characteristics. More recently, a unique type of feminine aggression has been identified, namely relational aggression (Crick et al., 2002). It is not always clear which type of aggression is presented, but all types of aggressive children need help.

Following the Well-being approach, it is my belief that these high-risk children deserve special treatment. But secondary prevention programs are rather scarce in comparison to primary prevention programs. Thus, although I highly value classroom and school preventive interventions, as presented in Chapter 9, the focus of the book has been on secondary prevention—in other words, on the specific treatment of aggressive children and youth, which is greatly lacking.

The program offered here is tailored to address the characteristics of aggressive children. As a group, they tend to be characterized by a verbal deficit, low empathy, perceptual problems, and lack of self-control. Aggressive children are often angry, but unable to express this anger verbally and so they act it out. The main reason they cannot express that anger is their need to appear strong, which is related to their deviant way of processing information. Being vulnerable, they are constantly on the offense, perceive others as acting against them, and select violence as their reaction. As empathy is low, they cannot recognize the suffering of others; they see the infliction of harm as a normal reaction of self-defense. This leads to uncontrolled behavior. Such patterns of behavior are based on their past experiencing and therefore quite difficult to change.

The varying types of aggression present somewhat different characteristics, and treatment must be adjusted to each. As proactive aggressors are goal-minded and endorse force, they particularly need an emphasis on empathy development and reconstruction of their information processing. Arnie is such a proactive aggressor; he likes to appear strong and enjoys hurting younger kids to show off. He admits at termination of treatment: "Before these sessions I would hit and feel nothing; now when I hit, I feel sorry for the victim." Reactive aggressors may need an emphasis on verbal expression and self-control. During a self-introduction game at his first treatment session, Sam, a fifth grader, says, "I like football, music, and dancing, and I have a bad temper. I would like to have more control over my behavior, but I can't." Bullies often express a high level of verbalization and are self-controlled, but are very low on empathy and morality. "I do not hit to hurt, I just play with this 'baby,' just like to see him cry," says Bill. Finally, relational aggression is by definition more indirect and requires the development of verbal expression and empathy. "I didn't tell the girls not to attend her birthday party, I just said I'm not going to such a dirty girl and they all followed me," says Patty. Despite the differences and the needed adjustments, the program offered here, with its four themes of anger management, empathy development, misuse of power, and self-control, is suitable for most aggressive children and youth.

The illustrations of treatments presented throughout the book suggest that changing child and adolescent aggression is quite a challenging endeavor. Changing well-established attachment styles, beliefs, norms, and habits is quite a demanding task. We need to provide a corrective socialization process, to offer corrective interpersonal experiences, to change perceptions, and to teach skills—all to a population of clients that is not particularly enthusiastic about therapy or change. It is especially difficult for aggressive youth to give up their sense of power. Bibliotherapy helps us achieve such demanding goals due to its unique features. It is offered as a major adjunct to psychotherapeutic treatment of aggressive children and youth.

The Rationale for Using Bibliotherapy

Why bibliotherapy? The idea of healing through books is not new, and is indeed applied in many helping professions, such as education, social work, and psychotherapy. However, at first, books were used to educate people and help them cope with a variety of difficulties in a rational way, assuming that the content of the literature in itself bears the healing power. To this day, cognitive bibliotherapy uses literature to guide people in understanding their situation and coping, even without the intervention of a therapist.

The program offered in this book is different; bibliotherapy is used as an affective mode of treatment and as an adjunct to a therapeutic process. Nossrat Peseschkian, a Persian therapist who practices in Germany, has stipulated, "With their playful character and their closeness to fantasy, intuitions and irrationality" (Peseschkian, 1979, p. xiv), stories can be used as mediators in therapy.

> They give the patient a basis for identification, and at the same time they are a protection for him; by associating with the story, he talks about himself, his conflicts, and his desires. Especially when there is resistance to be dealt with, the stories have proved their value. Without attacking a patient or his concepts and values directly, we suggest a change of positions, which at first has more the character of a game. This change of position finally allows the patient to see his own-sided concepts in relation to others, to reinterpret them and to extend them. (Peseschkian, 1979, p. xv)

In his therapeutic work with adults, Peseschkian uses fictional stories of Oriental origin as a tool in psychotherapy. The more fantasy oriented, the better, he claims.

Similarly, we use fiction to assist the therapeutic process with children and adolescents. Children like stories even more than adults; and sometimes it is the only way to reach them (Gurian, 1997). I once had a chance to help a youngster who suffered from anxiety attacks. Up to then, he had refused any help. I offered stories and he agreed. At the termination of the single session we had, he asked for more literary texts, which I didn't have with me at the moment. Through the stories, he experienced meaningful catharsis and felt much better at the end, but any attempt to move directly to his difficulties met a wall of resistance. Being a single session, his resistance was quite expected. However, it was clear that without the literature there would have been no therapeutic session at all. Many such examples can be found throughout this book.

However, I also believe that a therapeutic process with a trained therapist must follow the use of literature, particularly when dealing with aggressive children and youth. Although children like stories, they cannot use the literature effectively without some guidance. The therapist should make sure that the content is understood and not distorted. Moreover, literature on its own may not be able to challenge such a stable behavior as aggression or violence. A therapeutic process must take place to help children get in touch with their feelings, develop insight, and find alternative behaviors. Finally, a therapeutic alliance must be established with a counselor to help in the socialization process. Thus, while the literary texts are selected for this program in accordance with the unique difficulties of aggressive children and youth, it is the therapist who directs the cognitive and affective exploration, the development of insight, and the action to make a change. That is, the literature is used as a vehicle to achieve these noble goals—a stimulus for identifying emotions and developing a discussion, a medium for self-exploration through the identification process, and a guide for change.

The power of bibliotherapy largely lies in it being an indirect method of treatment. Because aggressive children are extremely anxious and self-defensive, dealing with their aggression directly may raise resistance to treatment. Therefore, the first step in bibliotherapy is to relate to the literary characters, their thoughts, feelings, and behavior; only later are children invited to engage in self-inquiry processes. As can be seen in the many illustrations of the process presented in this book, the literary text helps start the therapeutic process and is particularly effective in helping the children get in touch with their own feelings.

When I say "literature," I do not only refer to books. Films are another alternative to bibliotherapy, which children like even more. I can envision a good bibliotherapy process based on films alone. Indeed, when asked to reflect on their treatment, most children cited movies as their favorite and most effective medium. However, watching a movie requires longer periods of time than the 45 minutes we generally have available. Thus, we use short stories and poems along with films. Short stories are particularly effective in guiding a conversation or leading to a resolution due to their structured nature, whereas poems have the power to elicit strong emotions.

Whatever the type of literature we use, the common format is comprised of the following steps: getting familiar with the text, identifying the character's emotions, discussing the character's behavior, connecting to the character on a personal level, and, lastly, exploring one's own behavior. This is the basic format, but one should not be rigid about it; the order of these components may change. A child may make a personal connection to the character at the beginning of the process, or a guided discussion may not be needed when a child initiates discussion of his/her own behavior at the stage of identification. It seems important to explore further the nature of each component of the therapeutic process.

Reading to the children is important to capture their attention; watching a movie has a similar effect. Identifying emotions serves to enhance understanding of human behavior, including their own emotions, as well as to increase their repertoire of feelings. The discussion of the dynamics of human behavior informs clients of other people's behavior, as well as their own. Finally, self-exploration is the main chunk of the session, and rightly so, because we intend to help aggressive children change their behavior. In an optimal session I would like to see the greatest part of the time devoted to self-exploration. Research on groups with inpatient adults (Shechtman & Nir Shafrir, 2007) indicated that slightly more that 50% of each session was devoted to the literature and the other half to self-exploration. In groups with aggressive children, the ratio was 25% for literature and the rest to self-exploration (Shechtman, 2004b). This difference in the proportions between child and adult group treatment may be attributed either to the limited ability of children to discuss the literature or the limited ability of adult inpatients to discuss themselves. More research is definitely needed to establish the optimal level for literature exploration versus self-exploration.

Because the self-exploration process is so essential, and in fact is the heart of the therapeutic process, it requires further explanation. The main component of self-exploration is the *clarifying process*, aimed at identifying one's thoughts, feelings, and behavior. Thus, when children explore their aggressive behavior, we expect to hear what they think about aggression, how they feel when acting aggressively, and what are some other options for response rather than aggression. The clarifying process helps us move the client from a stage of lack of awareness, or a stage of unwillingness to change despite self-awareness, to the stage where a will to change is raised and the child is ready to take charge of his/her life. At this action stage, it is the therapist's role to help with alternative behavior. In a clarifying process, we seek discrepancies between the three components of the process: thoughts, feelings, and behavior. When a child thinks that power is essential to his/her survival but doesn't feel comfortable about acting aggressively, the therapist should work on this discrepancy. Alternatively, when a child doesn't like aggression and thinks it is a bad behavior, but cannot help it because he/she cannot control the impulsive behavior, we can work on that. Very often I use the continuum to visualize the discrepancy. When the gap is small, it is clear that the child is not ready for change. A large gap between the real and ideal situation suggests that the child is motivated to change and the therapist needs to work on the relevant discrepancy. Putting a number on a continuum forces the children to think more precisely about their behavior and the change needed.

Most of the time, our treatment of children reaches the third stage of Prochaska's (1999) change process, where motivation for change is raised. This is a turning point in the therapeutic process because the children are in a stage of hesitation, of confusion, of debate with themselves. They are not completely sure they want to give up their power yet they want to be good. It is the therapist's task to help them see the results of good and bad behavior, to weigh the consequences of each. In fact, we use this metaphor of measuring weights to help them arrive at a conclusion about what's best for them. Usually, the children themselves know what the pros and cons of nonaggressive behavior are and can name them; sometimes they need help in seeing the price they have to pay or the gains of more prosocial behavior.

The final step is discussing alternative behavior to aggression. This is indeed the ultimate goal of most therapists who treat aggressive behavior (Dodge & Schwartz, 1997). However, I do not find it effective to identify alternative behavior before going through the entire process outlined above. Until kids are motivated to take charge of their behavior, they have no reason to make a change. They become motivated because they establish a therapeutic alliance with a meaningful person or persons, explore their behavior, understand what makes them angry and aggressive, and see the price they pay.

The Implementation of Bibliotherapy

Several chapters in this book address the different formats of delivering the treatment. The same program can be provided in individual treatment, in pairs, and in small groups. We prefer group treatment for several reasons—first and foremost, for the obvious reason of cost-effectiveness; working in groups, we reach out to more children. As aggression is so common in school that every second child experiences some form of it (Benbenishty & Astor, 2005), cost-effectiveness becomes a major consideration.

Nonetheless, I would not recommend group treatment if I believed it were less effective than other types of therapy. Although some researchers caution against group treatment (Dishion et al., 1999), the fact is that our research found no treatment differences when comparing group and individual therapy (Shechtman, 2003b; Shechtman & Ben-David, 1999). Indeed, the illustrations of group treatment provided throughout this book show that, despite a few disturbances along the process, children were mostly helpful to one another, providing emotional and instrumental support. Positive interactions in a group occur in a supportive and intimate climate. When the therapist succeeds in establishing a therapeutic alliance with and among group members, outcomes are more favorable in counseling groups (Shechtman & Katz, 2007; Shechtman & Leichtentritt, 2008) and this includes groups of aggressive children. More-over, the discussion of the literature is much richer in groups, and so are the suggestions for alternative behavior.

Take the following feedback provided by Arnie about his experience in a group of three classmates: "I like it here because I get to know other children in depth and befriend them." Later Arnie mentions in the group that he also feels a bit embarrassed to need such help and the following dialog ensues.

Stan:	It doesn't matter as long as it helps, and everyone can see that you are more relaxed, yet you still have a ways to go.
Arnie:	What do you mean?
Stan:	Yesterday you were in a fight.
Dan (nonaggressive):	It doesn't matter, as long as he tries, we should appreciate that.

In this short conversation, there is honest expression of feelings, courageous feedback that was accepted, and support—all therapeutic factors in group counseling and psychotherapy.

Not all aggressive children are suited to a group format, however. Some are too disturbed to adjust to a group, whether extremely withdrawn or extremely acting out. One of the major roles of a group therapist is to protect group members and the group process (Shechtman, 2007). Therefore, for some children, individual or duo therapy is a viable alternative.

Duo therapy has similar features to group treatment. Children support and assist each other in overcoming their barriers to change. Working in pairs, close friends become even closer, and rivals learn to resolve the conflicts between them.

In individual therapy, the most important factor in the change process seems to be the alliance with the therapist. Here is how one teenager summarized his experience: "I have learned to relax because you [the therapist] listened to me; I could get the pain and sorrow off my chest. I know now what kind of person I want for a girlfriend, someone like you."

Treating the Caregivers

In working with children, we often ask ourselves who should be our client: the child, the caregiver, or other significant people in the child's life? Considering aggressive children, this question becomes even more relevant in light of the vast literature suggesting the impact of the social environment, and particularly parenting, on children's aggression (Connor, 2002; Dodge, 2002; Pettit et al., 2001). The optimal solution is to treat all parties—parents, teachers, and even classmates.

While classmates and teachers are accessible for some types of treatment, as demonstrated in Chapter 9, parents of aggressive children do not frequently participate in the treatment offered to them. Aggressive behavior of children is related to attachment style (Cassidy, 1994), parental reactions (Eisenberg et al.,

1996; Gilliom et al., 2002), and parental modeling (Connor, 2002). Parents of aggressive children tend to escalate conflict situations rather than help the child relax; they not only raise anger in the child, but also model the use of physical and/or psychological force. Indeed, much of the research to date suggests that family-based intervention is the key to maximizing change in children's aggression (Horne et al., 2007).

The question, though, is how to reach out to such parents. My experience in working with aggressive mothers is limited, but when practiced, it proved effective. Mothers were able to change their own perceptions and patterns of parenting, and some were even able to step into the role of a paraprofessional therapist and do an extremely efficient job. An empirical investigation (Shechtman & Birani-Nasaraladin, 2006) of mothers in group treatment with a bibliotherapy program indicated that treatment children whose mothers were also in treatment reported more favorable outcomes than those whose mothers didn't receive treatment. Moreover, treatment mothers reported less distress, less of a punitive response style, more encouraging of emotional expression, and less minimizing responses than did nontreatment mothers. Finally, an association was found between mother's gains and their children's decreased aggression. Hence, it is clear that children can be helped either directly or indirectly through the treatment their mothers get. More efforts in this direction are needed.

Teachers are another of the large population that requires treatment in order to be more helpful with aggressive children. Most teachers have been trained to teach, but rarely are they to taught to respond to challenging children and youth, especially aggressive ones. Coping with behavioral problems is their greatest challenge. Teachers see themselves as good people and want to be of help, but lack the skills to respond constructively (Almog & Shechtman, 2007). The aggressive behavior of students particularly upsets teachers, as it frightens them and puts them on the defensive. Understanding the helplessness of most aggressive kids may help teachers to befriend rather than fight them, to assist rather than reject them. Teachers' self-efficacy is of great importance in this respect; once they feel capable of coping with aggressive youngsters, they are likely to continue such efforts. We found two components of our intervention to help the most: understanding anger and aggression in an experiential way, and receiving tools, such as bibliotherapy. We lack systematic research on teacher training, but the illustrations and teacher feedback to such interventions speak for themselves.

The Evidence Base of the Bibliotherapy Intervention

Is all this effective? This is a major question in contemporary psychotherapy treatment (Norcross et al., 2006). A series of studies have pointed to positive outcomes of the treatment offered in this book. Most studies compared treatment children with no-treatment (control) children, showing that the former reduced their level of aggression, while the latter tended to increase it (Shechtman, 2000, 2003b; Shechtman & Nachshol, 1996). In those studies where a follow-up was possible, treatment gains were sustained after a few months. Following Deffenbacher and colleagues' (2002) distinction between absolute and relative gains, these are absolute outcomes.

Relative effectiveness can be gleaned from the three studies that compared bibliotherapy treatment with a similar intervention without bibliotherapy. In all the three studies, we found some indications in favor of bibliotherapy, but not on all measures. In the first such study (Shechtman, 2006a), results indicated no treatment differences for aggressive behavior; both interventions reduced aggression compared to a control group. However, the difference for empathy was significant: children in the bibliotherapy condition gained in empathy more than those in the no-bibliotherapy condition. In addition, aggressive boys in bibliotherapy reached a higher stage of change at termination and functioned more effectively as clients; that is, they resisted less frequently and reported more gains in insight and therapeutic change. Moreover, the therapists who used bibliotherapy in their treatment reported higher satisfaction than their counterparts who did not. Taking all the results together, the bibliotherapy treatment appears to be more effective.

The second study (Shechtman & Nir Shafrir, 2007) compared the same clients (adult inpatients) in two types of treatment, using a single therapist. Patients participated in two treatment groups a day; one included bibliotherapy, while the other did not. In such a study design, it is not possible to measure outcomes, because outcomes cannot be attributed to one of the treatment groups; only process measurement is possible. Results indicated that in the bibliotherapy condition, clients were less resistant, used simple responses less frequently, and demonstrated affective exploration more frequently than they did in the no-bibliotherapy condition. As simple responses are considered less constructive client behavior, the study suggests that literature helped clients function more constructively.

In the third study (Shechtman & Effrati, 2008), the same children participated in both treatments in an alternate fashion (similar to the preceding study). That is, every other session they received one of the two treatment types: with literature (bibliotherapy) or without (helping sessions). Results indicated that, overall, the less productive responses were more frequent in the helping sessions, while the more productive responses were present more in bibliotherapy. That is, the children worked more effectively in the bibliotherapy treatment, as they were engaged more in cognitive exploration and reported more therapeutic changes. This last finding is particularly important, as it points to behavior change as perceived by the children. Moreover, a comparison of the stages of change (Prochaska, 1999) revealed that more children remained in the precontemplation and contemplation stages during the helping sessions than the bibliotherapy ones (10 vs. 5 children, respectively), while more children in bibliotherapy were at the preparation and action stages (8, as opposed to 4 in the helping sessions).

In short, the relative comparisons suggest that treatment with bibliotherapy is superior to treatment without it, particularly on process measures. Resistance was consistently lower in the bibliotherapy conditions, a finding that particularly validates our rationale for using literature as a buffer of resistance to treatment. Moreover, affective exploration and insight occurred more frequently. These are two major goals in our therapy; we consider affective exploration the path to insight and to change (Hill, 2005). These positive outcomes could only be attributed to the unique features of bibliotherapy, as other than that, treatment was similar in theory and principles.

Taken as a whole, the research outcomes provide a strong evidence base for the bibliotherapy intervention offered in this book. Such empirical support for an integrative program that applies humanistic, psychodynamic, and cognitive-behavioral principles is of particular importance in a world that worships cognitive treatment. Based on the consistency of positive outcomes, it is safe to recommend the program for the treatment of aggressive children.

Concluding Remarks

This book may seem counterintuitive to some readers. Our society is governed by adults, and children are expected to obey. When they do not succeed, they are either punished or removed from mainstream education. How many adults are aware of the internal struggle of aggressive children, as evidenced in the many illustrations throughout this book? How many can see their pain, sadness, fear, and anxiety? It is hard to recognize the plight of these high-risk children, because they appear forceful and strong, threatening, and dangerous. Our intuitive reaction is to reject them, keep our distance, or engage them in battle, but their need is to be accepted, befriended, and embraced. In the Preface to this book I used the metaphor of driving on a wet road, when suddenly the car veers to the right. Our first instinct is to turn the wheel in the same direction, but actually we should turn it the other way. So, too, with aggressive youth; we need to act against our basic instincts, to love rather than hate, to accept rather than reject, to nurture rather than punish, and to reach out rather than avoid. To illustrate this argument, let me cite the reaction of one highly aggressive youngster: "I think that those people who initiated this group are very smart. Here we can talk and feel, and relieve the pressure, not like in everyday life in school."

My hope is that by listening to the voices of aggressive children and youth, so loudly expressed throughout this book, readers will develop the love for them that they so badly need. I also hope that coming to know these aggressive youngsters will convince the reader that they need much more than skill training and improvement of a deficit in information processing. While I do believe that information processing should be corrected and that better skills for coping with conflict are important, there is a sequence of experiences that must be present before behavior change can take place. Aggressive children are frustrated, disappointed, angry, and lonely for many reasons. They often feel intimidated and attacked, and they are just protecting themselves through their aggressive behavior. It isn't that they don't see the consequences of aggression, but they justify it in terms of being the victim.

These characteristics of aggressive and violent youngsters require a therapeutic rather than an educational approach. Only in a safe climate with intimate relationships will they dare peel off the layers of defense, the cloak of masculinity (Pollack, 1998), and reveal their vulnerability. Bibliotherapy addresses such needs; the stories, poems, and films serve as an indirect way to reach out to youth that reject treatment. It helps them see their conflicts from a distance, and in a playful way. Once they feel safe, we introduce the therapeutic process necessary to help them explore their own difficulties, develop insight into the price they are paying, and take charge of their behavior.

Such treatment, as we have seen in many illustrations, can be carried out not only by workers in the helping professions, but also by paraprofessionals, such as teachers and parents. Just as the literature helps the children, it is also useful to caregivers, helping them to navigate the therapeutic process with minimal difficulties. Indeed, the many illustrations throughout the book and the research outcomes lead me to the conclusion that such short-term treatment can be safely used by mental-health professionals, teachers, graduate students, and even parents.

Appendix A: Translated Stories and Poems

The Present/Y. Sade

Dad's palm was thin but strong, and when it hit, it hurt a lot. I did not experience it very often, but when I did, I couldn't forget it.

The event that I am about to tell you took place when Mom was still around. I was four when Dad taught me the ABCs. In 6 months, I was a fluent reader. Dad was very proud of me and would show off my reading skills whenever we had guests. As he succeeded with this task, he decided to upgrade my knowledge and teach me to tell time. One day he explained to me the two hands of a clock. I understood the hour hand at once and could read the numbers, and I was happy with that. It was clear to me that if the short hand points to 7, then it must be 7 'o'clock, and when it moved a bit to 8, then it must be 8 'o'clock. I really liked the hour hand because of its simplicity and clarity. But the minute hand was very different; I couldn't understand why it is 10 minutes when it points to number 2, and why it is 30 minutes when it points to number 6. Dad kept repeating the explanation over and over, but I just couldn't get it.

One day, following several attempts to explain it, he must have lost his temper. He told me I would be tested the next day and I must master this knowledge and be perfect. I truly wanted to succeed and satisfy him. But, I was so frightened I couldn't understand it at all. In the evening, when Dad came home, he set me on a chair and the exam started. We were all alone at home, Mom was out and my younger brother was playing in the yard. Dad started asking questions and I responded. As long as he asked about the hour hand, everything went well, but when he started asking about the minute hand it all began. I became so confused that I couldn't answer to the point at all. Out of fear I just murmured some sentences without hearing myself. Even the very little I knew was gone.

And so I was standing on the chair, all terrified, trembling and stuttering.

"Why do you tremble?" Dad shouted. "Just answer the questions!"

I felt that facing my terrified face and confused answer Dad was getting even angrier. I knew his anger attacks. I felt chilled and I just froze. I couldn't even open my mouth anymore.

I saw Dad's face piercing me, his eyes narrowing to two cracks, his teeth black, his fists contracting, and his hand raised. I closed my eyes to avoid seeing what was about to happen, and a scream slid out of my mouth. When I opened my eyes I felt his fist on my face, I fell off the chair, my head hit the floor, and I passed out.

The Smiley Face/Itzhak Noy

He arrived at school toward the end of the first quarter with a big smile on his face. A sense of strangeness characterized him from the first moment.

First, what is this smile? You come to a new class in a new school, a different world, you must be serious, your face frozen, and your look directed to an unknown point. It is clear that this is what every normal student would do. But no, he was smiling, not a simple shy smile, but rather a big happy smile. Not only that, he did something else, unbelievably: he looked straight into our eyes. His eyes were wide open, entirely open, with no sign of embarrassment. It was clear that he doesn't understand the rules of the game. What a student!

I hated him from the first moment, from his first glance at me, when he was looking at me with his big eyes and stupid smile. What could I do but lower my gaze. Me, the veteran, the one whose roots are here and is respected by his fellows, and he, the newcomer is looking at me, smiling.

I really hated him. We didn't exchange a single word; nevertheless, I hated him. Don't you sometimes hate someone only because of a glance or something like that?

When the bell rang and all the students entered the class, the smiling guy was standing peacefully, waiting for the teacher to come in. The boys' glances didn't seem to bother him at all, as he was standing quietly and smiling. Why the boy who always sat next to me was missing that day, I can't say, but it was clear to me why the teacher decided to seat the new smiley student with the big eyes next to me. This is a long-standing conflict between me and the teacher, a minor issue about grades that were too good to be mine, and the teacher suspected that my capable friend was helping me. In short, this particular teacher took great effort to discover the truth and, as he was not able to prove his point, he found other sneaky ways to give me a hard time. Having the smiley guy sit next to me was only one in a long chain of miserable episodes.

He sat down next to me, smiling of course. I snuck a look at him, he was very sensitive and looked at me openly and straightforward, with no fear, still smiling. What a character! I thought, and I lowered my gaze. I felt humiliated and my blood boiled. I instinctively drew a line between us on the table, made a clear boundary between us, murmuring "this line do not dare pass." The stranger looked at me calmly and smiled. "Is he an idiot or what?" I thought.

The class passed by quickly. I was so busy guarding my territory that I did not notice the time flying by. When I heard the bell ring, I was even a bit sorry.

Never mind, I thought, next lesson I will make sure that his feet do not go past the halfway mark.

Then, someone brought in a soccer ball! Normally we would play soccer outside on the playground and the class would be the place to study. However, that day the class became our playground. The game became wild, the girls left the class screaming, but the boys, the real boys, remained in class throwing the ball to each other. The smiling guy was standing near a window watching us, when I took the ball: "Catch!" I screamed and threw the ball at him. I put all my power into it. You could say, it was straight from my heart and contained great hatred for the smiling boy who never hurt me, but just stood there at the window and looked at us with his big eyes.

The ball went over his head into the window, a terrible sound was heard, and the ball disappeared. A deep, tense silence was present for a few moments and then questions such as "How did it happen?" "Who threw the ball?" "The window is broken," and then again silence. The teacher was at the doorway, demanding to know "Who did this?"

That's it! I thought. Now I'm in real trouble; trouble with my parents, detention from school. How do I get out of this?

"I did it." I turned my head in surprise. The smiling guy went forward and said: "The ball slipped out of my hands and went through the window."

"A shame the ball slipped out of your hands," said the teacher angrily, "you could play outside, not here. Take your things and go to the principal. What a nice start with us, who knows how many windows you broke in your previous school! Go to the principal, go!"

And I was silent. All that time I was silent. During class I didn't pass any notes, and I didn't bother Myra, I was also very quiet during the next class. I was 14 or 15 at the time, a grown guy. But when I came home from school, I went quietly into my room and burst out crying.

It seemed to me that a big smile was hanging in the room and a pair of big eyes was looking straight at me without hesitation.

Yaron Is Angry/Dvora Omer

Yaron was angry; he screamed and shouted. You should see him. And why?

Not because he wanted something from Mom and didn't get it immediately. No one bothered him on the playground. His younger sister didn't touch his toys. His father let him do whatever he wanted. His parents didn't go out. His older sister didn't insult or hurt him. Then what did happen? Yaron was angry, screaming, and shouting because he drew a picture and it didn't come out the way he wanted.

His face became red. Tears came to his eyes, and he was very very angry. He wanted to take apart the house if he only could. He would spank Yaron himself, although no one wants to hurt himself. He would be willing to hit his older sister but knew she would hit him back. He would pinch his younger sister if Mom would allow it. He would bite the pencil that made such a horrible picture, but the pencil seems too bitter; he knows, because he has done it once.

So, Yaron didn't do any of those things. Instead, he crumpled up the paper, tore it into pieces, and cursed it. He threw the paper on the floor and stomped on it, again and again. The paper was too ugly of course, and it didn't help the picture to look nicer; on the contrary, it became torn and crumpled.

Nevertheless, it did help. It helped Yaron to relax and start a new drawing. Maybe this time the picture will be more successful.

> *I am in charge of myself* (final) – Amira Bokek (final)
> Once if someone touched me
> Even by accident,
> Or called my mother "Fat"
> Or made a face at me and laughed
> Or simply didn't include me in the game...
> I would immediately get mad and "heated"
> Immediately react
> Chop chop
> At once biff bop
> My hand would strike
> Luckily no one got hurt
> A direct whop-whack
> Real hand-to-hand combat
> At once bang-bang
> And a smack
> Just like a crazy person
> The teacher would say:
> Why do you immediately get mad and "heated"
> Why do you react chop chop?"
> At once biff bop
> Strike with your hand
> A direct whop-whack
> A direct bang-bang
> And a smack
> Enough! "Just stop and calm down".
>
> Then one day I said to myself:
> "Wait a minute, wait a minute
> No one is going to tell me how to react.
> From today on,
> I am in charge
> Period
> From today on only
> I give

The orders
From today on I decide how to react
My hand won't spring up like a coil
And only I will tell it when to hit?

The Bad Boy/Leah Goldberg

I visited my aunt yesterday,
I said "thank you," "please," "is this OK?"
And Suddenly, I don't know how –
I said to her "You stupid cow!"

Mom turned as red as a tomato, maybe
And dad said "A first grader – acting like a baby!"
How can I explain that it wasn't me, I cried?
It was the bad boy that got inside -
Without warning he gets in,
The bad boy under my skin.

I played in the yard with Jane,
I gave her my car and a train
I let her win a bubble gum
As bright and shiny as they come
And I don't know how it happened, well –
I pushed a little, then she fell.

Her Mom got angry and she said:
"What a savage!" with such dread,
Her Grandma came and "Oy oy oy!"
"You know that Gad is a bad boy"
So I said "You ass!" just to annoy
They don't understand , I don't decide –
It was the bad boy that got inside.
Without warning he gets in,
The bad boy under my skin.

"Go away" I tell the boy
He is one thing that I wish I could destroy
But he stays there – ignores my voice,
I've tried it all, I have no choice
What do I do? Is there a way?
Maybe when I grow up, he'll just go away.

Appendix B: Stories from Teaching Pictures

The Bully/Sylvia Tester

Alan cut through the tiny park and along the back alley and sauntered into school just as the bell rang. "Made it," he thought. He took his seat and looked up just as Bruce entered the room. Bruce's eyes narrowed when he saw Alan already there. Nonchalantly, he walked up Alan's aisle, managing to kick Alan in the shins—hard—as he passed. Alan winced, but managed to keep from crying out.

"Is something wrong, Alan?" asked Mrs. Morrison.

"Oh, no, Ma'am," Alan said, improvising. "I just remembered something I forgot to do at home."

"Oh," said Mrs. Morrison. She watched the room carefully until everyone was seated. Alan wanted to reach down and rub his ankle. The pain seemed like a fire in his leg. But, by the time Mrs. Morrison quit watching, the pain had faded a little, so Alan decided not to give Bruce the pleasure of knowing his kick had hurt.

"And Bruce would take pleasure," Alan thought. "He sure likes to hurt people."

This was the third day now that Alan has escaped Bruce. All the boys in the class, and some of the girls too, knew Bruce was out to get Alan. No one knew why, though, not even Alan. No one knew what to do about it either. Bruce was the biggest kid in the room. He'd flunked 2 years, so he was older than anyone else. And he was mean. Everyone was afraid of him. Alan was about the littlest. He might be quick on his feet, but if Bruce ever caught him . . . well, no one liked to think about it.

At lunch time and at both recesses, Alan managed to stay in sight of the playground supervisors. That afternoon in class, thought, he made Bruce even madder by answering a question Bruce hadn't been able to answer. He couldn't help it. He hadn't even raised his hand. But he wasn't going to lie and say he didn't know when Mrs. Morrison called on him. Alan wished she'd given up that habit of calling on anyone who seemed to be not listening.

The bell rang and Alan headed for the door, hoping to be halfway home before Bruce made it out to the playground.

"Alan!" Mrs. Morrison called. "I'd like to talk to you, please."

Alan stopped and returned to her desk, his heart sinking. There was no way to beat Bruce out the door now.

Mrs. Morrison waited until the other children were gone before she began. "Alan, I know something is wrong. I know Bruce is involved. Now, why don't you tell me about it?"

Alan looked at the floor, then said: "You're mistaken, Mrs. Morrison. Nothing's wrong."

"Alan...," she watched him closely. "I saw Bruce kick you this morning. I saw him push you yesterday. I can tell there's trouble."

Alan remained silent, looking at the floor.

"Alan...I don't want either of you to be hurt. Bruce will be in bad trouble if he picks even one more fight. The principal has said he'll suspend Bruce. That would be the worst possible thing that could happen to him. His mother beats him, you know, every time he is suspended. Last time, she threw him against the wall and broke his arm. It's no wonder he's...." She paused, looking carefully at Alan. Alan stared at the floor. "And you," she said. "Bruce is much bigger than you. He could hurt you badly. I wouldn't want that to happen."

Alan could constrain himself no longer. "Tell him that!" he yelled. Then he shut up. He hadn't meant to tell her anything.

"Alan...why is he angry at you?" "Don't know," Alan mumbled, again staring at the floor. "Who said he was angry at me?"

"I did," Mrs. Morrison sighed. "Well, I'm going home your way. Would you like a ride?"

Alan thought about it. Riding with a teacher would get him home safely today, but it would just make Bruce that much madder.

"No thank you," he said. "If Bruce sees me riding with you he'll think I tattled on him...or something."

"I see. You may be right. If there's anything I can do...anything at all...." Her voice dropped off. She looked worried.

"It'll be OK," said Alan, not believing it himself.

Alan made it out the door without being seen. He cut through the back alley and across the little park.

"One more block," he thought.

But just then Bruce came from behind a tree, charged him, knocked him down, and began pounding on him. In a fury, Alan fought back.

The Underdog/W. E. S. Folsom-Dickerson

It has been a fine baseball season. There was a minimum of rain and the school and city playgrounds had been filled with youthful teams from boys' clubs and the Little League. Schedules had been played out, winners and losers nursed their joys or sorrows, and fathers and mothers not so quietly tried to recover from their emotional bruises.

Then suddenly it was over. One day it was baseball. The next day it was football. Bam! Just like that!

James Bolen, age 10, awake on the first cool day in August with the wish to feel the tough pigskin cover of a football in his hands. And he wanted to see how far he could kick it. He wanted, too, to feel the plastic helmet on his head.

He was no sooner out of bed and dressed than he ran to the garage. There a big box-like shelf served as a catch-all for balls, uniforms, old shoes, and socks.

The helmet was there. He put it quickly on his head. It felt good. Now he was ready for the football. But he could not find the football. He felt around on the shelf, but the pigskin surface eluded him. Quickly he looked around in the corners of the garage. Still no football.

There was only one answer. He dashed from the garage, ran down the side of the house, up the outside stairs to his younger brother's room, and burst through the open door. Charles, age nine, otherwise dressed, was lacing on his tennis shoes.

"Hey!" James spoke with a grim seriousness, "where's my football?"

"Where's your football? I don't know anything about your old football."

"Well, it's supposed to be on the big shelf in the garage where we keep our stuff. But it's not there. And you're the only one who could have taken it."

"I am telling you I didn't take it. Let's go look for it again."

So down the stairs they went, around the corner of the house, taking a sharp turn into the garage. Charles looked carefully over the shelf and found—no football! He turned about slowly to see the angry face of his older brother. James had thrown off his helmet, thus revealing more plainly the deep scowl on his features.

"So," he spoke venomously. "it's not there. So you got it. And you lied to me. Now where is it?"

He advanced on his smaller brother and seizing him by his arm, shook him vigorously. Charles lunged and broke away and headed for the stairs. But he never made it. James was on him, as they say in Texas where they lived, like a duck on a June-bug. He threw his brother to the ground, grasped him by the hair, and began to rub his face in the grass.

At this point one of those peculiar reversals of fate and circumstances occurred. Perhaps no one can explain how an underdog becomes a mad dog, nor how a smaller boy held by a larger one can be transformed into a squirming, wriggling, kicking, biting, spitting tornado of terror.

But James was compelled to face the problem immediately. And while he was trying to analyze this change in his little brother, he was stunned by a small fist landing like a hammer on his right ear. This blow was followed by another one squarely on his left eye.

While he was trying to decide where these two missiles came from, he was knocked almost breathless by a small hard head landing in his stomach like a battering ram.

"Hey!" he said to himself. "I've got to do something about this!"

So he took the logical way out. He had lost his anger and didn't really want to fight his little brother, who had suddenly developed surprising skill in that field. So using his greater reach he found if he stuck his arm out stiffly in front of him, he could hold off the attack of the little hornet.

The stand-off, however, did not stop the mounting rage of Charles. On the contrary, his wails, cries, and howls increased until the air was blue with his howling.

This brought Mrs. Bolen out of her kitchen where she had been banging pots and pans so vigorously she was unaware of the small war going on in the back yard.

"Boys! Boys!" she cried, at the same time using a mother's favorite trick. She took each boy firmly by an ear and held them securely apart. The howling ceased.

"What in the world is the matter?"

"Oh, he got my football. . .."

"No, I didn't. And he called me a liar. . ."

"Oh, so that's it. Well, Mr. James Bolen, your brother Charles didn't get your ball. And he isn't a liar either."

"Well, then, where's my football?"

Mrs. Bolden's face got surprisingly red. "I guess I'm the guilty party. You see, I called the Good Will man to come and get some stuff out of the garage. I forgot all about your ball, so I guess he took it, too."

The two boys wilted, their anger dissolved.

"But what will we do for a football?" asked James. "And will you please turn loose of my ear?"

"Sorry," replied the mother, surrendering her hold. "I'll tell you what we can do. I will go down to the Good Will store and if they still have your ball, maybe we can buy it back. And I guess we'll have to get one for you, too, Charles. Then no one can say that anyone else had his ball."

There was quiet in the back yard and peace in the air.

"Now, do you two fellows think you can get along without fighting?"

"I guess so," came from James the elder.

"I will try," said Charles the younger.

"Then shake!" negotiated their mother.

James extended his hand. Charles took it, and then the two boys walked away. The war was over.

He Did Not Come/Sylvia Tester

Samuel Jackson stood at the door. He watched the street. Surely, his dad would come any minute. Surely, he was just late. He couldn't have forgotten to come again! Not again! Finally Samuel Jackson gave up. "I don't care!" he said out loud. "I don't care if he didn't come! But Samuel Jackson did care!

Samuel Jackson lived with his mother. His father lived in another city. His father was supposed to come to see Samuel that day, but he hadn't come. And Samuel did care!

Samuel Jackson walked outside and down the street. He kicked a can. He kicked it again, then again. He picked up a stick. As he walked by a fence, he hit the fence with the stick again and again. "I don't care at all!" Samuel Jackson said. But Samuel Jackson did care!

Samuel Jackson leaned against the fence and watched as Kenny Chan and his father walked by on the other side of the street. They were laughing. They were having fun. Kenny Chan's father loved him.

Suddenly Samuel hated Kenny Chan. Samuel hated Kenny Chan's father. Samuel hated everyone, because he was so lonely. Samuel Jackson broke his stick. Then he ran down the street to his house. His mother saw him come in. She knew how he felt.

"Sammy," she called, but he didn't stop. He didn't want his mother, he wanted his father. His father hadn't come, and Samuel Jackson was the saddest, maddest, most lonely boy in the world!

References

Achenbach, T. M. (1991a). *The Child Behavior Checklist (CBCL)*. Burlington, VT: University of Vermont, Department of Psychiatry.

Achenbach, T. M. (1991b). *Teacher's Report Form (TRF)*. Burlington, VT: University of Vermont, Department of Psychiatry.

Achenbach, T. M. (1991c). *Manual for the youth self-report and profile*. Burlington, VT: University of Vermont, Department of Psychiatry.

Ackerson, J., Scogin, F., McKendree-Smith, N., & Lyman, R. D. (1998). Cognitive bibliotherapy for mild and moderate adolescent depressive symptomatology. *Journal of Consulting and Clinical Psychology*, *66*, 685–690.

Adler, A. (1956). The Individual psychology of Alfred Adler: A systematic presentation in selections from his writings. In H. L. Ansbacher & R. R. Ansbacher (Eds.). New-York: Harper.

Ainsworth, M. D., Blehar, M. C., Waters, E., & Wall, S. (1978). *Patterns of attachment: A psychological study of the strange situation*. Hillsdale, NJ: Erlbaum.

Ali, A. (1997). Hamishpaha hadruzit beIsrael: Tafkidim, coah, veihut hanisuim (The Druze family in Israel).

Al-Yagon, M., & Mikulincer, M. (2004). Patterns of close relationships and socioemotional and academic adjustment among school-age children with learning disabilities. *Learning Disabilities Research & Practice*, *19*, 12–19.

Almog, O., & Shechtman, Z. (2007). Teachers' democratic and efficacy beliefs and styles of coping with behavioral problems of pupils with special needs. *European Journal of Special Needs Education*, *22*, 115–129.

American Psychiatric Association (1994). *Diagnostic and statistical manual of mental disorders* (4th ed.). Washington, DC: Author.

Baker, J. A. (1998). Are we missing the forest for the trees? Considering the social context of school violence. *Journal of School Psychology*, *36*, 29–44.

Baker, R. L. (1987). *The social work dictionary*. Silver Springs, MD: NASW.

Bandura, A. (1983). Psychological mechanisms of aggression. In R. Green & E. Donnerstein (Eds.), *Aggression: Theories and empirical reviews*, Vol. 1. *Theoretical and methodological issues* (pp. 1–40). New York: Academic Press.

Barkley, R. A. (2002). Major life activity and health outcomes associated with attention-deficit/hyperactivity disorder. *Journal of Clinical Psychiatry*, *63*, 10–15.

Bauer, A. L. (2000). Violence prevention: A systematic approach. In D. S. Sandhu & C. B. Aspy (Eds.), *Violence in American schools* (pp. 139–152). Alexandria, VA: ACA.

Benbenishty, R., & Astor, R. A. (2005). *School violence in context: Culture, neighborhood, family, school, and gender*. New York: Oxford Press.

Berkowitz, L. (1963). *Aggression: A social learning analysis*. Englewood Cliffs, NJ: Prentice-Hall.

Bernstein, J. E. (1989). Bibliotherapy: How books can help young children cope. In M. K. Rudman (Ed.), *Children's literature: Resource for the classroom* (pp. 159–173). Norwood, MA: Christopher-Gordon.

Berry, I. (1978). Contemporary bibliotherapy: Systematizing the field. In E. J. Rubin (Ed.), *Bibliotherapy sourcebook* (pp. 185–190). Phoenix, AZ: Oryx Press.

Bettelheim, B. (1977). *The use of enchantment: The meaning of fairy tales.* New York: Random House.

Beutler, L. E., Engle, D., Mohr, D., Daldrup, R. J., Bergan, J., Meredith, K., et al. (1991). Predictors of differential response to cognitive, experiential, and self-directed psychotherapeutic procedures. *Journal of Consulting and Clinical Psychology, 59,* 333–340.

Bloomquist, M., & Schnell, S. (2002). *Helping children with aggression and conduct problems.* New York: Guilford Press.

Bohart, A. C., & Stipek, D. J. (2001). *Constructive and destructive behavior: Implications for family, school, and society.* Washington, DC: American Psychological Association.

Boulton , M. J., & Smith, P. K. (1994). Bully/victim problems in middle-school children: Stability, self-perceived competence, peer perceptions, and peer acceptance. *British Journal of Developmental Psychology, 12,* 315–329.

Bowlby, J. (1969). *Attachment and loss: (2). Separation. Anxiety and anger.* New York: Basic Books.

Broidy, L. M., Nagin, D. S., Tremblay, R. E., et al. (2003). Developmental trajectories of childhood disruptive behaviors and adolescent delinquency: A six-site, cross-national study. *Developmental Psychology, 39,* 222–245.

Bronfenbrenner, U. (1979). *The ecology of human development: Experiments by nature and design.* Cambridge, MA: Harvard University Press.

Burlingame, G. M., Fuhriman, A. J., & Johnson, J. (2004). Processesand outcomes in group counseling and psychotherapy: Research and practice. In J. L. DeLucia-Waack, D. A. Gerrity, C. R. Kalodner, & M. T. Riva (Eds.), Handbook of counseling and psychotherapy (pp. 49–61). Thousand Oaks, CA: Sage.

Burlingame, G., & Fuhriman, A. (1990). Time limited group therapy. *Journal of Counseling Psychology, 18,* 93–118.

Burns, D. D. (1980). *Feeling good.* New York: Guilford Press.

Buss, A. H., & Perry, M. P. (1992). The aggression questionnaire. *Journal of Personality and Social Psychology, 63,* 452–459.

Bybee, J., & Quiles, Z. N. (1998). Guilt and mental health. In J. Bybee (Ed.), *Guilt and children* (pp. 269–291). San Diego: Academic Press.

Capuzzi, D., & Gross, D. R., Eds. (2000). *Youth at risk* (3rd ed.). Alexandria, VA: American Counseling Association.

Cassidy, J. (1994). Emotion regulation: Influences of attachment relationships. In N. Fox (Ed.), *Emotional regulation: Biological and behavioral considerations* (pp. 228–249). *Monographs of the Society for Research in Child Development, 59* (2–3, Serial No. 240).

Cassidy, J., & Berlin, L. J. (1994). The insecure/ambivalent pattern of attachment: Theory and research. *Child Development, 65,* 971–991.

Chambless, D. L., & Cris-Christoph, P. (2006). The treatment method. In J. C. Norcross, L. E. Beutler, & R. F. Levant (Eds.), *Evidence-based practices in mental health: Debate and dialogue on the fundamental questions* (pp. 191–200). Washington, DC: American Psychological Association.

Connor, D. F. (2002). *Aggression and antisocial behavior in children and adolescents.* New York: Guilford Press.

Corr, C. A. (2003/4). Bereavement, grief, and mourning in death-related literature for children. *Omega, 48,* 337–363.

Crick, N. R., & Bigbee, M. A. 1998. Relational and overt forms of peer victimization: A multi-informant approach. *Journal of Consulting and Clinical Psychology, 66,* 337–347.

Crick, N. R., & Dodge, K. A. (1996). Social information processing mechanisms in reactive and proactive aggression. *Child Development, 67,* 993–1002.

Crick, N. R., Grotpeter, J. K., & Bigbee, M. A. (2002). Relationally and physically aggressive children's intent attributions and feelings of distress for relational and instrumental peer provocations. *Child Development, 73*, 1134–1142.

Crothes, S. M. (1916). A literary clinic. *Atlantic Monthly, 118*, 291–301.

Cunningham, B., & Sugawara, A. (1988). Pre-service teachers' perceptions of children's problem behavior. *Journal of Educational Research, 82*, 34–39.

Davis, M. H. (1996). *Empathy: A social psychological approach. Social psychology series.* Boulder, CO: Westview Press.

Deffenbacher, J. L., Oetting, E. R., & DiGiuseppe, R. A. (2002). Principles of empirically supported interventions applied to anger management. *The Counseling Psychologist, 30*, 262–280.

Denham, S. A. (1997). When I have a bad dream, mommy holds me: Preschoolers' conception of emotions, parental socialization, and emotional competence. *International Journal of Behavioral Development, 20*, 301–319.

Dishion, T., J., McCord, J., & Poulin, F. (1999). When intervention harms: Peer groups and problem behavior. *American Psychologist, 54*, 755–764.

Dishion, T. J., & Patterson, G. R. (1997). The timing and severity of antisocial behavior: Three hypotheses within an ecological framework. In D. M. Stoff, J. Breiling, & J. D. Maser (Eds.), *Handbook of antisocial behavior* (pp. 205–217). New York: Wiley.

Dodge, K. A. (2002). Mediation, moderation, and mechanisms in how parenting affects children's aggressive behavior. In J. G. Borkowsky, S. L. Ramey, & M. Bristol-Power (Eds.), *Parenting and the child's world: Influences on academic, intellectual and social-emotional development* (pp. 215–229). Hillsdale, NJ: Erlbaum.

Dodge, K. A., & Coie, J. D. (1987). Social information-processing factors in reactive and proactive aggression in children's peer groups. *Journal of Personality and Social Psychology, 53*, 1146–1158.

Dodge, K. A., Lochman, J. E., Harnish, J. D., Bates, J. E., & Pettit, G. S. (1997). Reactive and proactive aggression in school children and psychiatrically-impaired chronically assaultive youth. *Journal of Abnormal Psychology, 106*, 37–51.

Dodge, K. A., & Schwartz, D. (1997). Social information processing mechanisms in aggressive behavior. In D. M. Stoff, J. Breiling, & J. D. Maser (Eds.), *Handbook of antisocial behavior* (pp. 171–179). New York: Wiley.

Dollard, J., Doob, C. W., Miller, N. E., Mowrer, O. H., & Sears, R. R. (1939). *Frustration and aggression.* New Haven, CT: Yale University Press.

Durlak, J. A., & Wells, A. M. (1997). Primary prevention mental health programs for children and adolescents: A meta-analytic review. *American Journal of Community Psychology, 25*, 115–152.

Dwyer, K., Osher, P., & Wagner, C. (1998). *Early warning, timely response: A guide to safe schools.* Washington, DC: Department of Education.

Dykeman, C., Daehlin, W., Doyle, S., & Flamer, H. S. (1996). Psychological predictors of school-based violence: Implications for school counselors. *The School Counselor, 44*, 35–47.

Eisenberg, N., & Fabes, R. A. (1994). Mothers' reactions to children's negative emotions: relations to children's temperament and anger behavior. *Merrill-Palmer Quarterly, 40*, 138–156.

Eisenberg, N., Fabes, R. A., Murphy, B. C. (1996). Parents' reactions to children's negative emotions: Reactions to children's social competence and comforting behavior. *Child Development, 67*, 2227–2247.

Elgar, F. J., & McGrath, P. J. (2003). Self-administered psychosocial treatments for children and families. *Journal of Clinical Psychology, 59*, 321–339.

Elias, M. J., & Arnold, H. (Eds.). (2006). *The educator's guide to emotional intelligence and academic achievement.* Thousand Oaks, CA: Corwin Press.

Eron, L. D. (1997). The development of antisocial behavior from a learning perspective. In D. Stoff, J. Breiling, & J. D. Maser (Eds.), *Handbook of antisocial behavior* (pp. 140–155). New York: Wiley.

Espelage, D. L., & Swearer, S. M. (2004). *Bullying in American schools*. Mahwah, NJ: Erlbaum.

Fabes, R. A., Leonard, S. A., Kupanoff, K., & Martin, C. L. (2001). Parental coping with children's negative emotions: Relations with children's emotional and social coping. *Child Development, 72*, 907–920.

Farrington, D. P. (1994). Childhood, adolescent, and adult features of violent males. In L. D. Huesmann (Ed.), *Aggressive behavior: Current perspectives* (pp. 215–240). New York: Plenum Press.

Feshbach, N. D. (1997). Empathy, the formative years: Implications for clinical practice. In A. C. Bohart & L. S. Greenberg (Eds.), *Empathy reconsidered: New directions in psychotherapy* (pp. 33–59). Washington, DC: American Psychological Association.

Floyd, M., Rohen, N., Shackelford, J., Hubbard, K., Parnell, M., Scogin, F., et al. (2004). Two-year follow-up of bibliotherapy and individual cognitive therapy for depressed older adults. *Behavioral Modification, 30*, 281–294.

Forgan, J. (2002). Using bibliotherapy to teach problem-solving. *Intervention in the School and Clinic, 38*, 75–82.

Frankas, G. S., & Yorker, B. (1993). Case studies of bibliotherapy with homeless children. *Issues in Mental Health Nursing, 14*, 337–347.

Frankel, F., & Feinberg, D. (2002). Social problems associated with ADHD vs. ODD in children referred for friendship problems. *Child Psychiatry and Human Development, 33*, 125–146.

Frankl, V. (1959). *Man's search for meaning*. New York: Pocket Books.

French, D. C., Jansen, E. A., & Pidada, S. (2002). United States and Indonesian children's and adolescents' reports of relational aggression by disliked peers. *Child Development, 73*, 1143–1150.

Garbarino, J. (1999). *Lost boys*. New York: Free Press.

Gersie, A (1997). *Reflections on therapeutic storymaking: The use of stories in groups*. London: Jessica Kingsley.

Gilliom, M., Shaw, D. S., Beck, J. E., Schonberg, M. A., & Lukon, J. L. (2002). Anger regulation in disadvantaged preschool boys: Strategies, antecedents, and the development of self-control. *Developmental Psychology, 38*, 222–235.

Gladding, S. T. (2005). *Counseling as an art* (4th ed.). Alexandria, VA: American Counseling Association.

Glasgow, R. E., & Rosen, G. M. (1978). Behavioral bibliotherapy: A review of self-help behavior therapy manuals. *Psychological Bulletin, 85*, 1–23.

Goldstein, A. P. (1999). *Low-level aggression: First steps on the ladder to violence*. Champaign, IL: Research Press.

Goldstein, A. P., & Glick, B. (1987). *Aggressive replacement training: A comprehensive intervention for aggressive youth*. Champaign, IL: Research Press.

Greenberg, L. S. (2002). *Emotion-focused therapy*. Washington, DC: American Psychological Association.

Gurian, M. (1997). *The wonder of boys*. New York: Tarther/Putnam.

Hartup, W. (1993). Adolescents and their friends. *New Directions for Child Development, 60*, 3–32.

Heath, M. A., Sheen, D., Leavy, D., Young, E., & Money, K. (2005). Bibliotherapy: A resource to facilitate emotional healing and growth. *School Psychology International, 26*, 563–580.

Hill, C. E. (2005). *Helping skills: Facilitating exploration, insight, and action* (2nd ed.). Washington, DC: American Psychological Association.

Hill, C. E., & O'Brien, K. M. (1999). *Helping skills: Facilitating exploration, insight, and action* (2nd ed.). Washington, DC: American Psychological Association.

Hinshaw, S. P., & Melnick, S. K. (1995). Peer relations in boys with attention-deficit-hyperactivity disorder with and without comorbid aggression. *Developmental Psychopathology*, *7*, 627–647.

Holman, W. D. (1996). The power of poetry: Validating ethnic identity through a bibliotherapeutic intervention with Puerto Rican adolescents. *Child and Adolescent Social Work Journal*, *13*, 371–383.

Holmes, S. E., & Kivlighan, D. M. (2000). Comparison of therapeutic factors in group and individual treatment processes. *Journal of counseling psychology*, *47*, 478–484.

Horne, A. M., Stoddard, J. L., & Bell, C. D. (2007). Group approaches to reducing aggression and bullying in school. *Group Dynamics: Theory, Research, and Practice*, *11*, 262–271.

Horne, A. M., Stoddard, J. L., & Bell, C. D. (2008). *A parent's guide to understanding and responding to bullying: The bully busters approach*. Champaign, IL: Research Press.

Horvath, A. O. (2005). The therapeutic relationship: Research and theory. *Psychotherapy Research*, *15*, 3–7.

Howard, K., Flora, J., & Griffin, M. (1999). Violence prevention programs in school: State of the science and implications for future research. *Applied and Preventive Psychology*, *8*, 197–215.

Huesmann, L. R. (1988). An information processing model for the development of aggression. *Aggressive Behavior*, *14*, 13–24.

Huesmann, L. R., & Guerra, N. (1997). Children's normative beliefs about aggression and aggressive behavior. *Journal of Personality and Social Psychology*, *72*, 408–419.

Huesmann, L. R., & Reynolds, M. (2001). Cognitive processes and development of aggression. In A. Bohart & D. Stipek (Eds.), *Constructive and destructive behavior* (pp. 249–269). Washington, DC: American Psychological Association.

Jack, S. L., Shores, R. E., Denny, R. K., et al. (1996). An analysis of the relationship of teachers' reported use of classroom management strategies on types of classroom interactions. *Journal of Behavioral Education*, *6*, 67–87.

Kaukiainen, A., Bjorkqvist, K, Lagerspetz, K., et al. (1999). The relationships between social intelligence, empathy and three types of aggression. *Aggressive Behavior*, *25*, 81–89.

Kendall, C. K., & Morris, R. J. (1991). Child therapy: Issues and recommendations. *Journal of Consulting and Clinical Psychology*, *59*, 777–784.

Kilpatrick, W., Wolfe, G., & Wolfe, S. (1994). *Books that build character: A guide to teaching your child moral values through stories*. New York: Houghton Mifflin.

Kirschke, W. (1998). *Strawberries beyond my window*. Victoria, CA: Eos Interactive Cards.

Klee, M. B. (2000). Core Virtues: A literature-based program in character education. New York: Harper/Collins.

Kolbert, J. B., & Barker, W. F. (2006). Middle school students' preferences for anti-bullying interventions. *School Psychology International*, *27*, 475–487.

Kottler, A. A. (1986). *On being a therapist*. San Francisco, CA: Jossey-Bass.

Kramer, P. A., & Smith, G. G. (1998). Easing the pain of divorce through children's literature. *Early Childhood Education Journal*, *26*, 89–94.

Kubovi, D. (1993). *Bibliotherapy: Literature, education, and emotional health*. Jerusalem, Israel: Magnes Press (Hebrew).

Leichtentritt, J., & Shechtman, Z. (1998). Therapist, trainee, and child verbal response models in child group therapy. *Group Dynamics: Theory, Research, and Practice*, *2*, 36–47.

Lochman, J. E., Fitzgerald, D. P., & Whidby, J. M. (1999). Anger management with aggressive children. In C. E. Schaffer (Ed.), *Short-term psychotherapy groups with children* (pp. 301–349). London: Aronson.

Loeber, R., & Dishion, T. (1984). Boys who fight at home and school: Family conditions influencing cross-setting consistency. *Journal of Consulting and Clinical Psychology*, *52*, 759–768.

Loeber, R., & Farrington, D. P. (2000). Young children who commit crime: Epidemiology, developmental origins, risk factors, early interventions, and policy implications. *Development and Psychopathology*, *12*, 737–762.

Loudin, J. L., Loukas, A., & Robinson, S. (2003). Relational aggression in college students: Examining the roles of social anxiety and empathy. *Aggressive Behavior, 29*, 430–439.

Luft, L. (1984). *Group processes* (3rd ed.). Palo Alto, CA: Mayfield.

Mains, J. A., & Scogin, F. R. (2003). The effectiveness of self-administered treatments: A practice-friendly review of the research. *Journal of Clinical P*sychology, *59*, 237–246.

Maslow, B. (1998). *Toward a psychology of being*. New York: Wiley.

Mazza, N. (2003). *Poetry therapy: Theory and practice*. New York: Brunner-Routledge.

McGinnis, E., & Goldstein, A. P. (1997). *Skillstreaming the elementary school child*. Champaign, IL: Research Press.

McKendree-Smith, N. L., Floyd, M., & Scogin, F. (2003). Self-administered treatment for depression: A review. *Journal of Clinical Psychology, 59*, 275–288.

Miller, G. E., & Prinz, R. J. (1990). Enhancement of social learning family interventions for childhood conduct disorder. *Psychological Bulletin, 108*, 291–307.

Miller, P. A., & Eisenberg, N. (1988). The relation of empathy to aggressive and externalizing/antisocial behavior. *Psychological Bulletin, 103*, 324–344.

Miranda, A., & Presentacion, M. J. (2000). Efficacy of cognitive-behavioral therapy in the treatment of children with ADHD, with and without aggressiveness. *Psychology in the Schools, 37*, 169–182.

Moeller, T. (2001). *Youth, aggression and violence*. London: Erlbaum.

Natvig, G. K., Albrektsen, G., & Qvarnstrom, U. (2001). School-related stress experiences as a risk factor for bullying behavior. *Journal of Youth and Adolescence, 30*, 561–574.

Norcross, J. C., Beutler, L. E., & Levant, R. F. (Eds.). (2006). *Evidence-based practices in mental health*. Washington, DC: American Psychological Association.

Ogles, B. M., Anderson, T., & Lunnen, K. M. (1999). The contribution of models and techniques to therapeutic efficacy: Contributions between professional trends and clinical research. In M. A. Hubble, B. L. Duncan, & S. M. Miller (Eds.), *The heart and soul of change: What works in therapy* (pp. 201–226). Washington, DC: American Psychological Association.

Olweus, D. (1993). *Bullying in school*. Cambridge, MA: Blackwell.

Olweus, D. (2001). Peer harassment; critical analysis and some important issues. In J. Juveonen & S. Graham (Eds.), *Peer harassment in school: The flight of the vulnerable and victimized* (pp. 3–23). New York: Guilford.

Orpinas, P., & Horne, A. (2006). *Bullying prevention: Creating a positive school climate and developing social competence*. Washington, DC: American Psychological Association.

Pardeck, J. T. (1998). *Using bibliotherapy in clinical practice*. Westport, CT: Greenwood Press.

Pardeck, J. A., & Pardeck, J. T. (1984). *Young people with problems: A guide to bibliotherapy*. Westport, CT: Greenwood Press.

Patterson, G. R., Debaryshe, B. D., & Ramsey, E. (1989). A developmental perspective on antisocial behavior. *American Psychologist, 44*, 329–335.

Peets, K., & Kikas, E. (2006). Aggressive strategies and victimization during adolescence: Grade and gender differences, and cross-information agreement. *Aggressive Behavior, 32*, 68–79.

Pepler, D. J., King, G., Craig, W., Byrd, B., & Bream, L. (1995). The development and evaluation of a multisystem social skills group training program for aggressive children. *Child & Youth Care Forum, 24*, 297–313.

Pepler, D. J., & Rubin, K. H. (1991). *The development and treatment of childhood aggression*. Hillsdale, NJ: Erlbaum.

Perry, D. G., Perry., L. C, &. Rasmussen, P. (1986). Cognitive social learning mediators of aggression. *Child Development, 57*, 700–711.

Peseschkian, N. (1986). *Oriental Stories as tools in Psychothrays*. Berlin, Germany, Springer-Verlag.

Pettit, G. S., Laird, R. D., Dodge, K. A., Bates, J., & Criss, M. M. (2001). Antecedents and behavior-problem outcomes of parental monitoring and psychological control in early adolescence. *Child Development, 72*, 583–598.

Pfiffer, L. J., Jouriles, E. N., Brown, M. M., Etscheidt, M. A., & Kelly, J. A. (1990). Effects of problem-solving therapy on outcomes of parent training for single-parent families. *Child and Family Therapy*, *12*, 1–11.

Pollack, W. (1998). *Real boys*. New York: Penguin.

Pollack, W. (2000). *Real boys' voices*. New York: Penguin.

Potter-Efron, R. T. (2005). *Handbook of anger management*. New York: Haworth Press.

Prochaska, J. O. (1995). An eclectic and integrative approach: Transtheoretical therapy. In S. S. Gurman & S. B. Messer (Eds.), *Essential psychotherapies: Theory and practice* (pp. 403–440). New York: Guilford.

Prochaska, J. O. (1999). How do people change, and how can we change to help many more people? In M. A. Hubble, B. L. Duncan, & S. D. Miller (Eds.), *The heart and soul of change* (pp. 227–258). Washington, DC: American Psychological Association.

Rahill, S. A., & Teglasi, H. (2003). Processes and outcomes of story-based and skill-based social competency programs for children with emotional disabilities. *Journal of School Psychology*, *41*, 413–429.

Rebok, G. W., Hawkins, W. E., Krener, P., Mayer, L. S., & Kellem, G. (1996). Effect of concentration problems on the malleability of children's aggressive and shy behaviors. *Journal of the American Academy of Child and Adolescent Psychiatry*, *35*, 193–203.

Reynolds, M. W., Nabors, L., & Quinlan, A. (2000). The effectiveness of art therapy: Does it work? *Art Therapy: Journal of the American Art Therapy Association*, *17*, 207–213.

Riordan, R. J., & Wilson, L. S. (1989). Bibliotherapy: Does it work? *Journal of Counseling and Development*, *67*, 506–508.

Rogers, C. (1980). *A way of being*. Boston: Houghton Mifflin.

Rosen, G. M. (1981). Guidelines for the review of do-it yourself books. *Contemporary Psychology*, *26*, 189–191.

Rothbaum, F., & Weisz, J. R. (1994). Parental caregiving and child externalizing behavior in non-clinical samples: A meta-analysis. *Psychological Bulletin*, *116*, 55–74.

Salmivalli, C., & Kaukiainen, A. (2004). Female aggression revisited: Variable- and person-centered approaches to studying gender differences in different types of aggression. *Aggressive Behavior*, *30*, 158–163.

Salmivalli, C., Lagerspetz, K., Bjorkquist, K., Osterman, K., & Kaukiainen, A. (1994). Bullying as a group process: Participant roles and their relations to social status within the group. *Aggressive Behavior*, *22*, 1–15.

Scheidlinger, S. (2001). Mini-treatment groups for children. *Journal of Child and Adolescent Group Therapy*, *11*, 197–201.

Schwartz, D., Dodge, K. A., Coie, J. D., Hubbard, J. A., Cillessen, A. H., Lemerise, E. A., et al. (1998). Social-cognitive behavioral correlates of aggression and victimization in boys' play groups. *Journal of Abnormal Child Psychology*, *26*, 431–440.

Scogin, F., Hamblin, D., & Beutler, L. E. (1989). Bibliotherapy for depressed older adults: A self-help alternative. *The Gerontologist*, *27*, 383–387.

Scogin, F., Jamison, C. & Gochneaur, K. (1989). Comparative efficacy of cognitive and behavioral bibliotherapy for mildly and moderately depressed older adults. *Journal of Consulting and Clinical Psychology*, *57*, 403–407.

Seligman, M. & Csikszentimihacyi, M. (2000). Positive psychology: An Introduction. *American Psychologist 55*, 5–14.

Shechtman, Z. (1993). Educating for democracy: Assessment of an intervention that integrates political and psychological aims. *Youth and Society*, *25*, 126–139.

Shechtman, Z. (1994). Group counseling/psychotherapy as a school intervention to enhance close friendships in preadolescence. *International Journal of Group Psychotherapy*, *44*(3), 377–391.

Shechtman, Z. (1999). Bibliotherapy for treatment of child aggression: The program and a single-group study. *Child Psychiatry and Human Development*, *30*, 39–53.

Shechtman, Z. (2000). Short-term treatment of childhood aggression: Outcome and process. *Psychology in the School, 37*, 157–167.

Shechtman, Z. (2003a). Cognitive and affective empathy in aggressive boys: Implications for counseling. *International Journal for the Advancement of Counselling, 24*, 211–222.

Shechtman, Z. (2003b). Therapeutic factors in individual and group treatment with aggressive boys. *Group Dynamics: Theory, Research, and Practice, 7*, 225–237.

Shechtman, Z. (2004a). Client behavior and therapist helping skills in individual and group treatment of aggressive boys. *Journal of Counseling Psychology, 51*, 463–472.

Shechtman, Z. (2004b). The relation of client behavior and therapist helping skills to reduced aggression of boys in individual and group treatment. *International Journal of Group Psychotherapy, 54*, 435–454.

Shechtman, Z. (2006a). The contribution of bibliotherapy to the counseling of aggressive boys. *Psychotherapy Research, 16*, 631–636.

Shechtman, Z. (2006b). The relationship of life skills and classroom climate to self-reported levels of victimization. *International Journal for the Advancement of Counselling, 28*, 359–373.

Shechtman, Z. (2007). *Group counseling and psychotherapy with children and adolescents.* Mahwah, NJ: Erlbaum.

Shechtman, Z., & Afargan, M. (2008). Psychoeducational and counseling groups with aggressive children: A comparison of outcomes and processes. Unpublished paper.

Shechtman, Z., & Bashir, O. (2005). Normative beliefs supporting aggression of Arab children in an intergroup conflict. *Aggressive Behavior, 31*, 324–335.

Shechtman, Z., & Ben-David, M. (1999). Individual and group psychotherapy of childhood aggression: A comparison of outcomes and process. *Group Dynamics: Theory, Research, and Practice, 3*, 263–274.

Shechtman, Z., & Birani-Nasaraladin, D. (2006). Treatment of aggression: The contribution of parent involvement. *International Journal of Group Psychotherapy, 56*, 93–112.

Shechtman, Z., & Gilat, I. (2005). Groups for parents of children with LD: Outcomes and process. *Group Dynamics: Theory, Research and Practice, 9*, 275–286.

Shechtman, Z., & Dvir, D. (2006). Attachment style as a predictor of behavior in group counseling with preadolescents. *Group Dynamics: Theory, Research, and Practice, 10*, 29–42.

Shechtman, Z., & Effrati, R. (2008). A comparison of bibliotherapy and individual therapy sessions in the treatment of aggressive boys. Unpublished manuscript.

Shechtman, Z., & Gat, Y. (2008). Relation between verbal behavior as group leaders and as clients in a training group. Under review.

Shechtman, Z., & Katz, E. (2007). Therapeutic bonding in groups as an explanatory variable of progress in the social competence of students with learning disabilities. *Group Dynamics: Theory, Research, and Practice, 11*, 117–128.

Shechtman, Z. & Leichtentritt, J. (2008). Differences in outcomes and processes in groups with children with and without learning disabilities. Unpublished manuscript.

Shechtman, Z., & Nachshol, R. (1996). A school-based intervention to reduce aggressive behavior in maladjusted adolescents. *Journal of Applied Developmental Psychology, 17*, 535–553.

Shechtman, Z., & Nir Shafrir, R. (2007). The effect of affective bibliotherapy on clients' functioning in group therapy. Unpublished manuscript.

Shechtman, Z., & Tanus, H. (2006). Counseling groups for Arab adolescents in an intergroup conflict in Israel: Report of an outcome study. *Peace and Conflict: Journal of Peace Psychology, 12*, 119–137.

Shechtman, Z., Weiser, L., & Kurtz, H. (1993). A values clarification intervention aimed at affective education. *Journal of Humanistic Education and Development, 32*, 30–40.

Shechtman, Z., & Yanuv, H. (2001). Interpretive interventions: Feedback, confrontation, and interpretation. *Group Dynamics: Theory, Research, and Practice, 5*, 124–135.

Shrodes, C. (1957). Bibliotherapy. *The Reading Teacher, 9*, 24–30.

Skiba, R. J., & Peterson, R. L. (2000). School discipline at a crossroad: From zero tolerance to early response. *Exceptional Children, 66*, 335–347.

Southam-Gerow, M. A., & Kendall, P. C. (1997). Parent-focused and cognitive-behavioral treatments of antisocial youth. In D. M. Stoff, J. Breling, & J. D. Maser (Eds.), Handbook of antisocial behavior (pp. 384–394). New York: Wiley.

Stattin, H., & Klackenberg-Larsson, I. (1993). Early language and intelligence development and their relationship to future criminal behavior. *Journal of Abnormal Psychology, 102*, 369–378.

Sullivan, H. S. (1953). The interpersonal theory of psychiatry. New York: Norton.

Sullivan, K. (2000). *The anti-bullying handbook*. New York: Oxford University Press.

Tallman, K., & Bohart, A. C. (1999). The client as a common factor: Client as self healer. In M. A. Hubble, B. L. Duncan, & S. D. Miller (Eds.), *The heart and soul of change* (pp. 91–131). Washington, DC: American Psychological Association.

Taylor, E., Chadwick, O., Heptinstall, E., & Danckaerts, M. (1996). Hyperactivity and conduct problems as risk factors for adolescent development. *Journal of the American Academy of Child and Adolescent Psychiatry, 35*, 1213–1226.

Teglasi, H., & Rothman, L. (2001). STORIES: A classroom-based program to reduce aggressive behavior. *Journal of School Psychology, 39*, 71–94.

Todahl, J., Smith, T. E., Barnes, M., & Pereira, M. G. (1998). Bibliotherapy and perceptions of death by young children. *Journal of Poetry Therapy, 12*, 95–107.

Tolan, P. H., & Dodge, K. L. (2005). Children's mental health as a primary care and concern. *American Psychologist, 60*, 601–614.

Thompson, R. A.(1999). Early attachment and later development. In J. Cassidy & P. R. Shaver (Eds.), *Handbook of attachment* (pp. 265–281). New York: Guilford Press.

Tur-Kaspa, H. (2004). Social information processing skills of kindergarten children with developmental learning disability. *Learning Disabilities Research & Practice, 19*, 3–11.

Wade, N. G., & Worthington, E. L., Jr. (2005). In search of a common core: A content analysis of interventions to promote forgiveness. *Psychotherapy: Theory, Research, Practice, Training, 42*, 160–177.

Wade, N. G., Worthington, E. L., Jr., & Meyer, J. E. (2005). But do they work? A meta-analysis of group interventions to promote forgiveness. In E. L. Worthington, Jr. (Ed.), *Handbook of forgiveness* (pp. 423–440). New York: Brunner/Routledge.

Walker, H. (1976). *Walker problem identification checklist*. Los Angeles: Western Psychological Services.

Waschbusch, D. A., Willoughby, M. T., & Pelham, W. E., Jr. (1998). Criterion validity and the utility of reactive and proactive aggression: Comparison to attention deficit hyperactivity disorder, oppositional defiant disorder, conduct disorder, and other measures of functioning. *Journal of Clinical Child Psychology, 27*, 396–405.

Webster (1985). *Webster's new twentieth century dictionary of the English language*. Cleveland: Collins & World.

Webster-Stratton, C. (1994). Advancing videotape parent training: A comparative study. *Journal of Consulting and Clinical Psychology, 62*, 583–593.

Webster-Stratton, C., Hollinsworth, T., & Kolpacoff, M. (1989). The long-term effectiveness and clinical significance of three cost-effective training programs for families with conduct-problem children. *Journal of Consulting and Clinical Psychology, 57*, 550–553.

West, D. J., & Farrington, D. P. (1973). *Who becomes delinquent?* London: Heinemann.

Wied, M., Branje, S., & Meeus, W. (2007). Empathy and conflict resolution in friendship relations among adolescents. *Aggressive Behavior, 33*, 48–55.

Wilson, J. Q., & Herrnstein, R. (1985). *Crime and human nature*. New York: Simon & Schuster.

Woodward, L. J., & Fergusson, D. M. (2000). Childhood and adolescent predictors of physical assault: A predictive longitudinal study. *Criminology, 38*, 233–261.

Yalom, B. (1998). *The Yalom reader*. New York: Basic Books.

Yalom, I. D., & Leszcz, M. (2005). The theory and practice of group psychotherapy (5th ed.). New York: Basic Books.

Yogan, L., & Henry, S. (2000). Masculine thinking and school violence: Issues of gender and race. In D. S. Sandhu & C. B. Aspy (Eds.), *Violence in American schools*. Alexandria, VA: American Counseling Association.

Zeiss, R. A. (1978). *Prolong your pleasure*. New York: Pocket Books.

Literature

Anderson, H. (1843). *The ugly duckling*. Denmark: Reitzel.

Bang, M. (1999). *When Sophie gets angry—Really, really angry*. New York: Scholastic.

Bennett, W., Ed. (1998). *The children's treasury of virtues*. New York: Simon & Schuster.

Elsner, E. (1974a). Teaching Pictures (#13). Dealing with Bullies. In learning about Human Relationships. Elgin, IL: David Cook Publisher.

Elsner, E. (1974b). Teaching Pictures (# 12). Dealing with Anger. Elgin, IL: David Cook Publisher.

Folsom-Dickerson, W. E. S. (1974). The underdog. In S. Tester (Ed.), *Learning about human relationships* (pp. 21–22). Elgin, IL: David Cook.

Hinton, S. (1995). *The outsiders*. New York: Penguin.

Millman, D. (1984). *Secrets of the peaceful warriors*. Tiburon, CA: Kramer.

Silverstein, S. (1974). *When the sidewalk ends*. New York: Harper/Collins.

Spelman, C. (2000). *When I feel angry*. Morton Grove, IL: Whitman.

Tester, S. (1970). He did not come. In S. Tester, *Moods and emotions* (pp. 19–20). Elgin, IL: David Cook Publisher.

Tester, S. (1974). The bully. In S. Tester (Ed.), *Learning about human relationships* (pp. 23–24). Elgin, IL: David Cook Publisher.

Thomas, P. (2003). *Is it right to fight? A first look at conflict* (illustrated by L. Harker). New York: Barron's Educational Series.

Verdick, E., & Lisovskis, M. (2003). *How to take the grrrr out of anger*. Minneapolis: Free Spirit.

Viorst, J. (1972). *Alexander and his terrible, horrible, no good, very bad day*. New York: Aladdin.

Foreign Literature (Hebrew)

Benziman, H. (1992). Ma osym cshecoasim? [What do you do when you're angry?] In *Chsheima haita ktana [When mother was little]* (pp. 34–35). Tel Aviv, Israel: Dvir.

Biran, Y. (1994). *Gader, kivsa, vyesh ym beaya [A fence, a sheep, and a man with a problem]*. Tel Aviv, Israel: Saar.

Bokek, A. (1980). Any hamefaked shel azmi [I am my own commander]. Daily newspaper, Israel.

Goldberg, L. (1959). Hayeled hara [The bad boy]. In *Zrif katan [Little shed]* (pp. 30–31). Tel Aviv, Israel: Syfriat Hapoalim.

Goldberg, L. (1989). Tof boded [The lonely drum]. In *At telchi basade [You will walk the field]* (p. 137). Tel Aviv, Israel: Syfriat Hapoalim.

Nir, H. (2000). Slichot [Forgiveness]. In *Tapuah bedvash [Apple and Honey]* (p. 12). Tel Aviv, Israel: Syfriat Hapoalim.

Noy, I. (1995). Hahaihan [The smiley face]. In *Lahalom beeinaim pkuhot [Dreaming with open eyes* (pp. 120–122). Tel Aviv, Israel: Miscal.

Omer, D. (1978). Yaron koes [Yaron is angry]. In *Haneshika shehalha leybud [The kiss that got lost]*. Tel Aviv, Israel: Josef Serberk.

Rabikovitz, D. (1981). Eitan. In *Ima Mevulbelet* [*Mother is confused*]. Tel Aviv, Israel: Keter.

Rabikovitz, D. (1995). Caf yad reshaa [The evil palm]. In *Col hashirim ad co* [*All the poems till now*] (p. 23). Tel Aviv, Israel: Hakibbutz Hameuhad.

Sade, Y. (1990). Matnat yad [The present]. In *Ctavim* [*Publications*] (pp. 48–51). Tel Aviv, Israel: Hakibbutz Hameuhad.

Shilon, L. (1981). Mifletzet lo mutzlacat [The disastrous monster]. Col Hamiflazot sheani maker: *All the monsters I know* (p. 41). Tel Aviv, Israel: Josef Serberk.

Films

Bazz (1997). M. Shtern-Odavi, Tel Aviv, Israel.

Dumbo the flying elephant (1941). H. Aberson & J. Grant, Walt Disney Productions, CA.

Life is beautiful (1997). R. Benini & V. Cerami, Cecchi Gori Group, Italy.

Madi (1987). Paul Tourveur, Australia: Baar films.

Index

Printed in the United States of America